The RedEye to Paris

TIFFANY AKITA DOMORAD

ISBN: 979-8-218-54104-0

First Printing, 2024

THE RED EYE

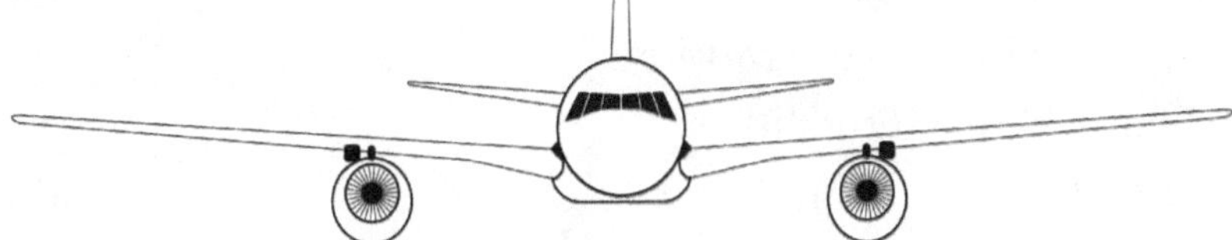

TO PARIS

TIFFANY AKITA DOMORAD

CONTENTS

Note from the Author

Part I
Prologue

1. The Redeye to Paris ... 4
2. Framed ... 15
3. The Run ... 22
4. The Safe House ... 37
5. Finding a Needle in the Haystack ... 49
6. Return of the Past ... 64
7. Going Through the Motions ... 79
8. The Flight Attendant ... 87
9. Time Equilibrium ... 105
10. Dreams ... 113
11. Looking for the Truth ... 117
12. The Engagement ... 125
13. Finding Balance ... 133
14. Finding Clarity ... 140
15. The Chase ... 151
16. Caught Between a Rock and a Hard Place ... 164
17. Everything Has Its Time ... 176
18. The Ceremony ... 186
19. The Ultimate Betrayal ... 193

Part II
Prologue

20. History   209
21. A New Life   224
22. The Trauma   232
23. Lost and Then Found   238
24. Iron Sharpens Iron   245
25. Unbalanced Equilibrium   255
26. Visions Beyond Me   261
27. Weeping Will Endure for a Night   272
28. Sorrow is Better than Laughter   279
29. The Grief of Wisdom   291
30. But the Greatest of These Is Love   304
31. But Joy Comes in the Morning   320
32. Lilith Rises   326
33. To Everything, There Is a Season   329

Acknowledgements
About the Author

NOTE FROM THE AUTHOR

What started as a project slowly transitioned into the book you see before you. I'm happy to say that with the help and support of those around me, I was able to produce this psychological thriller. I will preface with a warning—all that you read may not be "medically" true. There are parts I took creative liberties with to create the story I envisioned. Regardless, I hope you enjoy it for what it is—a story that embodies a kaleidoscope of emotions, constructs, and overall experiences we face in life—seven, to be exact. The seven categories that I believe drive people to either be the best versions of themselves or the worst, depending on the situation, are empathy, love, hate, joy, sadness, betrayal, and death. This book will capture these seven categories and cause you to indulge in a different way of thinking. We all have a story, and I hope I did justice to the characters in mine.

Throughout *The Redeye to Paris,* you will find yourself questioning, who can I trust? Then there will be times when the book pulls at your heartstrings, making you ask, how do I define true love? And can true love stand the ultimate test of life? And of course, there will be moments of pure surprise—it is a psychological thriller, after all.

But most importantly, out of all the questions to ask, the ultimate one is this: who can I turn to when I cannot trust myself?

Part I

Prologue

How would she describe herself? This was a question that had her feeling stumped for several years, both before and after she left home. Her name is Zuri Sierra Dawson, and she is a stone-cold killer. Correction, she *used* to be a stone-cold killer.

Who is she now? Zuri is a beautiful, bright, and educated kick-ass corporate lawyer for one of the biggest firms in the United States. She is gentle, kind, and caring after mostly shedding her stone-cold killer persona, but every now and again, that killer resurfaces. So, how would she define herself? Life has shown her she can easily define herself by the decisions she makes and the lessons she learns from her experiences. Zuri's various traumas at a young age shaped her into who she is today. The anger from those experiences shaped her killer persona, and her killer persona shaped her 180-degree change to the right side of the law.

In her lifetime, Zuri encountered many people, and each time she met a new crook or conman, she always seemed to come back to the same three questions, and she couldn't imagine she was the only one asking them. First, why do people do the things they do? Second, the things they do, do they do it for love, hate, or revenge? Third, do people do what they do because it gives them the ability to leave a mark in a world that knows vastly all this information about them? Therefore, their defining moment has to be uniquely chaotic to cause even the slightest ripple effect.

Needless to say, Zuri always went through life asking more questions than she could find answers to until she realized she knew the answer. Like so many people, destiny wrote her story with an iron pen and engraved it with a diamond point.

1

——————————

The RedEye to Paris

"**T**hank you for flying with us today—"

Zuri put her matte-black Beats Studio headphones on as she settled into her uncomfortable non-first class, premium economy, Delta window seat. It was midnight. She was on the red-eye to Paris, a dream in which she never thought she would be able to do. As she reached up to her headphones and pushed the button to play her music, smooth jazz reverberated into her mind and soul. This was all she needed to drift off to sleep.

Three hours later, she was abruptly awoken when the woman sitting next to her bumped into her arm while sitting down. If there was one thing that annoyed Zuri, it was being woken up abruptly, especially by a stranger. Zuri rolled her eyes and looked at the woman. The first thing she noticed was the vast amount of sweat on her forehead. The second thing was her racing heartbeat. The third thing was her lack of courtesy. Zuri rolled her eyes again then turned back to face the window, readjusting so she could be as far away from her neighbor as physically possible. She reached into her pocket to grab her phone. It was 3:03 a.m., which meant she had another four to five hours to go before she landed in Paris. Zuri was definitely feeling drowsy.

She knew the best remedy to combat drowsiness was to get up and stretch. She took her headphones off and placed them on the seat as she stood up. "Excuse me," she said to her neighbor as she shimmied past her knees. A quick trip to the restroom was all the stretching she needed, and killing two birds with one stone was always Zuri's preferred choice. She stepped into the aisle and looked in the direction of the bathrooms, in premium economy, which were located toward the front of the plane and there was a short line of people waiting. She then turned and looked in the other direction and noticed there was no line for the economy restrooms, located at the back of the plane, so she headed that way.

On her way to the restroom, she noticed how peaceful the flight was. Most people were either sleeping, watching movies, or getting lost in the alternate reality of a book. Zuri flashed back to a time when she and her ex-fiancé, Massimo, would sit on the couch and watch movies. Time moves fast when you're in love and slow when you're suffering—the irony in this.

Zuri used the bathroom, as unsanitary as it was for her, and when she stepped out of the restroom, she noticed two flight attendants sitting in the galley at the back of the plane whispering to each other. One flight attendant was crying, and the other flight attendant was comforting her. *Heartbreak*, Zuri thought to herself. She had only felt that pain twice in her life; once for her parents and the other when she parted ways with Massimo. She remembered the breakup so vividly. She had to ask herself several times that night, *what will I do for love?*

It was a long summer evening, and she had had enough. The anger in her face said it all. She really did not want to leave, but she realized there was no place for her there anymore. She had burned the last bridge, and there was no going back. She remembered pushing Massimo and hearing the sound of his back hitting the wall. She walked toward him to close the gap, grabbing his shirt and kissing him passionately, knowing deep down, she may never see him again. She turned to walk away, and Massimo caught her arm pulling her back. He hugged her tightly and whispered, "I love you, but right now, I hate you." As he slowly loosened his grip, she kissed his neck, pushed herself away from him, and ran out of the house. They had not seen each other since.

When Zuri had left, she ran straight to her car and drove off, not looking back. Three hours later, she found herself at the edge of a precipice. As heavy raindrops fell from the sky, Zuri got out of her car and let the rain wash away the hatred and disgust she felt for herself. Yelling and screaming to God, she was yearning to love who she was and all that she embodied, but she didn't know how. While those around Zuri perceived her to be a specimen of success and greatness, in Zuri's eyes, she saw herself as insignificant.

As the rain slowed down that night, so did Zuri's mind. Zuri thought about what she could do to right her wrongs.

How can I get on the right side of the law? It didn't take long for Zuri to put the pieces together. She knew who she needed to become. She hopped back in her car, drove to a hotel, signed up for the LSAT, and sent in several applications to some of the top law schools in the United States. The rest is history.

Zuri became a successful lawyer who was on her way to making senior partner. Her job gave her the ability to right her wrongs and this was how she defined greatness and success. This was the life she created for herself—the victory she earned and the treasure she fought to keep.

"Excuse me, Raven!"

Zuri's daydream was broken when the cute guy on the plane spoke. The first time she noticed him was when she was going through airport security at JFK. It was his medium-length blonde hair that caught her eyes because it made him look like a movie star. He had on khakis with a white t-shirt and a black Banana Republic trench coat—just what she liked. When she arrived at her gate, she saw him sitting alone, waiting to board the same flight as her. She had hoped he was sitting next to her on the flight, but sadly, he was not. As she was building up the courage to talk to him while they waited to board, he beat her to it and approached her before she could approach him.

It seemed like the world stopped as they talked about their jobs, life, and books. He was sweet, attractive, and funny. The flight was delayed, and the thought of being able to spend more time with him excited her. She felt a connection to him—as weird as it sounded—but a girl can dream.

"Sorry about that," Zuri chuckled. "I was having a serene moment, as they say."

"No worries, I figured you were lost in an alternate reality. It was the blank stare that gave it away. I see it now—it's one and the same," he said laughing.

She laughed with him as they squeezed past each other.

At the gate, she told him that her friends would sometimes call her Raven. Specifically, Raven Baxter from the TV show, *That's So Raven.* He asked why, and she proceeded to tell him that she, too, has a distinct blank stare when she is deep in thought. It was very similar to the blank stare Raven Baxter would have when she was having a vision.

Zuri went back to her seat smiling and hoping that he was still watching as she walked away. She dared not look back to see. When she finally arrived at her seat, she was annoyed to see her lovely neighbor was looking at her attentively. "How was the bathroom?" her neighbor asked.

"Fine, thanks for asking," Zuri replied with a confused look as she shimmied past the woman's legs to get into her seat. Zuri grabbed her headphones from the seat and sat down. *This is what happens when you're nice to someone.* This woman was a stranger to Zuri. Besides the simple pleasantries they exchanged, Zuri was not interested in making a new friend.

Zuri remembered standing behind her neighbor in the boarding line and observing the woman's dark brown hair mixed with white highlights. Zuri thought the color choice to be weird, but for some reason, it did not look bad on the woman at all. Her hair was cut in a bob that slightly grazed her shoulders, and she was shorter than Zuri with a plump body and round face.

Zuri got comfortable, put her headphones back on, and stared out her window, Watching the night sky go by. She started her music again and her mind drifted back to her earlier thoughts. God answered her prayer that night she left Massimo. God told her that she was on the right path. She always believed Massimo was everything she ever wanted. He was going to be her husband; they were going to build their own family and start an amazing life together. Zuri did feel that there had always been a hole in her heart for him. She realized that people come into your life for a reason and while they don't always see it at the time, it is all part of God's plan.

No regrets.

It had been ten years since they separated, and she never felt better. She finally loved herself as much as she loved others. She had been working, traveling, and enjoying every moment of everyday. She was fighting to heal her mind, body, and soul. Even though her work schedule was hectic, she still made time for herself. Pilates and working out five times a week were doing wonders for her mind and body. Her Sundays were focused on God and self-care, which was doing wonders for her soul.

Zuri found herself dozing off again. By the time she woke up, she only had twenty minutes left on the flight. She paused her music, reached down into her black Goyard bag that rested on the floor in front of her, and pulled out her compact mirror. Her face was still flawless. Zuri had long black hair, caramel skin, a perfectly oval face, almond-shaped eyes, naturally shaped eyebrows, and a slightly wider nose. She had an athletic physique that she often received compliments on and hazel eyes, which she believed were her best assets.

She started packing her stuff up and getting ready for what was going to be the greatest month of her life. During times of excitement was when Zuri missed her parents most. They were the center of her universe. Her mother was Ghanaian, and her father was Italian. She made sure she embraced both cultures in her day-to-day life. When she lost her parents, she found herself seeking to embrace both cultures more and more each day and clinging on to unfulfilled promises. Her father always promised to take her to Paris. Even though he did not fulfill that promise, she took it upon herself to fulfill it for the both of them and knew he would be there in spirit. Truthfully, she felt closest to her parents on planes because the plane was as close to heaven as Zuri could get.

As she put her compact mirror back into her bag, she noticed that her neighbor was not in her seat anymore. Zuri had concluded that this woman, upon first impressions, seemed like the type to be in the cockpit making out with the pilot while he was flying the plane. Right as the thought crossed her mind, her neighbor plopped down next to her. This time, she was cleaned up with a fresh set of clothes. She had a black long-sleeved top with light blue ripped jeans. Zuri only noticed because the holes in her jeans were quite big. Nonetheless, Zuri paid her no mind but thought the timing of her arrival was odd, especially because she just crossed Zuri's mind. It was only a matter of seconds before the seat belt sign turned off, so Zuri stood up in front of her seat to stretch and also to peek over a few rows back to see if she could spot the plane cutie.

She laid eyes on him as he was engaged in conversation with his seat neighbor—also another female—and it seemed as if they knew each other. Zuri remembered that when it came time to finally board the flight after their long conversation, the woman boarded first. She had not noticed his seat neighbor before, but she looked like a schoolteacher. Regardless, that was the lucky girl who got to sit next to him on the flight.

The man looked up from his conversation and noticed Zuri staring. She waved, and he waved back. She sat back down, petrified that he noticed her staring, but excited because he acknowledged her. *Why do I feel like a little girl in middle school waving at my school crush?* It did briefly cross her mind that he might be that beau she needed in Paris to make the trip that much better.

As the seat belt sign turned on and the plane descended, Zuri remembered that she dreaded this part of flying; the descent. She did feel a sense of freedom, though. Internally, she was flying higher than a plane could take her—she had the life she wanted—a life of serenity, harmony, and amazing experiences.

"Ladies and gentlemen, Air France welcomes you to Paris. The local time is 1:15 p.m., and the weather is sunny and clear. The current temperature is 60 degrees Celsius. For your safety and the safety of those around you, please remain seated with your seat belt fastened and keep the aisle clear until we are parked at the gate."

Excitement coursed through Zuri's veins as she looked outside the window to see Paris Charles de Gaulle Airport.

Zuri always wanted to be the first one off the plane, but in Comfort+, that was highly unlikely. As the seatbelt sign disappeared, she could hear the vast unclicking of seatbelts and see people rising from their seats, preparing for what lay beyond the doors.

Several minutes passed before the plane doors opened. As people began to deboard the plane, the line was slow but moving. Zuri was ready to get off the plane and start her new adventure. As she waited for her turn to get into the aisle and grab her carry-on bag, she looked over at her neighbor, who was fixing her makeup as if she had no clue that everyone was deboarding. After realizing that the woman would not be deboarding with the rest of the passengers, Zuri spoke up. "Excuse me! I have a connecting flight." Zuri grabbed her purse. Her lovely neighbor rolled her eyes realizing that Zuri was probably lying but moved out of the way so she could shimmy by.

Zuri stepped into the aisle, put her bag on her shoulder, and reached into the storage area above to grab her Louis Vuitton duffle bag. Ready to go, Zuri headed down the aisle toward her destiny. As she was walking down the aisle, she heard a man sneezing continuously a few rows up. Clumsily, he grabbed a stack of what looked like napkins as he passed by first class, and in the rush, mistakenly dropped them on the floor. He kneeled to pick them up and continued on his way, blowing his nose into one of them as he walked, stuffing the rest of the unused napkins into his pocket. She laughed to herself and thought, *that was weird yet mildly entertaining.*

Finally, off the plane, Zuri felt her spirits rise with even more excitement. Zuri decided to make this trip completely focused on self-love and maybe even real love—Paris is the City of Love, after all. As Zuri was walking to baggage claim, she felt someone tap her shoulder.

"Hey, you got off so quickly, I was unable to get your attention," the cute guy on the plane said to her.

Zuri blushed, trying to calm down the delight she was feeling. "Oh yeah, I'm excited to start this vacation. Don't be upset, but I told you at the gate, I'm terrible with names."

He smirked and said, "No worries, I was planning on calling you Raven for as long as you could stomach it. Name's Paul. Remind me again, yours is?"

"Zuri."

"Ah yes, I remember when you told me earlier, I thought it was such a unique name."

"Thank you." She looked around to see if the woman sitting next to Paul on the flight was anywhere to be found because they looked so chummy on the plane. She was not. Zuri started rubbing the scar on her hand, which she did when she felt vulnerable.

They made it down the stairs to the carousel and continued conversing, as the bags started to flow slowly in front of them.

"So, where are you staying while in Paris, if you do not mind my asking? And before you answer, I am not a stalker. Scouts honor," he said as he held up three fingers.

She laughed and said, "I am staying at the Ritz. You?"

Paul stared at Zuri like she had two heads. "No way! I'm staying there as well."

Zuri couldn't believe it. What were the chances that her crush, her flight cutie, Paul, would be in the same hotel as

her? Thirty minutes in Paris and Lady Luck was already on
her side.

2

Framed

I t was her first morning in Paris, and Zuri woke up in the fanciest hotel, with the most luxurious sheets, in the most comfortable bed. Zuri turned over to face the patio glass doors and smiled as she took in the beauty of the terrace's foliage. *Luxury.* Half awake, she grabbed her phone from the side table near the bed to look at the time—it was 7:26 a.m.—and then put her phone back down. The sun was rising and a calmness set over her. She was thrilled not only for the trip but also because she and Paul were really hitting it off.

After they grabbed their luggage last night, they decided to take the same car to the Ritz. During the ride, they delved deeper into learning about each other. There was a level of comfort that started to form between them when they realized how compatible they were. Zuri believed that Paul was attractive both physically and intellectually, and she was hoping that this could blossom into more.

After they both checked in, they made plans to meet back up. Zuri offered to have them meet in her room because she was staying in the Suite Grand Jardin, which had a private rooftop area. Paul agreed. They ended up ordering room service and talking until the wee hours of the morning. It was almost 3 a.m. when they finally decided to call it a night. Before he headed back to his room, he asked Zuri if they could meet for brunch. Gladly, she said yes, and Paul agreed to pick her up from her room at 10:15 a.m. Once Paul left, Zuri watched a little TV before heading to bed.

She dozed off while thinking of the night before with Paul and her eyes shot open, slight panic flooding over her. Quickly, she grabbed her phone and felt relieved when she realized it was now only 8:33 a.m. Wide awake, Zuri checked her phone notifications. Besides her normal influx of emails and a few texts from her friends, not much was happening. Just as she went to put her phone down, she received a notification from her International SOS app.

Prior to leaving the U.S., Zuri was told by some of her colleagues that this app would be helpful during her travels. She quickly read over the notification which informed her about the Paris airport strike. She had read about this briefly before she left but didn't do any research. She was just happy that this did not affect her travels to Paris. After seeing a second notification about protests, she put her phone down got out of bed and hopped in the shower. It was time to get ready.

After she showered and while she was getting dressed, she turned on the TV to get some more information on the strike. The news broadcast was in French, which was fine for Zuri because she was multilingual. She not only spoke English and French, but she was also fluent in Italian and Ga—one of the many languages spoken in Ghana. The news reporter continued filling Zuri in on the political climate of Paris.

Even though Zuri tried to stay out of politics, she couldn't. Politics fueled everything around her—like it did for most people—but because this was vacation and as much as she liked to be informed, she was really trying not to get too wrapped up in the politics of Paris. She did want to avoid these protests at all costs, especially since this trip was a getaway from her normal involvement in the world and in the law.

As the news played in the background, Zuri put on a matching pant set. It was a short-sleeved green ensemble with high-waisted wide-leg pants from one of her favorite stores in New York City—Madrag. She planned to match it with her green and white sneakers, which she had waiting in the hotel room from a Parisian boutique. It was one of the perks of having money and connections.

As she was putting on her sneakers, she heard a knock on the door. She briskly tied the laces, walked to the door, and checked the peephole, hoping it was Paul. When she saw she was right, she slowly opened the door so as to not show her eagerness. At the doorway, he stepped toward her and gave her a hug. She hugged him back and took a deep breath, intoxicated by Paul's Sauvage by Dior cologne. Paul was wearing a crisp white t-shirt with black cargo shorts and a pair of white Air Force One's.

"S'il vous plaît entrer," Zuri said, signaling for him to come in.

"Merci! Bonjour. Are you ready for brunch?"

Zuri giggled because she distinctly recalled telling Paul how she loved hearing him speak French and this morning was no different. "Almost ready, just finishing up the final touches and trying to get an update on these protests."

Paul nodded, following her into the living room, and sat down at the table near the TV. Paul turned to face her and stated, "I hope you don't mind my forwardness, but you're very beautiful."

"Thank you, you're not so bad yourself," she replied with a big smile on her face. Unconsciously, Zuri rubbed the scar on her hand. Just as she did, the TV lit up with a breaking news headline. A news reporter appeared speaking frantically.

"We come to you with breaking news, we have identified the three individuals who were found dead in the back restrooms on Flight RD4379 going from John F. Kennedy International Airport in New York City to Paris-Charles de Gaulle airport here in Paris."

Paul and Zuri both stared at each other and then back at the screen. Zuri ran to get the remote and raised the volume.

"Ces trois individus ont été—These three individuals were found dead in the restrooms located at the back of the plane. We are trying to locate all individuals who were seated on this flight. Police are going to start interviewing the flight attendants to see what they know. If you know anyone who was on this flight or has any information, please call our emergency line 112 or 17."

The news coverage switched to commercials. Paul sat in silence. Zuri stood in utter shock. *Three dead . . . in the bathrooms . . . What the hell is going on?*

Paul broke her internal rambling. "Holy crap! That was our flight. That's insane! Did you see anything while you were on the flight? Anything suspicious?"

Zuri thought back and realized all she really did on the flight was sleep or roll her eyes at her less-than-pleasant neighbor, except for the one bathroom break she took where she ran into Paul. "I didn't really see anything. You?"

"Not that I can recall."

Zuri sat down next to Paul. The news returned and Zuri moved to the edge of her seat.

"Breaking news: We are looking for these three individuals—"

Three pictures popped up on the screen. Zuri Sierra Mariano, Paul Black, and Marcy Evelien's faces were plastered all over the TV. Zuri stood up with her mouth agape. The news reporter stated that Zuri was a prestigious lawyer from NYC, Paul was a day trader for XEA Capital and Marcy Evelien was a flight attendant, specifically the one on Flight RD4379 that landed in Paris yesterday afternoon. The news report continued, "If anyone knows or sees these individuals, we are—"

Paul and Zuri looked at each other in disbelief for what felt like five minutes. She started to rub the scar on her hand. *Suspects in a crime.* Zuri was a lawyer, and she knew that France had a particularly scary legal system when it came to murder. A murder that occurred in Air space, which may be tried internationally, was even worse. The FBI and MI6 would be looking for them. This just became an international criminal investigation. She could not fathom the implications this would have in court—*what jurisdiction? What law? What venue? Will the U.S. send for her?* She had so many questions and not enough answers.

Zuri knew that this could be the end of her career. She needed to flee, but first, she needed to get out of the hotel. If there was one thing she learned from her past, it was that having your face plastered on national TV was the start of a downward spiral into being a suspect in an investigation. They knew something about Zuri, but she could not imagine what it was. She knew she was innocent.

Her mind started racing quicker than it had been before. Zuri knew she was being irrational in thinking that they would try to pin these murders on her, but for some reason, she had a gut feeling that things were not as they seemed. She had to go before they found her. Her first instinct was to flee, and she followed that. Her instincts had yet to fail her. Zuri turned around and grabbed her Louis Vuitton duffel bag, throwing her casual clothes and essential products in.

Paul was watching her frantically pack. "What are you doing? Where are you going? What's happening?"

Zuri kept quiet but kept packing. She left her larger suitcase and only grabbed necessities. She put on her Yves Saint Laurent beige cap and turned around to face the TV. Then she looked over at Paul and said, "Something isn't adding up. I am not sure why they are looking for us, but I know I didn't kill anyone. I need to get out of here."

Paul stared at the TV, distraught.

"Listen, Paul, you're a great guy, and I would love to see where this can go, but the reality is, if we do not leave in the next couple of minutes, we may find ourselves in a France prison. I, for one, will not be put in that predicament. You can get up, go pack a bag and join me, or you can stay here and explain the death of three people—the choice is yours." Zuri finished grabbing the remaining of her items and started for the door.

"Wait! I'm coming with you." They quickly ran to his room down the hall where he dumped all the items from his suitcase on his bed so he could re-pack his carry-on luggage.

Five minutes later, Zuri and Paul walked out of his room and headed straight to the staircase where they didn't stop running until a bright light hit their faces as they walked through the door at the bottom. It was a sunny and beautiful day. Zuri knew this was coming. She knew that eventually, *they* would find her, frame her, and kill her. Zuri did have the perfect life now, but only because she got lucky.

3

The Run

Zuri was ten years old when she noticed a shift in her parents' demeanors. It all started one afternoon when a black SUV pulled up to their house while Zuri was playing in the living room. Her parents were sitting in the dining room eating when they spotted the SUV through the window. Zuri heard angry whispers coming from her parents. They stopped eating and walked to the window.

Zuri could not see what they were seeing so she got up and walked to the dining room herself, hoping to catch a glimpse. She made it just in time to see the SUV, but a few seconds after, her parents rushed her upstairs. Her dad jogged to their room, while Zuri's mom ushered her to hers, telling her to hide under the bed. Zuri did not know what was going on at the time, but her parents knew this was just the beginning; the mold was breaking.

Zuri was born into a mob family on her father's side. When Zuri's mom was pregnant with Zuri, Zuri's father chose to make his own way by rebelling against his father, UQ. Why? Because Zuri's father was a trained assassin who was essential to the family business. Her father left the "family business" with the hope that Zuri could have a life that did not consist of control, anger, and death. Yet, little did they know, Zuri would soon pick up where her father left off—in line for the family business. When Zuri's father left, UQ was livid but allowed his son to go with a caveat that when UQ came calling—his son, Zuri's father—would answer the call.

Zuri's father knew that this was inevitable. Even though he had wished that UQ would leave them alone to raise Zuri as a normal family, deep down, he lived in fear each day, waiting for that call. He knew when the time came, he could never say no to UQ.

UQ was a dangerously quiet man. He built an empire, a syndicate, that many have tried to take, but none have succeeded. He was ruthless yet kind, dangerous yet gentle, and psychotic yet sane. UQ had the traits of a lion—power, bravery, fearlessness, and he was majestic. He only spoke when absolutely necessary and his voice, like a lion's roar, could strike fear into anyone. He was also protective and expected loyalty from all those around him, especially his family.

Two women and two men came out of the SUV dressed in black suits and wearing sunglasses. They looked identical. The females were wearing tight buns in their hair, and the men had low faded haircuts. All four individuals approached the house and knocked on the door. Zuri's mother stood at the top of the stairs while Zuri's father ran down the stairs, opening the door and stepping outside.

Zuri's mother waited patiently, still at the top of the stairs. After what felt like hours of talking, Zuri's father came back into the house, and the four individuals left. Zuri could hear her father running upstairs and whispering to her mother.

After a few more minutes, Zuri's father walked into her room and let her know it was safe to come out. Zuri crawled out from under the bed and stood up. Her father reached for her and hugged her tightly. Her father never wanted this life for her, but he knew he could neither escape fate nor UQ. Zuri's father loosened up his arms around her, sat on her bed, and patted the bed next to him so Zuri could sit down. Her mother stood in the doorway, quietly crying.

"I want you to remember that no matter what happens, we love you, and nothing or no one will change that. You're my greatest blessing, and the reason I get up each morning. I tried to build a life and shield you from the realities of this world, and at times like this, I feel as though I failed you as a father. I want you to know—*we* want you to know—that we love you so dearly." Zuri's father reached out his hand, a signal, for Zuri's mother to walk over and grab it. Her mother walked into the room, grabbed her father's hand, and sat down on the bed beside him.

Zuri hugged her father and said, "I love you too, Dad." She felt her mother also come into the hug. "I love you too, Mama."

There was something about this moment that felt finite to Zuri, but she did not understand why. Her parents released her, got up, and walked out of the room. Zuri did not notice, but her father had tears falling down his face as he left her room holding her mother's hand.

Zuri sat on her bed, confused. *Who were those people, and what could they have possibly said to make Dad sad?* That question floated around in her head for the rest of the night.

A few weeks passed by, and Zuri was stuck with the babysitter as her parents went on their monthly extravagant dinner. Zuri loved dinner nights for two reasons: one, because her mom would wear the fanciest of gowns, and her father looked like a prince in his three-piece suit, and two, because Zuri would get to play in her mom's closet and try on her mom's shoes which were three times her size. It was only on these nights that Zuri was allowed in the fancy part of the closet where diamonds and jewels were laid out and where the ball gowns were located.

The doorbell rang, and the babysitter arrived just as her parents were ready to head out. Her parents kissed and hugged Zuri, reminding her to behave. The babysitter said, "Bye," to Zuri's parents as she closed the door behind them. Zuri and the babysitter then headed to the kitchen to make her favorite snack; sliced apples and peanut butter. Then the two of them played rock paper scissors to decide which movie to watch. Zuri won so they sat in the living room to watch one of her favorite movies, *Flubber.*

When the movie ended, Zuri went upstairs to get ready for bed while the babysitter cleaned up the living room and kitchen. Zuri was putting on her pajamas when she heard a loud *bang*. She was startled and walked out of her bedroom, down the hall, and to the top of the staircase where she saw the front door being kicked open. The babysitter looked up the stairs to Zuri, with a frying pan in her hand, and mouthed *run*. As Zuri retreated from plain view of the stairs, she sat in the corner of the hallway and watched through the banister to see what was happening.

The door was finally cracked, and someone reached their arm through the hole to open the door from the inside. The babysitter slammed the person's hand with a frying pan and then ran toward the living room. Zuri closed her eyes, taking deep breaths. When she opened them again, she saw four individuals standing inside the house.

"Where is the little girl?" one of the men asked the babysitter.

"She's not here," the babysitter stated as she walked backward in fear.

The man grabbed the babysitter by the throat.

Zuri ran into her room, turned off all the lights, and locked the door. Her parents had always taught her to hide if there was ever trouble. She never understood why until now. She quickly slipped underneath her bed and waited. The house was quiet. As she lay there, she felt anger rise inside her. There was a doorway to the safe house in her parents' room, which was down the hall. *Stupid! Stupid! Why didn't I go in there? Mom and dad always told me to go in there first.*

Just as she was contemplating getting up and running to her parents' room, she heard a loud banging on her door. There was a moment of silence and then the wood splinters flew as the door was kicked in. Zuri lay perfectly still. Two individuals walked into the room slowly. They saw the closet doors closed and kicked the doors open. She could hear them deep in the closet, ripping the clothes off of the hangers. She took this moment as her only opportunity to run. She quietly crawled from under the bed and ran out the door. Her parents' room was right across the hallway, past the stairs. There was a chance she could make it.

That thought was quickly dashed as she saw the other two individuals waiting at the stairs. One of them ran up and grabbed her. They held a napkin over her face, and before she even knew what was happening, she passed out.

The next thing she remembered was waking up in a room that looked similar to hers but was not quite hers. She sat up on her forearms and was startled when she saw an older man sitting in the corner of the room. He smiled at her, but even through his smile, she could see his age etched across his face. Somewhere in those etchings, she saw fragility.

"Hi, Zuri. My name is UQ. I'm your grandfather."

Zuri sat up fully and wiped her eyes. *My grandfather?* She did not know about any other family besides her parents.

The sun was shining bright as Zuri and Paul continued to walk alongside the hotel. It wasn't long before they could hear the sirens. Zuri did not know if the sirens were for them, but she was not going to stick around to find out.

They passed by a trash bin and she stopped. Zuri looked at Paul and said, "Listen, I can understand if you don't want to go with me. I have a car that can take you anywhere you want, and I have people and ways to get you out of Paris. This has nothing to do with you."

Paul stared at her, contemplating what to do. Zuri pulled out her cell phone and tapped it against her left palm as she waited for Paul's answer.

"I'm not sure what you mean by *this has nothing to do with me.* My face was also plastered on that TV screen. I am choosing to come with you—deep down, something is telling me to trust you. We are now in this together."

"Okay," she replied while nodding. Zuri smiled at how naïve Paul sounded, but she enjoyed it. It had been a long time since she felt bubbly, but emotions were temporary in reality—she needed to be smart. She threw her phone on the ground, stepped on it, then tossed it into the trash bin. "Give me your phone," she said, holding out her hand.

Paul reached into his pocket and gave her his phone. She dropped it on the ground, stepped on it, and threw it into the same trash bin as hers. She turned to face the street and tried to hail a cab. Paul stood right next to her, checking their surroundings for fear that the cops would grab them at any second.

They flagged down a cab, and Zuri asked the driver if he could take them to the metro in La Campagne à Paris—the countryside in the 20th arrondissement. The driver signaled for them to get in. Zuri grabbed Paul's arm, slightly pushing him in front of her. Paul got into the cab first and Zuri followed, looking behind them one last time before she fully got in.

As the cab pulled away from the curb, Zuri knew that regardless of all her high-tech blockers, she could still be tracked. Stalkers are always one step ahead of their prey, and she was the prey for the second time in her life. Zuri understood that most stalkers—like hunters—watched their prey obsessively and stealthily so they could strike at the most opportune moment. She knew this because that is what she did when she was stalking her prey. Her fate was inevitable, and Zuri came to terms with it. It was finally time for her—the hunter—to be hunted.

During the ride, Zuri kept rubbing the scar on her hand and found herself in deep thought. She thought about how she ended up in this situation. Specifically, how her past landed her in this situation. She blamed herself but under-stood that it wasn't truly all her fault. This was a domino effect, and it started on that night, the night her parents allowed her to be hunted, which was the first night she knew what it felt like to be prey. She remembered a quote she had memorized by Mitch Albom because it resonated with her life so well: *"All parents damage their children. It cannot be helped. Youth, like pristine glass, absorbs the prints of its handlers. Some parents smudge, others crack, a few shatter childhoods completely into jagged little pieces, beyond repair."*

The cab came to a halt. bringing her back to reality. They had arrived at the metro. She paid the cab driver, grabbed her bag, and climbed out of the cab, Paul following closely behind her. She did not know why she brought Paul along. She knew there was a chance that he would not survive this. Paul was what Zuri wanted to normalize her life. She wanted someone ordinary, but it was not feasible because she was always on the run—just like her father. What she needed was someone who might be able to understand her situation, the way her mom understood her dad's.

Four years after Zuri was taken by her grandfather, she was no longer the girl she was when she first met him. Zuri was focused, trained, quiet, stealthy, and a stone-cold killer.

At the age of fourteen, she was something fierce. She spent the last few years on the family estate in Italy working with Massimo, UQ, and his carefully selected team to ensure that she was ready to be the best. They built her into a weapon—training her to be the best fighter, intelligence gatherer, and eventually, the best assassin. UQ wanted to not only instill morals and values in her, but he also wanted her to learn and embody important life lessons.

Zuri was homeschooled during this time, which made it easier for UQ to have her training five times a day. Her curriculum included advanced placement courses, such as trigonometry, chemistry, and most importantly, English literature. In her English lit course, she was required by her home school instructors to read a new book each week. Her regimen was strict, and it left little room for her to be normal, but then again, nothing about her situation was normal. The only normalcy she had was the time she spent with Massimo, her scheduled weekly time with UQ, and her bi-weekly phone and video calls with her parents, which helped build trust between them over time.

Regardless of what transpired, they were all family. She understood that as she got older and let the past stay in the past. Her focus was learning from UQ so she could lead the syndicate one day—worrying about her parents' past mistakes was a distraction from the overall goal.

Zuri and Paul's next destination was Zuri's hidden safe house in the middle of nowhere. The safe house was about six miles away from the bus stop, and the only way to access it was by walking.

When training with UQ, Zuri set up safe houses all over the world. They never knew when disaster or chaos would strike, so they were always prepared—always ten steps ahead. The safe houses were untraceable and scattered all over the world. Each of her safe houses was set up in a methodical way, her way, so she always remembered how to get to them.

When she left Massimo, it was up to her to hire security to ensure that the safe houses were stocked with food, weapons, and necessities for a one-year time span. UQ told Zuri, "Safe houses are meant to keep you safe for short periods of time. If you spend more than six months in a safe house, nine out of ten times, you are already dead." She never understood what he meant by this until she left Massimo. What he meant was, if you stay in a place for too long, eventually, the ones hunting you will find you—no matter where you hide. She thought about her current predicament. She had been hiding for years . . . and they finally found her.

Zuri had not spoken to Paul since they got out of the cab. Paul was confused and scared, but he continued to follow her lead. Zuri stopped when she heard Paul's breath starting to quicken. He was definitely panicking. She looked back at Paul and said, "Listen, try to remain calm." Paul only nodded, and they continued walking.

Zuri knew what he was feeling; it was the fear of the unknown. She could see it in his face. "Emotions should be felt and not seen. Fix your face." This was one of the other lessons UQ engrained in her. Zuri developed her poker face after that, and this was one of the things that contributed to her being a kick-ass lawyer.

Zuri led them into a wooded area where she had her safe house. The safe house was mostly built underground, and a beautiful three-bedroom two-bathroom custom-built log home sat above it. This was a way to shield the presence of anyone knowing what laid beneath. The home had cameras all around, which gave Zuri a panoramic view of the area. Behind the log home sat a large ten-foot by ten-foot shed. They walked past the home and into the shed. "Close the door," Zuri said to Paul as he looked around.

He nodded again and complied.

At first glance, the shed looked like a regular shed, especially to Paul. Zuri stopped in the middle of the space and looked around. If her calculations were correct, she was standing in the right spot. She moved around some equipment until she spotted the white button. She pressed the button, and a screen lit up on the left side of the wall. She walked to it as Paul stood there, mouth agape. The security system required her to do a retina scan, fingerprint scan, and voice recognition verification.

Once her identity was verified, the ground started to move, and Paul nearly screamed. Any other time, she would have laughed or even slowed down enough to tell him what was about to happen, but there simply weren't any seconds to waste. Nonetheless, she grabbed his arm to comfort him. The floor was a type of elevator that took them down, stopping at the top of a staircase. Zuri led Paul down the stairs.

During a reading session by the pool, Zuri decided it was time to use her persuasive skills to win favor from UQ. "So, Grandpa, my seventeenth birthday is coming—I would like to ask for two things."

UQ looked at her curiously. "What can I do for you, young lion?"

"First, I want to go back to the U.S. and be with my parents. Second, I want to be a normal seventeen-year-old and attend college. I'll train and study daily. I don't ask for anything, and I've never questioned you. I know this is less than ideal and not what you envisioned, but I'm asking for you to at least consider it."

UQ sat still, realizing that his granddaughter was not only conniving and smart, but she was also developing that stone-cold persona and mindset that he had. He would consider it, but not without her giving him two things he needed in exchange for her own request.

Zuri was a planner at heart. Everything she did was carefully evaluated and mapped out before she executed her vision. Her conversation with UQ was no different. Earlier that year, on one of the scheduled phone calls with her parents, Zuri asked her mom to put in several applications to some of the top colleges in the U.S., including the University of North Carolina Chapel Hill (UNC-Chapel Hill). Her parents heard back a few months later from UNC-Chapel Hill, stating that not only was Zuri accepted but that they would grant Zuri early admission. The day she asked UQ to leave was the day her parents told her she was accepted. Zuri was overjoyed, but she knew she needed to be methodical and strategic when talking to UQ. Zuri knew she needed to offer leverage to UQ—so she could get her way.

"What's your plan?" UQ asked.

After Zuri carefully laid out the plan to UQ, he thought for a few minutes before hesitantly granting her his blessing. "I am giving you fair warning, you need to hold up your end of the bargain. Between everything you mapped out and promised, plus the new responsibilities I will give you, you'll be a busy girl. But time waits for no man. If you don't hold up your end of the bargain, you will be pulled out of school and brought back here. Understood?"

"I understand. I give you my word."

It was summertime, and Zuri was ecstatic to be back in New York City. She missed her parents dearly and was so happy to enter into what she believed would be real normalcy. Even though she was intelligent—with an IQ of 140—UNC-Chapel Hill required her to have a high school diploma.

After careful evaluation from several professors at the University, Zuri was offered two options: she could take the General Educational Development (GED) test or attend one year of high school. Due to her lack of social interactions with people her age, she chose one year of high school. Upon completing the year, she would then attend four years at UNC-Chapel Hill.

After she made her decision about school, she called and updated UQ on what the next five years would look like. In turn, UQ paid several trusted advisors to train Zuri three times a week, six hours a day. She trained three hours before school and three hours after school. As UQ warned, these five years would prove challenging to Zuri. Not only was her schedule intense, but her training and trainers were ruthless—physically and mentally.

The trainers taught Zuri the ins and outs of the business, which was no small feat. As much as Zuri was learning about the business, she knew there were things she still had no idea about and that worried her. She knew the reigns would eventually go to her, and these next five years would prove if she was truly ready to take UQ's place.

Regardless of the uncertainty, Zuri knew her focus had to be in the present—taking it day by day and enjoying her new normal of being a teenager.

The summer flew by, and before she knew it, September arrived. Zuri was entering her senior year of high school. It took Zuri several weeks to make friends, and within her first two months of school, she found her two closest friends—Simon Palermo and Alice Reese.

Zuri, Alice, and Simon were inseparable. They spent weekends going to the movies, museums, and the mall. They attended Broadway shows and experienced all the food NYC had to offer. The three of them had big dreams and constantly talked about their plans for the future, including the lives they wanted for each other and themselves.

In all the time they spent together, Zuri developed a huge crush on Simon, and after bravely telling him how she felt, he told her he felt the same way. They decided to 'go steady,' as her parents called it. In her world, that meant he was her boyfriend. Luckily, Alice was so happy for them, and Zuri was grateful that this did not stop them from being the trio that they were.

The three of them spent both winter and spring break together. Winter break was filled with snow and skiing, while spring break was filled with lakes and jet skis. It might have been because her parents felt guilty, or maybe they were just happy to have her back, but they spoiled her to no end, including planning and chaperoning these two trips. They made it a point to get to know Simon's parents as well as Alice's. It was a year of new beginnings and new friendships.

4

The Safe House

Zuri loved this safe house the most out of the other ten she had around the world because this was the one she was able to fully customize to her specifications. This was her dream house, which aligned well with her dream to retire to Paris with Massimo one day and raise a family together.

This was her first time seeing it in person, and at that point, she realized that the pictures and video calls did not do the place justice. It was astonishing.

When they came off the elevator, there was a spiral staircase. Two-thirds of the way down, they could see the kitchen to the right, which sat directly across from the living room on the left. Then when they got fully down the stairs, they could see the dining room adjacent to the kitchen and across the game area, which had a pool table, dart board, PS5 gaming desk, and an old-school Pacman machine. Everything on the open-floor plan was nude and black.

At the bottom of the staircase to the left, past the game area and dining room, there was another staircase that led upstairs to the second floor. On the second floor was the main bedroom, which had a large walk-in closet and a bathroom. The bathroom had dual sinks as well as a shower and hot tub set up. Down the hall from the main bedroom were two smaller bedrooms. Zuri had made these rooms for the kids she always wanted.

Back downstairs on the first floor and down the hall, past the kitchen and living room, was the first guest bedroom on the left with a bathroom directly across. Further down the hallway was another full-size bathroom on the right with a gym beside it and another guest room on the left. At the end of the hallway was Zuri's tech room where she had a weapons room installed within it. This house had her favorite weapons, including her Smith and Wesson S&P shield. It was one of her more accurate guns—*then again, all guns are accurate when the shooter is.*

She walked over to one of the chairs in the dining room and dropped her bag down on the floor. She pulled out the chair, fell onto it, and sat there, gathering her thoughts. Paul came over and dropped his bag near the table as he looked around the safe house in amazement. "What is this place?" Paul asked. "It's remarkable!"

"One of my safe houses."

Paul looked at her in shock. "How many safe houses do you have? And why do you need multiple safe houses?"

Zuri ignored the first question but answered the second one. "Because I like safe houses. They keep me safe. Duh,"

Zuri said with a smirk on her face. "There is a lot you don't know about me, obviously . . ." her voice trailed out. "And you'll never find out," she whispered to herself.

Zuri was so thankful for her personal growth and friends. This one year of high school had been magical for her, and she was happier than she had ever felt. The year was coming to an end, and she was saddened by how quickly it had gone by but felt blessed by the experience. Even though she only knew these people for a year, it felt like a lifetime. The end of her senior year consisted of yearbooks, graduation, and of course, prom night.

On prom night, she and Simon were crowned Prom Queen and Prom King and, in the yearbook, she was voted Most Likely to Succeed. She would have given anything to have experienced four years of high school, but this one year gave her all she ever wanted, which was to be normal.

Zuri was so proud of herself as she put on her graduation dress and heels. She wore a beautiful black midi Zara dress that hugged her in the right places. She also wore glass slingback pumps that were her mother's. She felt so accomplished, especially juggling her crazy schedule, a boyfriend, and life as a teenager. She truly felt invincible, like nothing could stop her success. Looking back on it, she realized that this was one of the last times in her life that she truly felt a rush of happiness. It was one of the few times Zuri was proud of who she had become.

As she walked down the aisle with her best friends, she could feel the hot sun on her face.

"I cannot believe we are finally here," Alice said.

"Let's remember this moment when we make our way to college!" one of her classmates shouted happily and jumped on Simon's back.

"I still can't believe we all got accepted into UNC-Chapel Hill," Alice said.

As they walked to their seats, Zuri looked around to see where her family was sitting. She saw her mom and dad, the loves of her life. Regardless of what mistakes were made in the past, her parents kept her grounded and gave her the strength she needed to excel this past year.

Her parents were seated next to Alice and Simon's parents. She had invited UQ, but he was unable to make it. He had sent his regards through a gift, a beautiful diamond bracelet from Cartier, and a note that said, "To my dearest Lioness, congratulations. I am so proud of you. May you continue to hold the family name with pride."

Paul sat next to Zuri and gave her a hug. Then he kissed her forehead and asked, "Where do we go from here?"

Zuri was not sure how to feel about Paul's warm embrace and affection. On one hand, she wanted it, but on the other, she knew it was not going to last. Regardless, Zuri needed that push to come back to her senses. She quickly rubbed the scar on her hand, got up, and said, "Grab your bags, and let me show you to your room."

"Wait," Paul said, standing up to meet Zuri's gaze. Paul stared deeply into her eyes and leaned in slowly watching her expression.

Zuri held his gaze, trying to figure out if Paul was actually trying to make this a romantic moment. He moved in slowly, reaching for Zuri's chin, and angled her face upward so her lips were facing him. In anticipation, she closed her eyes and held her breath. Zuri felt his lips touch hers and electricity flowed through her body. She returned the kiss, allowing everything else to fall away. They kissed for a few minutes, having a full make-out session and allowing the built-up emotion to overtake them.

When Paul slowly pulled away, he was smiling. Zuri returned the expression. "Follow me," she said again. As they passed the living room, she opened the door to the first bedroom on the left. "You can sleep here. Drop your bags. I want to show you something else."

Paul looked around the room, impressed by the décor as he did as he was told. She continued down the hall to the doorway of her tech room. To get inside, it required a fingerprint scan as well as a retina scan. After completing both steps, she opened the door, which led to automatic lights turning on and revealing several seventy-inch screens connected to a computer with a touchscreen table encompassing the keyboard. In front of the table sat three rolling chairs.

Zuri walked over to the table and tapped it, making the screen light up. While the screens were loading, Zuri pulled out the middle chair and sat down. After a minute, the computer was ready for her to log into the system. She searched the case in the Parisian Police Database—a file on her, Paul, and Marcy popped up on the screen as well as some notes from the detectives handling the case. Paul stood back astonished and quiet as she tried to figure out where the Parisian police detectives were in their investigation. "This is going to take some time. If you want, you can go walk around the weapons room, and I will check what the police have on us," Zuri said. "Look—don't touch."

Paul nodded and wandered into the weapons room. She could hear him gasp when the lights automatically came on, and he saw the extensive, meticulous layout of weaponry Zuri contained. She knew this would keep him busy for a few minutes so she could see what the police had in her file. She clicked into her file and multiple items popped up. They had information about Zuri being a well-known corporate lawyer in the United States, who worked on many corporate deals with some of the largest firms in the world in locations such as Hong Kong, Mexico, Japan, Ghana, and South Africa, which unbeknownst to them, were all locations where she had safe houses. The file stated that she was quadrilingual and had the ability to blend in.

Upon further digging, Zuri stumbled across a file inside her file that came from an anonymous tip. In the notes, it said that an untraceable call came into the station for the acting commander around 6:12 a.m. that morning. On the other end of the phone was a disguised voice, stating, "The clock is ticking. Catch her if you can." The person also warned the commander that Zuri was armed and dangerous. Next to that note was the word 'mastermind' with a question mark. From the looks of it, the call came in hours before the news broadcast came on which meant that when her face was plastered on TV, they already knew she was a suspect. Zuri was so confused. She leaned back and intensively rubbed the scar on her hand.

She heard Paul's footsteps as he was entering back into the room, and she quickly exited the screen, replacing it with the file they had on him. The investigators had a few pictures of Paul and notes stating that he was a day trader who was working for one of the largest investment firms in the world. The file warned that Paul had a lot of money and connections, therefore, officers were ordered to stay vigilant at boating docks and private plane terminals. She clicked on some attachments in his file and found that they had pictures of her and Paul in the airport and walking from the airport to the shared cab they took. The license plate was unreadable in the picture, but she was sure they had surveillance video by now and already knew who the driver was.

Paul sat next to her on the left and read through the notes on the screen. After he finished reading, he leaned back in his chair. Zuri could feel his eyes burning a hole at the side of her face as she continued reading herself. Zuri stopped and looked at Paul. She realized that he was panicking, but she could not tell if it was because he was hiding something or was just scared. You could hear a penny drop with how silent the room was. The only audible sound was Paul's breathing, which began to pick up.

"What are you hiding?" Zuri asked.

Right when he started to speak, the screen flashed with an update being made in the system on the flight attendant. Zuri had completely forgotten about her. They both watched as updated notes appeared in Marcy's file. Marcy Evelien had a light complexion with dirty blonde hair that fell past her shoulders. She had a thin face with large eyes, high cheekbones, and dimples. She was five foot eleven inches and was skinny like a model. She did a few modeling gigs when she was younger but was never selected for any big fashion shows. Shortly after Marcy's last modeling gig, she decided to become a flight attendant. Marcy grew up in a small town and recently lost her entire family—her mom, dad, sister, uncle, and cousin—in a car accident when a tractor-trailer fell over and crushed their car. The cops were sent multiple files from the U.S. with Marcy's entire history as well as the police report and the investigative notes that stemmed from that night of the accident. They also had a surveillance video of the accident in the files caught by a highway camera.

Curiously, Zuri clicked on the video and looked at Paul. He nodded for her to play it. They watched in horror as they saw the happy faces of Marcy's parents, seconds before the tractor-trailer fell on them. They had no idea that this was the end. It all happened so fast that the video seemed unreal. Zuri closed the video and sat there, wondering what this poor woman went through, losing both of her parents at the same time. Zuri knew what that felt like, but this was no time for sympathy. This was time for information gathering.

Zuri continued clicking around the file. The cops did not have any hard evidence as to how Marcy was involved, but they noted that they were having a hard time locating her. Just as Zuri was about to click out of Marcy's file, a picture of Marcy when she was a teenager caught her eye.

She enlarged it on one of the screens. Something looked familiar about her that Zuri could not put her finger on.

Paul broke her concentration by starting to speak slowly. "Zuri, what I have to tell you is highly confidential, and I need you to swear to secrecy."

Zuri closed out of all the computer tabs and logged out of the database. She looked over at Paul and rolled her eyes. "I think we are past that point of needing to make such statements. You see where we are, correct?" she said as she gestured vaguely to their surroundings.

Contemplating if he wanted to continue, Paul took a breath. "Years ago, I was part of an undercover rescue team. I cannot tell you which organization, but this was before I became an investment banker. I left after a mission went sideways. I didn't know what the target was or who we were picking up. We got there and entered into a warzone. There were bullets flying and most of my team members were shot and killed." He took another deep breath. "We almost made it to the car. I was holding fire while my team member was loading the last person into the car. It was a family who had been in Witness Protection for over fifteen years. I was put on this detail because it was supposed to be a quick grab and move. My team member went to start the car, and he signaled for me to come. As I was running to the car, it exploded. I woke up in the hospital to find that most of my team was dead. Our rescue unit was disbanded—we were sworn to never speak of it again." Paul looked at her to gauge her reaction.

Zuri only stared at him, offering no feedback or clear reaction.

Her silence made Paul second-guess his decision. "I should have never told you this. I can't have you knowing this. I just figured with how easy you were able to get into the police database that you would just as easily be able to access those files about my past." Paul stood up, briefly pausing to see if Zuri was going to say anything but decided against it and walked out of the room.

Zuri was astonished and saddened by his confession. His voice sounded hurt and angry, yet numb. She heard his retreating footsteps and then the door to his bedroom slam. Zuri questioned the genuineness of Paul because even though he explained his reasoning, *why would he tell me this?* He could have waited for her to find it and question it before he blurted it out. Maybe it was the pressure of the unknown or the fear that this could potentially be his last few days on Earth—depending on how this all played out. Either way, she needed to do some research.

Zuri quietly got up and closed the door to the tech room for more privacy. It was time for her to do a deep dive into who Paul was. The great thing about her training with UQ was that with the right software, she was able to hack into any and everything. This was one of the reasons she was a great asset to the syndicate. With one click, files could disappear. She started with his time in the military and dug from there. Thirty-six minutes later, she found herself in a deep hole of who Paul Black was. She was a bit rusty with getting past certain internet roadblocks, so she made do with the information she was able to access. Regardless, she found out a lot about Paul; his family, friends, business ventures, military background, and medical records.

Within his medical records, she found two things that were intriguing. First, Paul had suffered from somnambulism, better known as sleepwalking. There were isolated incidents when he was younger and after leaving the military. Second, after the incident Paul mentioned, which she was still unable to verify for its truthfulness due to the access blocks, she found a diagnosis of post-traumatic stress disorder—PTSD—in his files. Besides these diagnoses, there were no additional surprises. "Great, another problem," she whispered to herself, annoyed. Zuri barely studied sleepwalking in college, but she had spent time learning about PTSD. She learned how it affects each individual differently and how it can go undetected by those around, including doctors, spouses, and children. She always heard stories from war vets, rape victims, and gunshot victims about how they struggled the first couple months, if not years, after the trauma. Several types of therapy and/or medication were effective in helping those who suffered from PTSD, though.

Zuri sat back in her chair in deep thought, rubbing the scar on her hand. Paul was a liability, and she needed to get rid of him quickly. This day had taken an emotional toll on her, and she was exhausted. Paul was going to have to be a problem for tomorrow. Her brain was feeling overloaded, and it was time for bed. She left the tech room and walked down the hall, past his room and up the stairs to her own room, locking the door behind her. She went into the bathroom and stared at herself in the mirror for what seemed like several minutes. "This is what you were trained for," she said to herself.

She grabbed pajamas out of the closet and got herself ready for bed. As she slid into her cold but comfy bed, she could not help but feel exhilarated and nervous all at the same time. Zuri knew that these next few days would be intense, especially with Paul around, but she was up for the challenge. She appreciated his honesty, but after everything Paul told her and everything she found, it further reiterated why you cannot trust anyone because people always have secrets. The question is, once you know the secret, can you live with it and accept it?

Truthfully, in this situation, it didn't matter. Paul was a pawn and his life was worth nothing to her in the grand scheme of things. But in the *rarest* of chances that they made it out of this alive and together, she believed she could accept his secret. That kiss made a bit of a difference in her judgment. She believed she could live with his secrets and accept him for who he was. It was probably because she had so many secrets of her own. She thought about all of them as she drifted off to sleep.

5

Finding a Needle in the Haystack

Zuri woke up the next morning and felt sore, which usually only happened after a workout or when she was under a lot of stress. She already knew the only way to relieve some stress would be to get herself back into parts of her normal routine, which meant it was time for a workout, followed by a good soak in the bathtub. She rolled out of bed, got dressed in her workout gear, and headed down the stairs to the workout studio. She walked past Paul's room and saw his door was closed. She assumed he was still sleeping.

In the studio, she put on her Beats Studio headphones and completed a thirty-minute full-body workout, followed by a fifteen-minute full-body stretch. When she was done, she headed back down the hall, up the stairs, and into her bedroom. She locked the door behind her and went straight into the bathroom. She adored this house, and the very best feature was her bathroom. The shower contained multiple shower heads with a glass door, and the whirlpool tub had hydrotherapy jets. When she designed this bathroom, it was a bit pricey—but totally worth it.

She took a shower, embracing the strong water pressure which loosened her muscles, and then drained the stress from her body by soaking in the tub, allowing the jets to relax her even further. Fifteen minutes later, when her stomach started to rumble, she decided it was time to get out. She realized she could not remember the last time she ate.

She dried off, proceeded to get dressed, and went downstairs to the kitchen. She glanced over at Paul's room again and saw that the door was open. She detoured to his room and saw him standing, facing his bed with a knife in his hand. Zuri froze. "Hey Paul, you doing okay?" she said as she quietly took a step into the room.

There was no answer, just heavy breathing. She remembered what she had seen in his files that previous night. He was a sleepwalker—maybe that was what was happening at this very moment. He finally turned around to face her, and there was a dead, cold look in his eyes. He had to be sleepwalking because there was no other explanation for what was happening.

"Paul, put the knife down," Zuri said loudly as she slowly walked toward him. She should have done more research. *What am I supposed to do in situations like this? How should I approach him? If I shake him, will he wake up?* Zuri had more questions than answers. She stopped when she was about five feet away from him. It was enough distance for her to be out of harm's way in case he swung the knife.

Paul did not move. She knew she could disarm him in five seconds but wanted to do this in a less combative and hostile way because she was not sure the repercussions of being aggressive while he was in this state.

"I can't have you knowing as much as you do," Paul said without moving.

Zuri was confused.

"My past is mine alone. I was not supposed to say anything. If they find out I told you, I could be facing serious jail time—" His voice trailed off and his hand twitched.

Based on his body language, Zuri was unsure if Paul was going to try to stab her. She knew she would have to disarm him before he could get the chance. Zuri continued to walk toward him. She went for the knife, but he swung his arm around. She punched him in the face and kicked the knife out of his hand. While he was off-balanced, she pushed him hard, and he stumbled backward before he steadied himself. He charged at her, grabbed her arm, and threw her across the room. She landed on her side but was unfazed as she stood up and charged back at him. She slid in between his legs, turned around on the floor, and kicked the back of his knee. His knee gave out, and he landed on it. She took this split second to stand up and jump on his back, putting him in a chokehold. He pushed himself off his knee and took several steps backward until her back slammed into the wall. She held on to his neck tighter and used her left leg to kick and push them off the wall. She locked both legs around him, her weight making him fall backward.

Zuri remembered this exact situation with Massimo when they were practicing with one of the trainers. She had held Massimo in the same position she was holding Paul in now. "Paul, snap out of it. I am not trying to hurt you. You're here with me in the safe house! Paul! Stop!" She used all her strength to choke him, and he began tapping her arm several times. She loosened her grip on his neck. He started coughing. She slid from underneath him and fully let him go.

He looked petrified. "What the hell is wrong with you?!"

"You were trying to hurt me," Zuri said. "You had a knife, and I did not know what was happening. You were rambling on about how I was not supposed to know the information you shared yesterday about your mission. Paul, I believe you were sleepwalking."

Paul caught his breath and his facial expression changed from confusion to acceptance when he heard her say sleepwalking. "How do you know about that? You looked at my files more after I left the room?"

"Yes," Zuri said annoyed.

Paul's eyes darted to the floor, and a sadness washed over him. "It does not happen often, just when I am under a lot of stress. I'm sorry—truly."

"Don't sweat it. I'm making brunch, you want some?" she said as she stood up, grabbed the knife off the floor, and headed to the kitchen.

After brunch, Paul kept his distance. Besides asking her to use the gym, he stood clear of her. Zuri could sense that Paul felt bad for the incident that occurred that morning. She left him alone because, realistically, she had her own problems to worry about.

Zuri went back to her tech room and closed the door. First, she went into a wall safe that was located behind a replica Jackson Pollock painting where she retrieved money and a burner cellphone. She closed the safe, sat down, and activated the phone, taking the time to hook it up to the security system for visibility on what the cameras outside were seeing. After the phone was set up, she then touched the table to bring the computer to life. She checked and noticed that the Parisian investigators did not get any further than the day before. This made her happy, but she knew after a while they would be able to find out more about her.

Zuri racked her brain trying to figure out who was behind all this. That was always the logical answer for illogical situations. *Who would want to frame me? Who would rejoice at my demise? Who are my known enemies?* She knew there were three people who could have been setting her up—her ex-best friend, Alice Reese, her ex-boyfriend, Simon Palermo, or her ex-fiancé, Massimo Mariano. She started analyzing each connection carefully to see the likelihood of it being any of them.

First on the list—Alice Reese.

When Zuri was working for UQ, she ended up killing Alice's uncle. Alice's uncle was a sadistic man. He was on UQ's radar because he was known for trafficking both drugs and girls. When Zuri was tasked with killing him, high school wasn't even a thought in her mind. Zuri had enjoyed learning how to kill as well as training to be an assassin. To say she was surprised when she ended up in high school and became friends with Alice would be an understatement. Zuri believed that karma was punishing her for what she had done years earlier.

Zuri recounted the conversation between her and Alice vividly. They were sitting in Zuri's dorm room, and Alice was sad because it was the anniversary of her uncle's death. She spoke to Zuri about how it was growing up and the things she remembered. She was also saddened by the things she forgot. As she continued on, she mentioned a syndicate and how her uncle was found shot dead in an alleyway on his way home from poker night. Zuri listened intently as the details of his murder sounded familiar, and by the end, she couldn't deny the truth any longer—she had murdered Alice's uncle. Zuri kept her past very vague for obvious reasons so she knew there was no way Alice could make the connection herself.

It ate Zuri up inside for weeks, and she tried to distance herself from Alice but often failed seeing as they were best friends. One night, they fell asleep in Zuri's dorm room watching a movie. Zuri had a tendency to talk in her sleep, and that night was the worst timing possible. Alice's 6 a.m. alarm went off, so she got up to head back to her dorm room and get ready for class. Alice tried to wake Zuri up, but she realized Zuri was in a deep sleep when she heard

Zuri mumbling. She stood up to walk out of the door when she heard Zuri say in an audible low voice, "Alice, I'm so sorry. I killed your uncle—"

Alice stopped dead in her tracks and looked over her shoulder at Zuri. "What did you say?"

Zuri was still fast asleep, but Alice saw a tear drop travel down her face. Confused, Alice left and their relationship struggled after that.

Alice never confronted Zuri, but in anger, she told Simon that Zuri's family is full of murderers. When Zuri found out about Alice's comments, she asked her directly where they were coming from. Alice finally told her what had happened, but Zuri couldn't believe that she would have said something so incriminating in her sleep. Alice laughed it off, but Zuri knew their relationship had run its course because Alice would never trust her now. When Alice told Zuri to lose her number, she knew she was right. And that was the last time they spoke.

Zuri spent days contemplating how to handle this new situation. *Kill her because she's a liability or leave her alive?* Zuri decided that killing her would bring about a whole new set of problems, especially with UQ. Instead, Zuri decided that if Alice had any information—like all young people—she would google it or create a word document on her laptop. Zuri decided to hack into Alice's laptop remotely. Upon hacking it, Zuri found information in a Microsoft Word document that detailed Zuri's sleep confession that Alice heard as well as further information about UQ's syndicate. Alice knew about the family connection and was trying to find out if Zuri was indeed responsible for the murder—all Alice had were theories on the connection between Zuri's family and her uncle's death. Even though there was nothing concrete, Zuri knew, in the wrong hands, this could be a problem, so she put a virus on Alice's computer. A few days later, she heard from Simon that Alice had to buy a new computer because of an irreversible virus. *Mission accomplished.*

Next person on her list—Simon Palermo.

Simon was the middleman between Zuri and Massimo's love. Simon hated Massimo from the first day he met him on a video call, and his hate for Massimo continued to grow, especially when Simon was dating Zuri. Simon swore that Zuri could not truly love him because she was in love with Massimo. It was the truth, but Zuri never admitted to it. Honestly, it was the love Zuri and Massimo had for each other that drove Simon away. She remembered the night quite vividly.

Zuri and Simon were in her dorm room about to have a movie night when there was a knock on the door. "Pizza's here," Zuri yelled as she jumped up to grab the door. While she was paying the delivery man, her phone rang. Simon went into Zuri's bag to retrieve the phone, but by the time he got to it, the ringing had stopped. He saw on the home screen that Massimo had called. Just as he was about to put the phone down, Simon heard her phone *ping* and saw that he had left a voicemail. He opened her phone and listened to it:

I'll be your knight in shining armor
if you'll be my serenity.
A fire lit on a candle, for whenever you can't see.
A piece of a puzzle that's always been missing—
been missing.

I'll be the one standing there with a hanky
whenever you're crying,
Standing there telling you to keep on trying.
Just thought that I should let you know—
just thought that I should let you know.

Simon was outraged when Zuri walked back in the room with the pizza. "Your husband called and left you a voicemail. He has a nice voice. This is over. I hope you both have a great life together."

That was the last time she saw Simon as he raced out of her room, in an anger she had never seen before.

Looking back on it now, there was the good and the bad that year of college. The bad was that she lost her two closest friends in a matter of months. All the normalcy she was striving for was short lived and eventually destroyed by the life she was trying to escape from. The good was that she had only tolerated Simon, and yes, maybe she did love him—but truthfully, Simon, like Paul, was a filler. Massimo would always be her one true love and hoped the feeling was still mutual.

Last on the list—Massimo Mariano.

Massimo knew everything about Zuri. He knew what she was capable of, and he understood that he was also capable of the same things. They fell in love with each other during the time she was training with UQ on the family estate in Italy. Their life together, their engagement, and their zeal to build a family was the highlight of her life. Some would say that this was who UQ chose for her, but she never knew, and Massimo never said anything about it. Regardless of the conflict that they were dealing with, she loved him. She loved him not only because he loved her for all she was, but because he loved her for all she was not. Fate brought them together—tragedy tore them apart.

She was responsible for the demise of UQ, and Massimo never forgave her. The irony is that this was her grandfather, but to Massimo, UQ was the only father he truly knew. Massimo's parents abandoned him, and UQ took him in, raising him as his own since he was eight. UQ loved him as a son and took care of him ever since. Some would say Massimo was the son UQ wished he had versus the one he did—Zuri's father.

Zuri reminisced on the last time she saw UQ and Massimo. It was a chilly summer night when Zuri found herself face to face with UQ. She was livid with UQ because he constantly lied and kept secrets. That night, she believed that she had uncovered the truth—UQ was responsible for her parents' death. Zuri did the only thing she knew how; she shot him. After she shot UQ, Massimo walked into the room. With tears running down her face, she whispered, "I had to do it."

Massimo ran across the room, and Zuri jumped out of the way, startled. She could see the anger in his eyes and the pain he was feeling because she felt both emotions too. Massimo went to UQ to check for a pulse but couldn't find one. Massimo turned and grabbed Zuri, slamming her against the wall. "What did you do?!" he shouted as tears ran down his face.

Zuri tried to get out of Massimo's hold, but she couldn't. Feeling trapped, she headbutted him, and he stumbled back. He ran toward her again and threw a punch, causing Zuri to duck down. She followed with a punch of her own to his stomach. Massimo stepped back, wiped his tears, and stood up. He got into his fight stance, and so did she. He threw a fist and she returned his blow with a kick. This fight went on for what felt like forever. They had fought and trained before as per UQ's wishes so this was a normal thing, but it felt more emotional this time around.

Five minutes later, Zuri stepped back and said, "I'm done."

Massimo put his hands up to show he was done too. Before he could react, she pushed Massimo one more time, and his back hit the wall. She planted a passionate kiss on his lips. Their lips separated, but Zuri stayed so close to Massimo's face that they could feel each other breathing. She reached for his left hand without breaking eye contact and placed the engagement ring in his palm. Abruptly, she turned to walk away, but Massimo grabbed her arm and pulled her back. He hugged her tightly and whispered, "I love you, but right now, I hate you." She kissed his neck, pushed him one last time, and ran out the house. They had not seen each other since.

After going down memory lane, Zuri was content with those three choices of suspects who could be framing her and began to research their locations. She worked backward, starting with Massimo, who was now head of the syndicate—taking over for UQ after Zuri left. His last known sighting was in Italy earlier that morning leaving the estate.

Zuri paused on his picture and stared. Massimo still took her breath away. He was always so well put together and handsome. Massimo had jet-black hair that was long and always slicked back. He had heterochromia—his eyes were two different colors, green in the left eye and hazel in the right eye. He always had a lightly shaven, scruffy goatee. He was six feet tall and had caramel skin. His body was athletic. He dressed only in the finest clothing as a businessman with power does, and he always held himself in a high regard. She moved the picture to another screen and went on to look up Simon.

Simon was traveling. His last known location was in Côte d'Ivoire, also known as Ivory Coast. He was doing work for Samaritans Purse, a Christian organization providing spiritual and physical aid to people all around the world. She was surprised to see that Simon was doing this but happy to see he made something of himself.

Simon was an average guy, height and build. He had a dark Caesar haircut, but he never grew facial hair, so he always had a baby face. He had dark brown skin with brown eyes. His chin was chiseled, and his face was perfectly symmetrical. Zuri remembered that Simon was the jokester among their group of friends, but when it came down to it, he was truly a sweetheart. She closed out of the search for Simon and went on to look for Alice.

Alice was in Greece with her husband and three children. From the looks of it, they had been living there for the last ten years. Alice was a short, beautiful women. She had long black hair and dark brown eyes. Her face was full, and she had high cheek bones. She also had a loud personality and was boisterous but had a caring side to her as well. When she walked in the room, people could not help but stare. It was the same situation for Zuri—so when they were together, it was double trouble.

Zuri sat back in her chair, pondering. She was not sure what to make of her findings. While everyone seemed to be living their lives, she could not help but wonder if they were plotting against her. Because truthfully, if it was not one of them, who could it be? Zuri always followed her gut, and her gut was telling her that something was not right.

Zuri sat forward, moving the different windows on the screen until she found the police database. She went back into the police files again to see if there was anything new. She did not see anything on her or Paul, but in reviewing the files, she became curious about Marcy, so she checked her whereabouts. Marcy was last seen near the Ritz in the city's 1st arrondissement. This was good because that meant she was either resting to board another flight, or she was in Paris to stay. Zuri was happy to know she may still be in Paris. Either way, she knew she had to get to Marcy before Marcy disappeared. It was imperative that Zuri did so before someone else did. She needed to develop a plan for herself, which included finding Marcy. Marcy could probably shed some light on any connections they might have to each other or any connection she might have to the deceased.

Zuri looked at the time; 8:07 p.m. She realized she had spent hours in the tech room. She definitely needed to take a break so she got up from the computer and opening the tech room's door as casually as possible and stepped into the hallway. The house was quiet. She closed the door behind her and turned to head down the hall, just as Paul came out of the bathroom with his towel around his waist. He was muscular and athletically built. His six pack was glistening on his perfectly tan skin, and his dimples made him that much more handsome. His black short hair was still damp. He walked to his room, not realizing that

Zuri was behind him. "Looking good," she said. Paul spun around to see Zuri admiring his body. His face turned red, and he walked slightly faster to his room, closing the door behind him.

Zuri could not help but laugh. As she continued down the hall and entered into the kitchen, her phone vibrated. She pulled her phone out of her back pocket, and the screen had several 'Motion Detected' notifications. "Someone's here," she whispered to herself.

She ran to the tech room, did her verification, opened the door, and went directly to her weapons room. She grabbed and put on a bulletproof vest as well as a leg and hip holster. She ran out the door and to the living room. Her living room table was a hidden safe with a RFID lock. She opened the safe and grabbed two handguns, extra loaded magazines, and two switchblades. She put one of the handguns in the leg holster, the extra magazines in the slots on her bulletproof vest along with one of the switchblades. The other switchblade she put in her back pocket. She grabbed the second gun and held it in her hand.

She ran to Paul's door and knocked. He answered quickly, astonished when he saw the gear on her and the gun in her hand. "Someone's here," she said. "Do not come out until I tell you it's safe. If you do not hear from me in five minutes, then something happened to me. Wait for an hour, leave this safe house, and try to find a safe location."

Paul nodded, too nervous to say anything else, and closed the door as Zuri walked away.

She ran up the spiral staircase and took the elevator. She quickly grabbed her phone to see if she could spot the individual on the camera while she was on the elevator, but she couldn't. "Focus," Zuri said to herself as she quietly walked out of the shed.

The moon was rising in the sky while the warm night breeze hit her, causing a shiver to go down her spine. She had her handgun in front of her as she slowly continued toward the back of the house, walking alongside the perimeter. She saw movement from the corner of her right eye. It looked like multiple figures headed her way. She pointed her gun to the sky and sent a warning shot. She brought her gun down to chest level, aiming it toward the figures in the distance while cautiously walking in their direction.

"If I shoot again, I'm taking all of you with me," she shouted. "Ask yourselves, are you prepared to die tonight and meet your maker?"

"That's cute, but not if I shoot you first," a voice yelled back.

Zuri stopped dead in her tracks. She knew that voice. "Massimo," she whispered.

6

Return of the Past

Massimo walked out from around the side of the house and headed straight toward Zuri. He turned his flashlight on and pointed it in the direction of her voice. She kept her gun raised as he walked toward her. He lowered his weapon as he got closer, and when he was a few feet away, he said, "I come in peace."

It was like seeing a ghost—she had not seen him in ten years. Zuri was even more confused because when she checked his whereabouts this morning, it said he was in Italy.

Zuri lowered her gun fully, holstering it on her hip. She took a few steps forward to close the gap between them and then she went in for a hug. Massimo hugged her back. Zuri was so happy to see him and did not realize she could feel this way by his presence. She felt safe. Emotions did not matter to her when it came to Massimo because he could read her like a book. They let go of each other, and

Zuri grabbed his hand. "Come inside," Zuri said as she led him toward the shed.

Massimo spoke to his team through his earpiece, "Stay alert."

"Alpha Red, copy. Beta Blue, copy—" using call signs, his six-man team confirmed their presence.

Zuri was not surprised to know he had a team with him but she was surprised to hear how small the team was. It was imperative that when you get into positions of power, specifically the position Massimo was in, a tactical team was exactly what you needed in case of emergencies or threats. She was glad to see Massimo learned a thing or two from UQ.

They walked into the shed, and while on the elevator, Zuri looked down at her hands and started rubbing the scar. For some reason, she couldn't make sense of Massimo being right next to her. She looked up to see Massimo noticing her rubbing the scar, and she quickly stopped. Before Massimo could say anything, Zuri got off the elevator, walked past him, and started heading down the stairs. She sighed a breath of relief. *Am I more relieved to see him, or am I more relieved that death isn't in the plans for me tonight?*

Zuri put her gun on the kitchen island and went to the guest room. She knocked on the door and let Paul know it was safe to come out. "It's okay," Zuri said as the door opened. "It's someone I know. Paul, this is Massimo. Massimo, this is Paul."

Massimo joined Zuri across the room. Paul smiled, slightly stepping out of the room and putting his hand forward to shake Massimo's. When Massimo reached them, he completely ignored Paul's greeting, stared him down, and then headed down the hallway to the tech room. Zuri looked at Paul apologetically. He nodded as if to reassure Zuri that it was alright then headed back into his room and closed the door. Zuri followed Massimo to the tech room.

Zuri knew Massimo was not the jealous type and was unsure why he had been rude to Paul. The only time he ignored someone completely was if he knew who they were and had a reason to dislike them. *Have they met before?* She had no idea, but she could feel the energy was unsteady between them.

Massimo pushed the door of the tech room open. In the rush, Zuri realized she had forgotten to close it fully. She stood in the doorway and watched as Massimo walked up to the computer, pulled out a USB drive from his bulletproof vest, and plugged it into Zuri's computer. He opened the only file on the USB drive, and a program began downloading onto her computer.

Massimo stared at the screen as the download continued from fifty percent to fifty-two percent and so on. He did not move or say a word to Zuri; he just kept his focus on the screen. The silence was deafening. Zuri knew Massimo couldn't bring himself to look at her, but she couldn't help but drool at the sight of him. He had aged like fine wine, and she still was not able to fully comprehend that he was standing in the same room as she was. Her mind started to race. All she could think about was the good times.

Massimo finally took a deep breath, breaking the silence as well as her concentration. Massimo started taking off his bulletproof vest, which he put on one of the tables, and then sat down in one of the empty chairs by the desk just as the program reached ninety-nine percent. Files began popping up on the screen.

Zuri watched and read the files and was surprised to see that Massimo had tracked the source of the investigation and was narrowing down who killed the three individuals. He had a lot more information than she could access. This proved even more how long she had been out of that lifestyle. She was so used to others doing the research and reports as she grew in her legal career that it did not occur to her that she was losing the skill she was once a teacher.

"I came to get you out of here," Massimo said, still facing the screen. "When I saw your face on the news, I knew this was not good. I knew you would come to this safe house—it was the closest one." Massimo turned around in the chair and stared directly into Zuri's eyes.

After what felt like sixty long seconds, Massimo grabbed the empty chair next to him and said, "Come here," signaling for Zuri to sit.

Zuri walked over and sat down, not breaking eye contact with him. She was glad he asked her to sit because her knees were starting to buckle at the intensity of the deep stare they were sharing.

Massimo leaned toward her and grabbed her hand. "I have another safe house a few miles away. Let's go there and figure out our next steps."

Zuri gave him a confused look. "What do you mean?"

"When you first got the houses built over a decade ago, UQ made me set up safe houses next to yours. He said it would give us a better chance at survival if either of us were ever compromised. All my safe houses are within ten miles of yours. Plus, if I could find you, I'm sure that it'll only be a matter of time before someone else finds you."

Zuri was not that shocked to hear that Massimo had a safe house nearby, especially because UQ always made sure to have additional measures in place, and he taught them to always do the same. Reluctantly, Zuri nodded to Massimo and said, "You're right." She knew that they had to go but was saddened at the idea of leaving this place so soon. In the short time she had spent in the safe house, she felt it could truly be home for her. She hoped one day, she could come back to this safe house, but for right now, she knew she was living with a false sense of security.

"I'll tell Paul the change in plans, and we can leave in the morning," Zuri said. She got up from the chair and headed down the hallway. Massimo stood up and watched from the doorway as she knocked on the door and spoke to Paul. "We're going to have to relocate in the morning. Massimo and I had a discussion, and he brought up a few great points that I agree with. Get yourself gathered tonight because we will not be returning to this house. And trust me when I say, we will get through this."

Paul stood there and stared at Zuri, a look of worry in his eyes.

"You don't have to go. We're not going to bring you against your will. You can always go back to the city and pretend this trip didn't happen. I'm sure a conversation with the cops can lead to you clearing your name. Regardless, I'm going to need you to make a decision right now."

Paul thought about it and then said, "I will go with you guys in the morning."

Zuri nodded and Paul closed the door. Zuri turned around to head back down the hallway, toward the tech room and saw Massimo still watching her from the doorway. He gave her a look, and she knew that if Paul had given a different answer, Massimo would have killed him. *No loose ends.*

Zuri walked within two feet of Massimo and said "C'mon. It's time for bed." Zuri reached out and grabbed his hand, gently pulling him closer to her.

Massimo smiled. "Lead the way." He closed the tech room's door and followed Zuri.

She led him down the hall and upstairs to her bedroom. As Massimo took in the sight, Zuri went into the closet and changed into pajamas. After she changed, she grabbed a pair of her oversized sweatpants and an oversized t-shirt for Massimo. She knew that at one point, these clothes belonged to him. Back then, Zuri always took his clothes and would tell him that his clothes looked better on her.

When she came out of the closet, she handed the clothes to Massimo. He changed right in front of her, and she couldn't help but blush. Zuri walked over to the far side of the bed and got under the covers. Massimo followed suit. Naturally, Zuri cuddled up to him, laying her head on his chest. He smiled at the warmth of her skin. She had missed this, more than she ever realized, and her mind started to reminisce.

When she pictured herself coming to this safe house for the first time, she had imagined it being with Massimo and their kids. It was interesting having him here with the dream half fulfilled. She hated to admit it—she was still in love with him.

She had spent so much time focusing on her career so she would not have to feel the void that Massimo left in her heart. Deep down, she also knew that no one would ever compare to him, so she did not bother setting herself up for disappointment. He was her person, and she was his.

Back then, there was a detriment that came with their love and relationship. Maybe it was the fact that they knew each other so well or maybe it was the fact that circumstances caused a strain. Either way, they had grown so accustomed to each other that she felt like they had become stagnant. At least that is what she told herself to make the emotional pain subside.

It was not until she left that she could breathe and learn who she truly was. She hoped he changed as well—but most people don't. People will always disappoint you, therefore, she had no expectations that he was different. Something did seem different about him, though—outside of her cynicism. When he first started training with UQ, he was careless, reckless, and angry. Now, he seemed controlled, calculated, and calm. It was weird to think of him as a different man. He reminded her so much of UQ.

Zuri had fallen asleep thinking about her past and woke up startled. Noticing that Massimo was still holding her, a calmness fell over her mind and body. *It wasn't a dream. He's really here.* She looked over at the clock, it was 6:18 a.m. She actually felt rested because, for the first time in years, she felt safe. She savored this moment because she was unsure how many more she would have with Massimo holding her like this.

Her mind started to betray her as thoughts floated in about the reality of her situation. They had a long day ahead of them, and Zuri knew it was time to get up and start planning their relocation. She moved slowly out of Massimo's embrace, and once she got out of bed, she looked over at him. The dimmed light from the wall sconces illuminated Massimo's face. He was sleeping as if he had not slept in years. *He must feel it too. Safe.*

She quietly left the room, closing the door behind her as she tiptoed downstairs in her pajamas. The motion-censored stair lights turned on as her foot touched each stair. Once she reached the bottom, Zuri turned on the living room light and dimmed it significantly before continuing down the hall toward the tech room. Zuri stopped dead in her tracks when she thought she heard whispers down the hall. She moved slowly toward the sounds and listened more closely, realizing it was coming from Paul's room. She tiptoed until she was a few inches from his door.

"He just showed up unexpectedly. I can deal with him now or once he shows us the other safe house. I was hoping to have her alone. I told her the story, and she believed it—but I don't know how long I can play this role."

Zuri was confused and outraged. *First off, where did he get the phone? Second, is he a part of this frame job? Has he been setting me up this whole time?* She moved away from the door and quietly hurried down the hall to the tech room. She did the verification, opened and closed the door, and sat at the computer, doing a deeper dive into Paul using Massimo's program. Massimo's encrypted program was able to get past any and all security roadblocks. She was astonished at what she found.

Paul was a Navy Seal. He was part of some of the most challenging search and rescue operations that happened outside of the United States. After he left the military, he became a hired investigator. He answered private ads for anything specializing in search and rescue.

Upon further research, Zuri found ties to terrorists, cartels, and underground groups she had never even heard of. She realized if Paul was this far gone into the underworld, he was probably there to kill her. Zuri got up, walked into her weapons room, and grabbed her gun and two additional magazines with ammunition in it. She put the magazines in her pocket. *How could I be so stupid?*

As she slowly opened the door to the tech room, she realized the house was dark and quiet. The light she turned on previously was now off. She closed the door behind her, making sure it latched this time, and walked down the hall. She put her ear to Paul's room, but there was complete silence. She raised her gun in front of her when she heard a shuffling sound coming from the living room. Right as she caught movement—*bang, bang, bang.* Paul fired three shots at Zuri. She ducked down and lost all eyes on him. She rolled behind the kitchen island.

"You're dead!" Paul shouted. He emptied his magazine.

Zuri returned fire. She was so mad that she trusted him. *Deception is a man's greatest talent.* "Who the hell are you?!"

Paul did not answer but she could hear him moving and dropped her empty magazine on the floor so she could reload.

"Typical woman. Cute face, fake personality, and you lose your mind. I knew who you were when I saw you going through security. Did you think you would go unseen forever? We've been looking for you." Paul stopped talking when he realized Massimo was walking down the stairs, the motion lights being an immediate giveaway. "Oh, Massimo, did you think that because you were here, I would not kill you both?" Paul said tauntingly as he turned to face Massimo.

For a brief moment, Zuri heard Paul's voice shift forty-five degrees to the right, and she quickly flashed back to her days in training when UQ taught her how to utilize and heighten all her senses in times of pressure—this was one of those times. She stood up and fired a single bullet. That's all she needed. The bullet went through Paul's cheek. He fell to the floor, so she jumped over the kitchen island, not wanting to lose eyes on him again. He was writhing around on the floor, grabbing his bloody face. She stood over him and fired one bullet into his head and another one into his heart. For extra measure, she checked his pulse to confirm he was dead. Zuri stared at him with disgust.

She kneeled over his body to search his pockets and found the phone he was talking on along with his wallet. She put the phone in her left-side pocket and the wallet in her right-side one. She stood up to see Massimo at the bottom of the stairs watching her. They didn't say anything to each other but knew what came next.

They ran down the hall into the tech room. Zuri wiped all the hard drives while Massimo grabbed a duffle bag that was in the weapons room and put as many weapons, bullets, and extra magazines that would fit into the bag. Zuri then ran upstairs and changed clothes into a white t-shirt with denim light blue jeans and black Ugg sneakers. She grabbed her Louis Vuitton bag and packed it with the items she had arrived with along with a few extra items from her closet. She also made sure to grab Paul's phone and wallet from her pajama pants and put them in her back pockets.

As she was coming down the stairs, she heard Massimo on the phone with the clean-up crew. He didn't have to say much because they would do what needed to be done. Once Massimo hung up the phone, it was his turn to run upstairs to change back into his clothes. He emerged from the room with anger in his face, walking down the stairs and nodding to Zuri. He grabbed the Louis Vuitton bag that Zuri packed with her items and the duffle bag with weapons. It was time to go.

They left Paul's body lying on the floor as they rushed to leave the safe house. Sadness fell upon Zuri because she knew this house would forever go abandoned. Paul had ruined the serenity and sanctity of the safe house. Luckily for them, the safe house was so secluded that no one would ever find it unless they actually knew the location and were looking for it. Zuri looked back one last time as they walked up the stairs to the elevator.

As the elevator took them up, she rubbed the scar on her hand. Zuri wanted nothing more than to stay, but it was not possible. She knew they were compromised, and whoever Paul was talking to on the phone would probably have the location of the safe house. The elevator stopped, and they got off and headed to the door of the shed.

The bright light of the sun illuminated the shed as Massimo pushed the door open. Zuri felt the warmth of the sun through the gaps in the tree branches. A light breeze was in the air, and Zuri took a deep breath, welcoming in the freshness. Her serene moment was cut short as Massimo whistled. She realized he was signaling for his team to come out of their positions. Zuri watched as his six security men emerged from inconspicuous hiding places. They had blended perfectly with nature. Massimo dropped the bags near Zuri and then walked over to meet his team. Zuri stood in one spot, enjoying the view of the log house and shed for the last time.

After a few minutes of getting lost in the beauty, Massimo walked up behind Zuri and grabbed her waist, startling her. She quickly relaxed as Massimo wrapped his arms around her. Zuri held onto his arms and leaned her head back, resting it on his shoulder.

"Let's go," Massimo whispered in her ear.

She lifted her head as he released his arms from her waist. He grabbed the two bags from the ground, and they started walking to his safe house.

They arrived at the safe house, which took Zuri's breath away. She thought her safe house was amazing, but Massimo's was astonishing. It was a beautiful above-ground two-story house with a basement, equipped with bullet-proof glass as windows. Outside, it had a terrace and a backyard. The house had four bedrooms and two bathrooms.

As they walked through the front door, Zuri looked around and was in awe of Massimo's taste. He had simple but elegant décor. He had several extra-large canvases by Craig Tracy all over the walls of the house. The living room sat to the right of the house, and the kitchen was all the way down the hall and to the left. There were two staircases, one going from the kitchen to the second floor, and the other from the living room to the basement.

"Custom made, just like yours. It was a hassle having the right people come to create this masterpiece, but you know nothing is impossible for people like us," Massimo said to her as she walked around, admiring the house. "Come with me. Bedrooms are upstairs, and I have a computer up there, so you can take it easy."

They walked upstairs and into the main bedroom. In the room was a long beige couch with a king-sized bed that had a black comforter and pillows. The room had an extended wood desk where a laptop, firearm, and cellphone were laid. There was a white bedside table on each side of the bed, both adorned with an antique lamp on top. To the right of the bed were two doors. One door led to a closet and the second to a bathroom.

Massimo put the two bags on the floor as she collapsed onto the couch. She realized she was sitting on the contents in her back pocket. She reached to take out Paul's phone and wallet. She looked over at Massimo and pointed to the laptop. He walked over to the desk, grabbed the laptop, and handed it to her.

"I'll be right back. Need to coordinate with my security team," he said as he kissed her forehead and headed back downstairs.

Zuri put the laptop next to her and turned on Paul's phone. She realized he must have turned it off after he hung up with whoever he was on the phone with. The phone was unlocked, and Zuri started reading through Paul's messages. She uncovered an airplane love triangle. She could not believe what she was reading.

Paul was dating two women. One girl looked similar to the woman sitting next to Zuri on the plane. From the pictures and text messages, this was going on for a few weeks. Zuri thought back to when her flight neighbor sat down next to her on the flight—she was sweaty and breathing hard.

The other woman, who looked like one of the flight attendants, said in a text how disgusted she was to find him making out with someone else on a flight she was working on. From what Zuri could discern, Paul was on the flight because he and the flight attendant were supposed to be on vacation together. Paul was cheating on the flight attendant with Zuri's flight neighbor. Zuri remembered seeing the flight attendant crying and realized now that must have been the reason why. *Paul was a scumbag.* Zuri was flirting with Paul, not realizing what was right in front of her face. *That's what a cute face will get you. Nothing but trouble.*

She kept reading and saw a few texts from random numbers that were coded. She could not decipher them, and without Paul, it would be useless to try. She checked the call log and saw the recent calls were wiped. The only numbers saved in the phone were the flight attendants and her airplane neighbor. *Weird.*

She turned the phone off and put it down next to the laptop just as Massimo walked back in. He knelt in front of Zuri and said, "Let me take your mind off of the chaos . . ."

7

Going Through the Motions

The next forty-eight hours were a blur for Zuri and Massimo. They barely left the bedroom. It was a relief to be lost in a different world, considering the craziness that reality had lined up for them. There was something exhilarating about Paul's death, or maybe it was just the fact that they were reunited after so long—they were hot for each other.

Words could not describe how much they missed each other. Zuri was reminded of what she loved about him. She felt complete again—this man was the love of her life. She tried to run, not only from the relationship, but from her feelings, but fate brought them back together. She knew Massimo was the only person who could understand her and the only person she wanted to be with at a time like this.

Zuri spent her entire adult life trying to find a replacement for Massimo. She would entertain a cute face and a lousy conversation if any part of the guy reminded her of him. Zuri was starting to get lost in the thoughts in her mind when Massimo walked back into the room. It was his cologne that brought Zuri back to reality.

Massimo strolled back into the room wearing just sweat-pants. He sat down on the edge of the bed. "Z, is everything okay?"

"All good. We just need to figure out our next move," she replied as she got out of bed, wearing his white but-ton-down collar shirt.

"Alright. First, let's get some gear together so we can have our go bag ready and by the door. We can grab what we need and then we can work on a plan for our next steps."

"Let me get dressed," she said as she playfully kissed his cheek and headed for the closet.

Massimo nodded. Zuri walked away slowly as if walk-ing down a runway, and she turned back to see Massimo watching her. She giggled when she saw the smile on his face. She retreated into the closet and got fully dressed. She walked out in a pair of black leggings and a black t-shirt with *Burberry* written across the front. Massimo smiled when he saw her. He had put on a plain black t-shirt during the time Zuri was getting dressed. He stood up, kissed her on the lips, and grabbed her hand as he led her downstairs, all the way to the basement.

The basement was where Massimo kept all his weapons and computers. They stopped in front of the only door in the basement, which had a fingerprint scanner. "Go ahead," he said, signaling for Zuri to use her fingerprint.

She put her thumb on the scanner, and to her surprise, the door unlocked. She looked at Massimo and smiled. She stood there coming to the realization that regardless of all that transpired, he truly loved her. He was her knight in shining armor and time or distance could not change that.

"If there was ever a doubt in your mind, and I know there was some doubt in my mind, I want us to forget it. How we left things is in the past, and we have another chance to change the future. You're my true love, Z. Your safety, your life, your heart, and your love—mean the world to me," Massimo said, staring into her eyes.

She wondered why she ever wanted to let him go. *He is worth fighting for.* The memories from the past began to circulate in her mind. There were good times but then came the bad times. The darkness of the past occupied her thoughts, shifting her mood. Her smile slowly turned into a frown, and she quickly turned away, pushing open the unlocked door and proceeding into the room.

The lights in the room automatically turned on, and Zuri was intrigued by the complexity of the room. His walls were covered with firearms. To the back left of the room sat computers. Next to the computers were monitors that looked bigger than the ones Zuri had in her safe room. *Maybe it is just the size of the room that makes it look bigger.* On a table adjacent to the monitors were images from the surveillance cameras that surrounded the perimeter of the house. There were several glass-enclosed tables that held all the weapons and gear one could imagine.

Zuri walked around and saw a glass table with smaller weapons and bulletproof vests. She looked until she spotted the smaller-sized ones. Zuri grabbed one of them and put it on. She knew this could be a war. Whoever was targeting her would not stop until she was dead. There were people out there who hated her, and it was time for her to go out there and face them. In order to do that, she needed to get geared up and start making plans for the road ahead. She believed if you stayed ready, you didn't have to get ready—Massimo taught her that.

Massimo walked over to her and helped her strap the vest on. Then he grabbed a vest to fit on himself. At the firearms, Zuri grabbed four pieces along with additional magazines for each. One gun was on her hip, her favorite, the S&P Shield. She put another one on the front of her vest, a Glock 17, one on her thigh, a Sig Sauer P210, one on her ankle, a Kahr P380, and one on her back, a Beretta APX. She was geared and ready to go.

Just as she put the last gun in the holster and Massimo had finished grabbing his own weapons, they heard an alarm go off, signaling that someone had breached the perimeter. Zuri ran to the cameras to see how many people were out there and counted seven. She noticed a flash of a decal, but she could not make out what type of decal it was. She wondered if this was who Paul was on the phone with. *How the hell did they find me? Shit, the phone.* After she checked the text messages, she turned the phone off, but she should have destroyed it from the beginning. They probably tracked the phone when Zuri turned it on to read the messages.

Zuri deviously looked at Massimo. "Tell your team to stand down. I want us to take care of them. It will be like old times."

"Luckily for us, my team is away. I told them to stand down shortly after we arrived because I wanted you all to myself. Plus, we are a dynamic duo. Hundreds of kills under our belt, we're unstoppable," he said, winking at her. "It will be like old times. This is what we trained for, and honestly, we could do this in our sleep."

"And the timing couldn't be any better. We are ready to go." Zuri smiled, grabbed her S&P from her hip holster, and held it by her side. "Get in front of me, babe."

Massimo stood in front of her, and she put her left hand on his right shoulder. They had not worked together this way in years, but he was right, they trained for this and much more. *This really does feel like old times.*

Zuri double-tapped his shoulder, signaling for him to advance, quietly walking out the door and starting up the stairs to clear the house. Zuri could not believe how in sync they were.

As they slowly continued, she realized some of the individuals were already in the house. They could both hear the footsteps regardless of how quiet it may have been to a normal person. The darkness heightened their senses.

"Clear," Zuri whispered as they made it halfway through the first floor.

"Clear," Massimo said.

A few seconds later, there were numerous gunshots—*bang, bang, bang, bang.*

They had killed eight people so far, including Paul, and were not any closer to finding out who killed the unaccounted-for individuals on the plane. After they finished clearing the house and taking care of the intruders, they went back into the basement, cleaned the weapons, refilled the magazines, and packed the go bag, as they had initially planned to do.

They walked upstairs and placed the bag in the living room. Zuri could smell the gunpowder in the air. Before they headed upstairs to the bedroom, Massimo made another call to his clean-up crew, so they could come over and take care of the mess Massimo and Zuri left in the kitchen where most of the bodies were, with the exception of the two near the bottom of the staircase. Once Massimo hung up the phone, he headed for the bedroom. Zuri followed suit, stepping over the bodies.

The bodies didn't bother her. What really bothered Zuri was her carelessness when she allowed Paul to come to the safe house with her. Either way, they were no longer compromised, and no one else had visibility into her and Massimo's whereabouts—Massimo made sure of it. Zuri was happy that Massimo was with her and she was not doing this alone. She was exhausted again but his presence made her feel relaxed.

As they entered the bedroom, Massimo went to the bathroom, and Zuri closed the bedroom door before following Massimo into the bathroom. The main bathroom had a similar setup to hers. There was a huge tub and shower combo with marble-heated floors and double sinks. Massimo walked over to the tub and turned on the faucet. *He knows me so well.* Zuri undressed and got into the bath to get cleaned up after what seemed like a productive day of killing. Massimo's phone rang, and he picked up the call, leaving the bathroom and closing the door behind him.

By the time Massimo returned, Zuri was lying in the tub, soaking her physical pain away. When he entered the bathroom, Zuri's head whipped around, breaking her preoccupation with what had transpired earlier that day.

"You okay, Z? These last seventy-two hours have been rough."

"You can say that again."

Massimo walked over and noticed her rubbing the scar on her hand. He leaned over to give her a kiss and then knelt by the tub. "Take all the time you need. You deserve some relaxation." Massimo kissed her again, stood up, and walked out of the bathroom. A few minutes later, he returned with a filled glass and an opened bottle of Château Latour, Pauillac. No words were exchanged as he gave Zuri the glass, put the bottle on the floor, and left. Zuri was so happy that he remembered that after a kill, she liked to enjoy silence and a soak. The wine was a bonus.

Zuri sipped the wine, and after she finished the glass, she put it on the floor next to the bottle and laid the back of her head on the tub, closing her eyes. *Four days later and I am not any closer to finding out what is happening to my life.* Zuri began to doze off as the thought floated into her mind.

8

The Flight Attendant

It was a rainy fall day when Zuri turned over to look at the clock, 3:10 a.m. She hated when she woke up earlier than her 6 a.m. alarm, but a quick bathroom break and a glass of water were usually what she needed to get back to sleep. She rolled out of bed with her mind feeling foggy but did her best to shrug it off as she headed to the bathroom.

When Zuri came back into the bedroom, she heard a noise but ignored it. This was UQ's house, so she was used to people coming and going at all times of the night. She trekked downstairs to get a drink of water, and this time, she heard voices. Zuri wandered toward them. It was coming from the meeting room on the second floor. Zuri sat on the stairs and listened.

She knew she could always learn things from listening to her grandfather. UQ spoke like a poet. Zuri admired the way he could make the room fill up with emotion, whether it was sadness, happiness, or anger. UQ had a way of commanding the room with his words. She hoped that by being around him, she could learn to speak like he did, walk like he did, and grab attention like he did. She tried to duplicate his persona every so often when talking to people, and she started to notice her ability to command attention. It was exhilarating.

Most of all, Zuri admired UQ's attention to detail and his reasoning for doing the things he did. UQ was a man of few words. His philosophy was that he may be a mobster, but he was working to rid the Earth of scum. UQ only killed people who did bad things—murderers, rapists, pedophiles, and drug dealers. Zuri knew that UQ had a complex. He believed that even though he may not have been running the most lawful organization, he was running an organization that the world needed. Even though some would say he wasn't doing good in the eyes of the public, he was doing this work for the greater good—a necessary exterminator.

UQ started raising his voice, causing Zuri to get out of her thoughts and listen intently. "Never come back into this house and talk about this again. She does not know—and can never know." Zuri was confused about what was happening. Usually, these conversations were business, not personal. *Who is he referring to?*

"Death is a part of life. In this business, I have to be ruthless. There is no room for emotion—she'll understand when she takes over," UQ stated. The room fell silent.

Zuri looked up and saw no movement. She slowly got up and walked back to her room. *Death? Who died? Or better yet, who was killed?* Zuri knew that she was in line to take over the business. She rubbed the scar on her hand, annoyed by her oblivion. *Was someone else supposed to take over?*

The sun had just come up, and Zuri was in the computer room looking through files over and over again. She was replaying the plane ride in her head, trying to figure out what details were missing. Zuri pulled the manifesto from the flight and was looking for familiar names or aliases. She was looking for anything that would jog her memory. She circled the three names of the dead individuals, then she circled Sophia's and Paul's names. Then she went back to analyzing the lists.

Zuri was able to pull the list of flight attendants who were on the flight. There were six flight attendants on the plane that day. Zuri did not remember seeing all six, but she did fall asleep pretty early on. She was able to identify four of the six flight attendants, specifically the two who were embedded in her memory—the one flight attendant who was crying and the other flight attendant who was comforting the crying one. She knew now this was probably due to Paul's shenanigans.

Zuri heard Massimo's footsteps coming toward her, so she started to speak. "I remember seeing Marcy Evelien crying on the flight and another flight attendant was comforting her. This was shortly after I went to the restroom, around three. At that time, three of the bathrooms were already occupied. I am assuming that this means the murder happened between midnight and 3 a.m. During that time,

I was pretty much sleeping because you know I love my sleep! The only constants on the flight were Paul—who is now dead—and Sophia, the girl in the seat next to me."

Massimo considered this as he stood in the doorway. "You mentioned her being all hot and sweaty as well as changing her clothes—maybe she was involved in one of the murders . . . or all of them. She obviously isn't a suspect in the investigation that the police are currently working on, just based on the files they have in their database. Let's take this one step at a time, though. First, let's find this flight attendant, Marcy. Then we can worry about Sophia." Massimo walked over, pulled a chair out, and sat next to Zuri. He started to dig for information on where Marcy would be staying. He came across the name of Marcy's Aunt, who lived in the 5th arrondissement near the Pantheon but couldn't find Marcy. Massimo printed a list of all the hotels in that area. They had a feeling that she had to be staying close to her aunt for comfort but not *with* her aunt because police officers would definitely have checked there first.

Massimo and Zuri both knew that she had not been tracked down by officers yet, which meant she had to have moved around Paris under a different name—if she even was still in Paris. Massimo searched for any aliases Marcy may have had, but the search yielded no results.

After an hour of investigating, they came across a news article about a brutal beating and rape that took place years ago. It was a young girl named Rachel Antoinette Myers who had similar attributes to Marcy. Zuri looked over at Massimo. "If she was this Myers girl, she would want to stay hidden."

"There is only one way to find out. Let's go get ready," Massimo said as he stood up, grabbing the printed list.

"Let's do it. But first, I need your help with something."

"Sure, anything."

"I think it's time for a new haircut," Zuri said as she tugged on her hair. She stood and kissed him.

Massimo smiled and followed Zuri up to the second-floor bathroom. Standing in front of the mirror, Massimo helped Zuri cut her hair into a bob. When he was done, Zuri curled her hair so the bob had volume. Content with her new haircut and style, Zuri got dressed, wearing a black pant suit with white Louis Vuitton pumps and a white Louis Vuitton bag. Zuri was unrecognizable with makeup, shades, and a new haircut. She loved wearing her hair in a bob because it was usually down her back, so this was a nice change of pace. Massimo, in turn, wore a navy-blue Louis Vuitton suit, accompanied by a black dress shirt and black Velasca Giacalustra Oxford leather shoes. Zuri looked over at Massimo and grinned. Somehow, they always found themselves unintentionally coordinated.

After they checked themselves out in the mirror one last time, Zuri and Massimo walked back downstairs. When Massimo opened the front door for Zuri, she gasped. In the driveway sat a beautiful white BMW M5 with tinted windows. Zuri was ecstatic. She was starting to feel like how she did years ago when she was young and in love, parading around Italy with Massimo in beautiful cars.

They made their way to the car, and Massimo opened the door for Zuri to get in. Inside the car were black leather seats. *Royalty.* Massimo got into the car, and they headed to the 5th arrondissement. It was a short drive so Zuri spent time calling the hotels on the printed list. Zuri knew Marcy would not use her real name or her pseudonym, so she tried to brainstorm what name to ask for. She had no idea, so she settled on asking for a Ms. Marcy Myers. She lucked out because only one hotel had a Myers staying in it. *Jackpot.*

Massimo got out of the car and opened the door for Zuri. He put his hand out, which she grabbed. They walked into the Hôtel des Grands Hommes. She remembered book-marking this hotel when she was preparing for her trip to Paris. She greeted the man at the front desk and explained to him that she was surprising Ms. Myers. "She's our sister," she told the attendant. Massimo nodded. "Today is her birthday, and we told her we would not be able to make it, but here we are. We would like to surprise her in her room, so please don't tell her we've arrived."

Before the man could answer, Zuri pulled out two pass-ports. One with her name, well *one* of her names, Zuri Myers, as well as Massimo's passport. It had the name Maximus Myers. Zuri looked back at Massimo and smiled. Massimo returned her smile with a weird look, trying to figure out where the passports came from. Zuri turned back around and handed the attendant the passports.

The attendant checked both passports and suddenly beamed. "What a nice surprise. Let me get you a room key. We also had a complimentary bottle of wine we were going to bring up as a thank-you, since she was staying with us for an extended period. Would you like to take it up?"

"Yes, please," Zuri said. "We just flew in from London. This is going to be such a great surprise. We haven't seen each other in several years."

The man handed Zuri the key and the wine, and in return, Zuri handed the man five hundred euros. She and Massimo got on the elevator and went up to the sixth floor, going straight to Marcy's door.

Massimo was looking around and whispered, "There is a camera at the end of the hall."

Zuri nodded but did not say anything as she proceeded to key into the room. She carefully tried not to knock the 'Do Not Disturb' sign off the handle when she turned it to enter.

They were startled when they saw how messy the room was. Zuri walked in further, and Massimo closed the door behind him, double-checking the 'Do Not Disturb' sign was still in its rightful place. They looked at each other, then back at the room. It looked as if Rachel was in a hurry to go somewhere.

The room was a suite. It had a lounge sofa area to the right. Across from the front door was a door to the balcony area, which contained tables and chairs as well as a view of the Pantheon. Once in the room, there was a desk, a set of drawers, and a bed. Past the bed was the bathroom, which had a shower and tub ensemble.

Zuri and Massimo started searching the room, looking for anything that could unveil the mystery of who Marcy was and what her connection might be to either the victims from flight RD4379 or Zuri. Massimo walked over to the closet and opened it. He saw a safe and was overjoyed because he was an expert at cracking safes. Thirty seconds later, the safe was open. In the safe were three stacks of ten thousand dollars in cash, a Cartier diamond ring, and a few miscellaneous documents.

"There is thirty thousand dollars here and a diamond ring that costs about one hundred and fifty to two hundred thousand dollars. What was she doing with this amount of money and this custom ring?" Massimo looked at Zuri. "Something is not right. She is a flight attendant, and honestly, she should not be able to afford these items."

"Maybe these documents can explain the reason for her having these items," Zuri said as she walked past Massimo and grabbed the miscellaneous papers. While reading, Zuri strolled over to the bed to sit down. Some of the documents were in French, which she knew how to read, but the rest were in English. There was information on one of the men who was murdered. The man's boarding pass, passport picture, the names of all his family members, and his home address were also with the documents. Marcy had an extensive file on this guy. Right as Zuri was about to give up her search, seeing nothing that would explain the ring or money, she saw a final page that revealed a little more than his flight schedule—the man was a sexual predator, and Marcy had a list of females who had been attacked by him.

Zuri looked at Massimo, smiling. *We are finally one step closer to solving this puzzle.* "We found motive. Marcy has to be this Rachel girl or why else would she have all this information on one guy?" Zuri pulled out her phone to take pictures of the files in case they were interrupted and had to flee. She then kept reading. Not only was this guy a sexual predator, but he was also wanted by numerous underground mobs for murder, arson, and a dozen sexual assaults. Zuri looked at Massimo. "Have you heard of this guy before?" She extended the picture in her hand toward Massimo's direction.

He walked over to where Zuri was sitting and studied the photo. "Yes actually. He is a low-life criminal. I came across him when we were in Washington D.C. I decided he was not worth the trouble of killing. There were so many murder contracts on him—and he personally did not interfere with our business—so I left him alone. I knew someone would get to him eventually."

Zuri looked at Massimo suspiciously. *That response was not like him.* If there was one thing UQ was, it was proactive. He never let a kill go nor allowed other people to take what he believed was his. *UQ instilled that into both of us, so why would Massimo let this man go?* In all these years, Zuri could still tell when Massimo was lying. His tell, the movement, was so faint that only Zuri ever noticed that his left nostril flared slightly when he lied. Eyes narrowed, she continued staring at him and said, "Try again. Why are you lying to me?"

As Massimo was about to answer, they heard the door click. Marcy walked in and threw several shopping bags on the sofa to the right. She had her dirty blonde hair in a ponytail and was wearing a beautiful red collared jumpsuit and white flat leather Prada sandals.

Massimo and Zuri were by the bed and realized there was no point in hiding. Massimo slowly walked toward Marcy whose back was turned to them as she was ruffling through the bags she threw down. Massimo paused as Marcy started to turn around. She saw them both and froze. She looked at Zuri who cautiously stood up, then at Massimo, then at the door, which was only a few feet away from her. The room fell still before Marcy panickily lurched for the door. Massimo was just as fast and stood in front of it, blocking her from leaving. He grabbed her hand off the handle.

Marcy stepped back toward the balcony and said, "Please don't hurt me. I did everything you asked."

Zuri walked over to Marcy with the files in her hand. "Calm down. We're not here to hurt you. We just want to know what is going on. What do you mean that you did everything we asked? Do you know who we are?"

Marcy did not say anything. From the look on her face, they could tell she was petrified. Zuri walked closer and dropped the files on the floor in front of Marcy's feet, which had the picture of the man paperclipped to the front of the file. "This guy was found dead on our flight. I'm assuming you killed him. My question is, if you killed him, why did you do it?"

Marcy relaxed her shoulders and spit on the man's picture. "He was scum. I reached out to have someone kill him. You know, a contract killer on the dark web. Instead, they sent me a package. No name and no return address. The box was just sitting on my front doorstep one evening. Inside the box was money, the ring, a gun, and a note with instructions. The money was to buy what I needed to carry out the killing. They told me to pawn the ring so I could use that money to disappear. The gun came with a silencer. At the end of the note, there was a warning that said 'Take care of it yourself. Stop making other people clean up your mess. You have seventy-two hours, or you'll be dead.'" Marcy stepped on the man's picture and walked to the bed where she sat down.

"What did they mean by that?" Zuri asked.

"That guy," Marcy said, pointing to the picture on the floor, "was responsible for the rape and murder of multiple women. The pattern started with me. I was the first one. My name is Rachel Antoinette Myers, but I changed it to Marcy Evelien when I was older. I could not stand the look people gave me when they realized I was *that* girl." She stood up and started pacing back and forth near the foot of the bed. "I will never forget that day. He was ready to kill me, but he got startled when my neighbor came to check in on me. She knocked on the door, calling my name. It was dark out, and I feared that if she used the key to come in, he would attack her. But he did what I did not expect him to do—he ran out the back door."

Anger flashed on Zuri's face as Marcy continued.

"He brutally raped and beat me. I could not walk for six months. I needed multiple surgical procedures to fix my broken leg and arm. I need several rounds of plastic surgery to fix my face from the extensive beating that left harsh bruising—I'm lucky to be alive." As Marcy said that last sentence, a glimmer of hope spread across her face, but it quickly disappeared. "The police got involved, and there were two detectives who were working the case. Because of the multiple surgeries, I was heavily sedated for a number of weeks. The detectives tried to work through the crime scene and find out what they could, but they needed me to fill in the blanks for them. There were no fingerprints and no DNA left at the scene."

Marcy paused and pulled her hair out of the ponytail, allowing her hair to fall gracefully down her back. She stopped pacing and didn't make eye contact with Zuri or Massimo but just stared at the photo on the ground. "By the time I was finally able to talk, my rapist had become more creative and was actually killing people. There were seven other teenage girls; each attack more gruesome than the last, and each one burned to death except for the sixth girl. When he set her house on fire, she mustered up the energy to crawl to the kitchen. By a miracle, she survived but suffered severe burns to her legs and arms. She was in a coma for weeks, which was enough time for him to strike again. *But* the silver lining was when she came into the hospital, they were able to pull DNA from her body. She was the only reason they caught the guy. He was arrested, tried, and sentenced to fifteen years for the attempted murder, rape, and arson of that one girl. While they were able to match his modus operandi, they could not get him on any of the other murders because he burnt the victims in their apartments, and he had strong alibis for each incident. She was the only one besides me to live."

"Wait, I heard about this guy. They called him "The Fire Rapist" and I remember when they found the DNA evidence. The authorities were finally relieved to have caught the guy even if he was only charged for one girl" Zuri said.

Marcy sat back down on the bed. Tears started to form in her eyes, and she allowed them to fall down her cheek. "Yes. That was him. So, imagine my disappointment when I think they finally got the guy, only to find out it was the wrong one. It was a setup. A fall guy. My thoughts, the real killer hired the fall guy to take his place. I spent years trying to find my rapist, and after paying several private investigators, we found the real perpetrator. I found out he was flying to Paris—I knew I finally had him."

Zuri and Massimo looked at each other. Zuri sat down on the chair by the desk, and Massimo moved the bags from the sofa to the floor and sat.

"I knew a corrections officer who would see the fall guy every shift. This C.O. would report back to me what this guy was doing, who he was hanging out with, who he made phone calls to, and everything else to keep me intertwined in his life. I felt this need to be close to him without him ever knowing. Trauma bonding, they call it. Anyway, after a while, I mustered up the energy to pay this fall guy a visit at the prison. Once I visited him, I knew they got the wrong guy. It was his eyes; his eyes were filled with hope—the man who attacked me had the eyes of the devil.

I spent ten years in my house, caged like an animal. I did not leave for fear of being attacked again. I spent countless hours searching for this guy. I kept reaching out to one of the detectives every few months trying to see if there was a break in the case. For some reason, the case haunted him as much as it haunted me because he eventually started working the case off the clock with me. He kept reassuring me that he was dedicating his free time to trying to find this guy. It was against the rules, but he told me a story about how all detectives have at least one case that keeps them up at night—one case that haunts them."

Marcy paused and stared at the ground. She looked lost in thought. Massimo looked at Zuri, and Zuri met his gaze.

They knew exactly what the detective meant. Between Massimo and Zuri, they had several "cases" like that—people who they killed that showed up in their dreams and haunted them. They quickly turned back to face Marcy when she started speaking again. "Little did I realize that with the detective's support, I began feeling like myself again. I was going to counseling and group therapy. It was working until I found out who and where my rapist was." Marcy started crying again so she signaled to them that she was going to the bathroom. She rose from the bed and walked to the bathroom, her shoulders moving uncontrollably with her cries. They could hear her blow her nose, and she walked back out picking up right where she left off.

"I decided to become a flight attendant so I could travel and get out of the United States. Every now and again, I fly back to New York to watch a Broadway show, but most of my flights are in Europe. One day, the detective called me and told me there might be a break in the case. He said he found a pseudonym that my rapist was using, and he told me the name. He also told me that this man would be on a flight coming to Paris. After a lot of negotiating and a few white lies, I was able to switch with another flight attendant so I could be on the same flight as this man. It was time to face him once and for all. After realizing I could not get someone else to kill him, I knew I had to do it on the flight. Some would call it luck or a coincidence—my belief, I think the person who sent me that note made sure that we would be on the flight together. I know it makes no sense, but I needed to believe that this was meant to be. I had to believe that the powers that be put this in play for me."

Marcy started pacing again. Zuri and Massimo knew she was about to talk about the murder. They both shifted to the edge of their seats, listening even more intently. "He didn't recognize me. I knew I had to set a honey trap, so I was kind to him, flirted with him, winked at him each time I walked by, and that was all it took to lure him to the back of the plane when everyone was sleeping. I was the only flight attendant awake because we were taking shifts. I told him that I was looking for some fun, and him being a man, he agreed. I pushed him into the bathroom and locked the door. We started making out. My skin was crawling, and when I couldn't take it anymore, I pulled out the knife and stabbed him in the neck three times. He looked at me shocked while he grabbed his neck—he bled out in a matter of seconds. I left him in there and marked the stall as occupied. We have showers toward the front of the plane, so I took a shower and washed the blood off. I put on a new uniform and threw the soiled clothes into my duffle bag."

Marcy walked toward the closet, dragging out the duffle bag and placing it on the floor. She kneeled down and unzipped the bag, pulling out the bloody clothes to show Zuri and Massimo. "I don't know what to do now. I only killed him because he needed to die or I would . . . I still don't feel . . . I feel more trapped. I thought this would give me closure—it didn't. I just don't know what to do."

Zuri stood up and took off her blazer and shoes so she could be more comfortable. She walked over to Marcy, knelt beside her, and hugged her tightly, feeling Marcy's tears fall on her shirt. "I'm sorry for what you went through. We'll help you." Zuri released Marcy who seemed relieved to have these two strangers be her guardian angels. Zuri grabbed the papers that were on the floor along with the duffle bag as she stood up. She walked the papers and bag to Massimo before she turned back around to address Marcy. "Marcy, thank you for your honesty. Before we figure out next steps, I just need to ask you a few questions. First, do you know a Paul Black?"

"I don't. Who is he?" Marcy said as she stood up, wiping the remaining tears from her face.

"No one who you need to be worried about. Second, on the flight, I remembered seeing you crying with another flight attendant. Do you mind sharing what that was about?"

"Oh, yeah. I remember that. It was because of my mom. One of the passengers in economy reminded me of my mom, and it made me miss her. That flight attendant is one of my close friends, and she had been there for all the funerals. It was hard for me. Still is."

Zuri nodded as the pieces of the puzzle were becoming clearer. "Third, do you remember if you saw anything suspicious on the flight?"

"Not that I recall. After my crying episode, my friend, the other flight attendant, told me to take over first class while she took economy. It was for the best because I don't think I would've been able to serve passengers with tears running down my face," Marcy said, cracking a smile.

"Last question, how many people know about the assault?"

"Only the detectives and district attorney who worked on the case. They interviewed me hoping that my case would be used, but between the alibi and the statute of limitations—there was nothing they could do."

"Okay, good. No one knows what this man did, but maybe we need to get this information out to the media so it can show that he made a lot of enemies. You need to disappear. Is there anywhere you can go? Lay low until this blows over? Once they realize his past, they will investigate, but no one will feel sorry for this man," Zuri said.

"I can stay at my aunt's place," Marcy replied.

Massimo stepped in and said, "Let's change the narrative. Marcy, you should turn yourself in and let them know what happened. Tell them that he recognized you and was trying to finish what he started. He pushed you into the restroom and tried to kill you. You were able to get the knife out of his hands, and you stabbed him."

Zuri looked at Massimo and then to Marcy. Deep down, Zuri knew Massimo was right, and she trusted his judgment, sometimes more than her own. She was thinking impulsively, while Massimo was thinking strategically. "He's right. That might be your best bet," Zuri said. Zuri proceeded to talk Marcy through what to say and how to say it. Zuri worked with a lot of international lawyers and had a connection to one in Paris. She called him and told him what was going on, and he agreed to represent Marcy. "You'll be okay," Zuri said to her as she grabbed her hand. "I have worked with this attorney before. He will help you and keep you safe. I trust him."

Marcy started crying and profusely thanked them for their help. "I was just so scared. I didn't know what to do."

Zuri grabbed her tight and reassured her again that it would be okay.

After a few hours of conversation, strategizing, and planning, Massimo and Zuri left Marcy in her hotel room, drunk and sleepy. As per their discussion, on their way out, they grabbed the duffle bag, the files, and the note, and left her with the bloody clothes, the money, and the ring. They put the bloody clothes into a plastic bag so the lawyer would have the evidence for her case. They left the money so Marcy could pay for the lawyer, and they left the ring so Marcy could pay for a fresh start.

Zuri and Massimo got into the elevator in silence.

Massimo grabbed Zuri and kissed her forehead. "If anything happened to you, I don't know what I would do. I am so thankful that your grandfather gave you the tools to survive. I worry less because of it."

Zuri smiled and hugged him. "Ditto."

9

Time Equilibrium

Massimo and Zuri headed back to the safe house. *This day was not wasted.* It had been almost a week since the murders. They had been able to solve one, but it took them longer than she expected. Zuri would say that since Massimo arrived, it had been better for her thought process and investigative skills. They needed to figure out who the last two people were, and why Zuri of all people was being framed for a crime she did not commit.

After a long day, both Zuri and Massimo liked to listen to music and ride in silence. Zuri enjoyed car rides with him; they were connecting and bonding without even saying a word. Her mind went further away than usual as she softly rubbed the scar on her hand. She thought back to a time when she almost died. The memory was so vivid. Zuri was in the second grade, and her father was driving her to school. She remembered that they stopped at the final stop sign just before her school, and that is when "Dance with

My Father" by Luther Vandross started playing. She loved that song—it was such a classic, and it reminded her about how awesome her own father was.

Anytime that song came on when they were together, her father always teared up. At the time, Zuri did not understand why, she just thought it was because he loved the song. Her father, on the other hand, knew the inevitable would happen. Eventually, he and Zuri would be apart, and that song and their memories would be the only thing she would have to hold on to. If anything, it would be a reminder of the love they had for each other.

The car came to a halt as Zuri's father parked in front of her elementary school. Zuri kissed her father on the cheek with excitement, said goodbye, unbuckled her seatbelt, and opened the door. Zuri had one foot out of the car when a white van with tinted windows crashed into the back of their car. Zuri was ejected from her seat. When they brought her to the hospital, they found she was suffering from severe brain swelling and a broken hand and leg and ended up being in a coma for two weeks. It was touch and go for a while, and the doctors believed she might not make it. Both her parents were Godly individuals, and she remembered hearing her mother pray for her while she was in a coma—faint sounds, but sounds nonetheless.

Zuri believed the prayers were what kept her alive. She also clearly remembered the pain she felt, both physically and emotionally. It was one of her first traumatic memories. It took her months of physical therapy to get back to her normal self. She still had the scar from the hand surgery. It was the scar she always rubbed when she felt vulnerable or anxious.

Massimo grabbed her arm. "Don't worry, babe. We will get through this."

Zuri knew that Massimo knew what it meant when she rubbed her scar. He always knew what she was thinking and what she needed for her anxiety levels to go down. She grabbed his hand and kissed it. "I know babe. We always do."

Night had come quickly and Zuri was exhausted. It felt like days since she slept. When they got home, Zuri went straight to the bedroom and noticed the time, 9:18 p.m. She went into the bathroom for a shower. After her shower, she went and grabbed the gun from the desk and put it on her nightstand. She always slept with a gun there. Zuri then proceeded to get into bed and cry. *I fought so hard to leave the life of being an assassin behind, but it seems like the life won't let me go.*

Massimo walked into the bedroom and noticed the tears on Zuri's face. He climbed into the bed and held her close, causing more tears to fall down her face.

"You make me feel safe," Zuri told him between the sniffles.

He kissed her forehead and said, "I will never let anyone hurt you again, I swear. Get some rest. I have a few calls to make, then I will join you."

It was 10:56 p.m. when Massimo tucked her into bed and she dozed off. Zuri was a light sleeper at times, but when she was really tired or feeling depressed, nothing could wake her up.

Zuri woke up groggy and disoriented. She turned to look at the time and saw it was 9:02 a.m. She turned to feel for Massimo, but he was not there. Zuri laid on her back and stared at the ceiling. There was something weird about her dreams that night. She remembered a vision of Massimo trying to kill her, a dream about UQ dancing with her on her wedding day, and another dream about Massimo and UQ when they were younger. Zuri wiped her eyes and attempted to clear her mind. She hated vivid dreams like that; they always made her think something bad was going to happen.

As she got up to stretch, she heard a loud *bang*. Zuri grabbed her gun from the nightstand and headed for the door. She held the gun in front of her, maneuvering through each doorway. Silently, she shifted from area to area, not seeing or hearing anything. She cleared the entire second floor and then headed down the stairs. She heard movement at the bottom of the stairs, coming from the kitchen. She got to the bottom, gun pointed, and stopped when she realized it was Massimo. Zuri lowered the gun. "You scared me, dummy. What are you doing?"

"Trying to make you breakfast, beautiful. I dropped the pancake on the floor while trying to flip it. Then the frying pan smacked against the stove. It burnt me, but I'm fine. I definitely am a better cook than I was when we were together, but flipping pancakes is the one thing I haven't mastered."

Zuri giggled and put her gun on the kitchen counter. "Thanks, baby. I cannot wait to taste what you put together." Zuri kissed him on the cheek and walked down the hall and into the living room. She sat on the sofa and turned on the TV, flipping through the channels, looking for a mindless soap opera. She realized it was too early in the morning for soap operas, so she put on the news. The news coverage was talking more about the protests, and it was just about to change to the meteorologist's report when a breaking news banner flashed on the screen in French. "Breaking news, police officers are one step closer to finding all the individuals who were involved in the flight murders. We turn it over to Lieutenant Grey, who is leading the search."

"Good morning. As of last night, we have made major updates in the investigation of the flight murders. We have one individual in custody, who has confessed to killing one of the individuals found dead. The D.A. has declined to press charges due to the overwhelming evidence of self-defense. Through our investigation, we found that one of the dead individuals we originally suspected as a victim was actually *not* a victim at all, but a perpetrator. He is said to be responsible for multiple rape and murders that occurred in the United States. We have teamed up with the Federal Bureau of Investigations and local police to get a better understanding of the extent of his crimes. Due to the severity of his crimes, we will not reveal the identity of the perpetrator until all victims and their families have been notified. We will also not reveal the identity of the individual who confessed because she was one of his victims as well."

Zuri stood up but kept staring at the TV.

"There was a second individual who was found dead earlier this morning. After help from the FBI, we were able to find incriminating information in his emails, specifically pointing to a plan and scheme to carry out a murder. He was responsible for the death of the second victim on the plane. His name was Paul Black, and the victim's name was Sherry Moore. Paul Black was a day trader at XEA Capital. Sherry Moore was a schoolteacher and mother of two. There is still one suspect at large who we believe killed the final victim on the plane. If anyone has any information on Zuri Dawson, please give us a call. Back to you Alexandre—"

Zuri muted the TV. "Massimo!"

Massimo came running down the hall. "What's going on?"

"Why did the police just find Paul's body on the street?" she asked, looking at him furiously. "You did this?" She pointed to the screen. "You took his body and did this?!"

"Yeah, I did. We needed him to be found to throw the detectives off of you. I thought we were on the same page about this, so why does it matter that I did that? Also, if I remember correctly, he was trying to hurt you. I don't know why you seem so bothered by it. It's your name we're trying to clear."

Zuri sat down and thought about what Massimo said. *There is more to this than clearing my name.* "Who was he to you? The day you arrived, you didn't acknowledge him.

There was something going on there. Be honest with me. How did you know him?"

Massimo sat on the coffee table directly in front of Zuri. He grabbed her hands. "Here is the true story—no bullshit. A year after you left, I was spiraling. But I had an organization to run, and there was no time to waste. After I was settled in, I decided I had enough resources to find out what happened to my mom. I had already lost everything that was dear to me, most importantly, you, and I just wanted some closure. So, I went and tried to find my mom, and I actually did. She was in Wisconsin. I found out that she was a government agent who was on the run. When she left me, with my alcoholic dad, it was only because she was snatched up and transferred to a safe location. I called her, but she didn't answer. I proceeded to leave her a voicemail, giving her my address and personal phone number, saying if she changes her mind and wants to get in touch, this is how she can find me. She never called me back but instead, she sent me a coded postcard.

Under the stamp, at the upper right-hand of the postcard, was a microdot. In the dot, she wrote a message where she discussed what happened, where she had been, and where she currently was. She asked me to come get her and free her from her life. I went because I knew I could keep her safe in Italy. I had the ability to get her out and off the grid. I gathered my team, and we went to the safe house. We arrived at the same time the first of Paul's team arrived. We started shooting, they shot back. All we were doing was trying to rescue my mom, but Paul and his team thought we were trying to kill them. Paul's team got them out of the house, and they ran to an unmarked SUV. I tried to call out to her, but the gunfire was too loud. Paul's team got her and a few other people into the SUV. As Paul was running to the car, it exploded. At that very moment, I had truly lost everything." Tears fell down his face.

Zuri's eyes were watering. "I am so sorry. I am so sorry, babe. I had no idea." Zuri hugged him tight then let go and wiped the tears from his cheek. "I'm sorry that I was not there for you. Please forgive me," Zuri pleaded.

"Forgive you for what?"

"Forgive me for not being there for you. I had no idea the pain Paul caused you and losing your mom after finding her after so many years—I should've been there for you."

"It's not on you," Massimo said as tears continued to fall down his face. "I have forgiven you for everything. I love you, and I haven't been the same since you left. But seeing you the other night made me so happy. Everything about you makes me so happy. You complete me," Massimo said as he leaned in to kiss her.

10

Dreams

Zuri yawned as she woke up to her alarm going off. She reached her hand to the nightstand to shut it off, 8 a.m. She turned over to see Massimo fast asleep. Her alarms never bothered him. She got up and went to the bathroom. As she glanced in the mirror, she saw how tired she looked. Even with the sleep she was getting, it did not feel like enough. These last few days had been so emotionally, mentally, and physically draining, especially with the new information she received from Marcy and Massimo.

Yesterday, Massimo told her how Paul was part of the team that was supposed to transfer his mom to safety, but instead, he watched as the SUV his mother entered blow up. Now, she was starting to understand why Massimo had changed so much. UQ hit his peak after grandma died and Massimo hit his peak after he lost everyone—just like Zuri had.

Zuri showered and got ready, putting on a light sweatsuit and heading back downstairs to the tech room. Yesterday, after they finished talking and eating breakfast, they decided to do some more research into the third and final victim. They figured out who he was—his name was Ethan Sparrow. Sparrow was a European diplomat, responsible for breaking the tech world into the EU sector and for the deaths of multiple high-profile families across the world. He was well known but had a nasty past that the U.S. government covered up. They called him "Le Boucher," translating to "The Butcher." Though never proven, The Butcher was known for killing and maiming people the government had an issue with. If you were in the way of the elite, The Butcher was who you had to watch out for—not only did he chop limbs, but he also ate them.

The Butcher was untouchable and heavily protected by the government. Him being dead meant that Zuri was in for a long prison ride. Zuri put her head in her hands, got up, and punched the wall. *Who would frame me to this extent? People will be looking for me at every turn.*

Massimo strolled into the room and sat down next to Zuri. "You okay?"

"Yeah, just frustrated. I am usually able to narrow down suspects and motives. For some reason, I don't understand. This guy was a European diplomat. Whoever did this knew that I would get additional time for killing a diplomat. They knew what they were doing. This is smart. It's strategic. It's diabolical. They also knew that he was tied to the U.S. government, which means he was connected. Why him? Why me?"

"Let me take a look. You might be missing something because you're too emotionally involved and exhausted. Go eat something, and I will try my best to figure it out."

Zuri rolled her eyes because she hated when Massimo called her emotional. "Who wouldn't be emotional at a time like this? Your entire life snatched from you in the blink of an eye. If we don't find the killer soon, my life will be over." Zuri got up, stormed out of the tech room, and went upstairs to the bedroom, leaving Massimo sitting there alone. She grabbed a pillow and screamed into it. *I'm so over this shit!* Zuri laid down, trying to ease her mind while she rubbed her scar. Slowly, she drifted off to sleep.

Zuri was woken up by the smell of food. She sat up, realizing she had fallen asleep, and looked at the time, 2:56 p.m. She must have been really tired and frustrated. She got up and walked downstairs to see that Massimo had prepared a spread for her; bacon, pancakes, eggs, toast, hash browns, corned beef hash, and her all-time favorite, mimosas.

They didn't exchange any words, but she looked at him, and he nodded to the mimosa and plate he had put together for her. She grabbed both, went into the living room, and saw that Massimo had *The Office* on. It was her favorite show and always calmed her down. She sat on the sofa and ate. *Massimo was right. He definitely is a way better cook than when we were together.*

After eating and four mimosas in, she snuggled up and felt her body relax. She missed times like these when she was a regular person with no worries in the world. She didn't remember dozing off again, but she was woken up by a gentle kiss on her forehead. Massimo climbed onto the sofa behind her, cuddling up next to her, and she fell back asleep as Jim Halpert dressed like Dwight said, "Bears. Beets. Battlestar Galactica."

It was 6:16 p.m. and Zuri jumped out of her sleep because someone was about to kill her. Massimo, who was startled, grabbed her and realized she was just having a bad dream. Her heart was racing, sweat dripping down her brow, and she was trying to catch her breath. "Hey, it's okay. It was only a dream," he said as he rubbed her back.

She realized she was lying on his chest and grabbed him tight, not wanting to let go. *Why would my grandfather want to kill me?* Zuri stopped her mind and noticed where she was. Her grandfather was dead. She hated dreams like that.

11

Looking for the Truth

Massimo was able to find that The Butcher had ties in Versailles—a home, a supposed family, and a bunker—so he and Zuri were back on the road, heading to Versailles. Versailles was less than an hour from where the safe house was. If they could just get inside, there may be clues as to who wanted him dead and why. Obviously, someone was able to get to him in a moment of weakness; they just needed to figure out who.

They arrived at the house. It was quiet and deserted as if no one had been there in months. The grass was high and unkept, the yard was trashed, and there were no cars in the driveway. They exited the car, and Zuri grabbed her gun, which was holstered on the side of her right hip. They moved slowly toward the house, searching to see if anyone was around, but there were no movements or sounds. Zuri walked up to the front door and tried the handle—the door was unlocked. She pushed the door open and raised her gun. Massimo signaled to her that he would go around back, and she nodded.

Massimo was able to get into the back door, which was also unlocked. He came inside and cleared the back end of the house. Zuri slowly walked around the house, searching rooms and staying vigilant. She stopped in the kitchen and looked around at the mess that was left behind. Massimo came around the corner.

After clearing the house, they started searching for anything that might point them to clues on why The Butcher was dead. The house looked like it had already been turned over by someone else who may have been looking for the same thing they were. While there was a chance that they would not be able to find anything, they decided to search anyway. The littlest clue was all they needed to find a connection between Zuri and The Butcher. Zuri searched high and low, but besides random papers and junk, she could not find anything.

"Hey, you got to see this!" Massimo yelled from downstairs.

Zuri walked down the stairs toward him, where she saw that he found a hidden door ajar that led to a bunker. The light was on so they pushed the door open further and walked inside to find monitors sitting on a desk and papers scattered everywhere. Zuri's face was on one of the monitors. She stopped dead in her tracks. This was a setup, and The Butcher knew all about it. She walked further into the room toward the monitor. She scrolled through to see what they had on her. They had *everything*. They knew her whole life story—who her family was, the moves she made in the last ten years, and even her different aliases.

One thing Zuri admired about herself is that she was able to scrub her digital footprint at any time. She was confused about how they had access to all this information because she scrubbed often, the last time being right before she left for Paris. This meant she was on their radar for years. She looked through the papers on the floor and saw her grandfather's name. The document was dated twenty years earlier. It seemed as though UQ hired The Butcher to kill a few people. There was a payment receipt for one million five hundred thousand euros wired to The Butcher's account. Zuri held up the paper and asked Massimo, "Did you know?"

He walked over to see what she was talking about. He grabbed the paper and started reading. "Holy crap! I had no idea. UQ stayed away from people like this—but I also know he had a dark side. This must have been one hell of a job for him to reach out to The Butcher."

Zuri continued to look through the papers on the floor, coming across a picture she noticed in the corner of the room. It was a picture of her parents. Zuri started to tear up.

It was a snowy Christmas Eve almost ten years ago, and Zuri's family was getting the house ready for what was going to be one of the largest Christmas celebrations they ever had. Everyone was invited, and Zuri was ecstatic. The days leading up to Christmas were always magical because it was filled with food, decorations, music, and a gathering of friends and family. Her mom ran around the kitchen like always, and her dad helped Zuri finish the last of the decorations. The house looked like a winter wonderland.

Zuri's phone rang, and she pulled it out to see that Massimo was calling. He was checking in and told her that he and UQ would not be able to make it for the holidays. While she was disappointed when she hung up, she understood. Honestly, UQ was never leaving Italy. Italy was his home, and he never spoke to his son, her father, so why would he come down for the holidays? He was a stubborn, old man who only forgave when it was beneficial for him.

Zuri walked over to her mom. "Mom, Massimo said hi and apologized that he may not be able to make it. On the other hand, a few of my friends from college are on the way."

Zuri's mom smiled and nodded. "Let the celebration begin," she said.

The house was packed with people talking, drinking, and having a good time. Zuri lived for days like these—there was nothing more important than family and friends. She always appreciated how close her mom and dad were to her friends' parents. It made for enjoyable dinners and sanctioned sleepovers. The doorbell was ringing constantly as more people joined the party. The night was young, and she was young, which only meant that they would be partying for the next two days.

Zuri grabbed her friends and retreated to her room. They played some music and gossiped about their lives. Simon, her ex-boyfriend, was working for a large tech company, and even though he was not invited due to their fallout, it was nice to hear from her other friends that life was going well for him. One of her friends was doing nothing but shopping and living her best life. While two others were preparing for new journeys—one moving to New Zealand while the other was starting a new job at a law firm in January.

Zuri was about to start working as a financial analyst at one of the largest law firms in the country. After several threats from UQ, Zuri was able to persuade him to let her do one more year in the States so she could become a better leader of the syndicate. Zuri was astonished that she was even able to pull it off, but she did—UQ accepted. Zuri had graduated with a degree in mathematics. Numbers were her specialty, and after graduating with a 4.0 GPA, the sky was the limit for her. Their lives had become picture-perfect, and nothing was going to stop them now.

Zuri looked around the room. "This is probably going to be one of the last Christmases that we are all in the same area. We need to cherish this moment because it is everything."

They all raised their glasses and said, "Sláinte is táinte," which meant health and wealth in Irish. It was a saying they learned while spending St. Patrick's Day at her Irish friend's house. Her friend's parents said it one year over dinner, and it became their motto.

Zuri's phone rang, and it was her mom. "Hey, sweetie, come down for dinner."

Zuri hung up the phone and excitedly let everyone know it was time to eat. They all went downstairs and ate their hearts out. The menu was extravagant; lasagna, baked ziti, chicken rice, seafood paella, chicken parm, pho, penne alla vodka, fish, chicken, steak, vegetables, champ, redang, rice—the list kept going. Zuri always admired her mother's love for cooking, especially her focus on international dishes. Her mom was amazing at what she did—no chef could beat this spread. They ate, drank, and partied well into the night.

Christmas day arrived, which meant presents and relaxation. The ritual every Christmas morning was to catch the parade, watch *A Christmas Story*, and open gifts. Dad always made Christmas brunch, and it was truly an intimate time for them. For Christmas dinner, they would be joined by a few of their closest friends and family to celebrate.

The doorbell rang, and Zuri's mom went to grab it.

"Who is it?" Zuri yelled to her mom, thinking her friends were stopping by early. Her mom walked back into the room, her face petrified. Behind her mom was a masked man holding a gun to her head. Her dad walked into the room, slowly realizing what was happening, and looked over at Zuri. She would never forget the way her parents looked right before the man shot and killed them. The man said nothing, had no distinguishes factors, but wore an all-black attire. His face was covered with a ski mask, and all she could see were his eyes. It happened so quickly—he shot her parents in cold blood.

The man left, and Zuri sat there frozen and confused. She realized with all her training, there was no time to react. She was caught completely off guard with no chance to plead for their lives. She ran to her parents, but she knew from her work with UQ that they were dead. She sat in the room and rocked back and forth with tears running down her face as she rubbed the scar on her hand. Her whole life was just ripped out from under her. She had just lost the two people who meant more to her than anyone else.

That day played in Zuri's head on repeat. That was her weakest moment, the day she let some man come in and kill her parents. She always thought back to how the situation could have been different, but she knew that their fates were sealed the moment the doorbell rang.

Zuri wiped the tears from her face and kept looking through the documents on the floor to see if there was anything else that contained familiar information. A moment later, there was a light consistent beeping sound coming from upstairs. Zuri and Massimo looked at each other with horror because they knew what that beeping sound was—it was an explosive device.

Zuri grabbed as many files and papers as she could, Massimo doing the same, and they ran through the bunker door, up the stairs, and out the back. They kept running until the bomb detonated, sending them flying forward a few feet, papers going everywhere. They rolled over and looked at the destruction.

"Someone was trying to destroy the information in that house," Massimo said as he caught his breath.

"Yeah, seems like The Butcher was a busy man. At least these files can point us in the direction of who hired him and hopefully give us some information on how my parents and I are involved."

They got up, dusted off their clothes, and gathered the papers that were scattered from the blast. Avoiding the burning house, they walked around to the front, hoping the car was in one piece. Thankfully, it was.

"I think we finally have a substantial lead in figuring out why me," Zuri said as Massimo pulled off.

As they drove, Zuri felt as if a weight was lifting off of her shoulders because they were one step closer to the end of this nightmare. *At this point, The Butcher no longer matters. What matters is how he acquired so much information about me and who he was working for.*

12

The Engagement

More than a decade earlier, Zuri and Massimo shared a truly magical weekend together which jumpstarted the beginning of a new chapter in their lives. First, Massimo woke Zuri up with breakfast in bed. This was no ordinary breakfast in bed either. This was breakfast in Arosa, Switzerland, at the Tschuggen Grand Hotel. The view was breathtaking. Massimo flew them in the night before on UQ's private plane, and they landed just as the sun was setting. Zuri could not think of a better way to spend the long Valentine's Day weekend. She always admired Massimo's attention to detail and his willingness to cater to her because he truly believed she deserved nothing but the best.

After an amazing breakfast in bed, Massimo took them snowboarding in the Alps, which they had learned to do years ago as part of another one of UQ's training instructions. Those weekends away during training gave them the

ability to free their minds on the slopes. The life of an assassin was mind-numbing, and the slopes were therapeutic
for them, giving them the ability to be competitive and
allowing success to be measured distinctly.

"Let's make a bet," Massimo said to Zuri.

"Game on."

"If you make it to the bottom first, we will fly anywhere
in the world, and I have to plan the most romantic evening
for you. If I make it to the bottom first, you have to do the
same for me."

Zuri laughed. Their competitiveness was not about being
better than the other—it was about loving the other person
through all wins and losses and praising those wins and
losses so they could be better for each other. Zuri smiled.
"Bet."

They got to the top of the slope—it was quiet, beautiful,
and serene. "Ready?" Massimo shouted.

"Set!" Zuri shouted back.

"Go!" they both yelled, and they were off.

Five minutes later, the winner was declared as Zuri made
it down the slope first. Massimo will never admit it, but
Zuri knows he let her win. She had beaten him before but
because of what happened next, she knew it to be true.

After the day of skiing, Zuri soaked in a bath as Massimo
was off planning the amazing, romantic event. Little did
Zuri know, it was already fully planned. Twenty minutes
later, Massimo came back into the hotel room and told
Zuri she had thirty minutes to get ready.

Thirty minutes later, Zuri walked out of the bathroom
wearing a well-known black off-the-shoulder dress by
Christina Stambolian and matched the dress with Yves

Saint Laurent Opyum pumps. If there was one thing Zuri loved, it was an all-black ensemble, and Massimo loved it even more.

Massimo helped Zuri put on a Michael Kors double-breasted princess coat with fur cuffs. Then Massimo escorted Zuri out the door, to the car, and into the private plane. The plane ride was filled with laughter, champagne, and an assortment of chocolate-covered fruit.

As the plane neared the destination, Massimo blindfolded Zuri. Before he could sit back down, Zuri reached her hand out, and he grabbed it. "I love you," she said. "Not only for all you do for me but for the way you love me."

Massimo leaned in and gave her a kiss. "You're my world, and therefore, I promise to always cater to you and treat you like the queen you are to me."

Zuri sat back and thought about these words. *How did I get so lucky?*

As they stepped off the plane, Zuri could feel the warm breeze on her skin. Massimo told her to remove the coat because they had arrived in a different country with warmer weather. Carefully, Massimo escorted a blindfolded Zuri into a car. To Zuri, the car ride seemed like forever, even though it was only twenty minutes. Being blindfolded made everything move so slowly in her mind. It was probably because Zuri was anxious to know what was going on and where they were going, but Massimo refused to tell her any information.

The car stopped, and Massimo stepped out. "Count to thirty," he said right before he closed the car door.

"One . . . two . . . three . . ." Zuri counted slowly all the way to thirty.

Just as she finished, Massimo opened the door. "We are almost there, my love," he said as he grabbed Zuri's hand to guide her out of the car.

Zuri held onto Massimo's hand and arm tightly as she walked slowly, wishing he would take the blindfold off already. Zuri heard a door open and close.

"Are you ready?" Massimo whispered in her ear.

"Yes," she replied, smiling.

Massimo removed the blindfold, and what she saw took her breath away. Massimo had completely decorated a room with rose petals, candles, and balloons. She looked straight ahead to see words asking, "Will you marry me?" Zuri turned around, and Massimo was on one knee, looking completely magnificent in his fully tailored Brioni black suit. Massimo grabbed her hand and said, "Zuri, I have spent so many years learning how to grow into the man I am today, thanks to UQ. He has taught me the value of love and family, and most importantly, he taught me the value of an amazing woman. You're a queen and will always be treated as such. I want to build a life of wealth, not only for us but for generations to come. I want you to be by my side, the way you always have. I want to make sure you're happy, motivated, and loved every day. I want the privilege to be your fiancé and then husband. I know your parents are not here, and this has been a hard time for you. I want to help you heal, and I want to be your strength. I want to grow old with you and have Nerf gun fights every Thursday night after we eat junk food. I want to be safe with you and do what we do best. I want us to build an empire. I say all this to say, will you do me the honor of becoming my wife?" Massimo pulled out a Tiffany box, which held a teardrop-shaped diamond-encrusted sapphire engagement ring.

Zuri could not remember a time when she felt so many emotions all at once. "Yes."

Massimo put the ring on her finger and then he got up to hug and kiss her. She held him tightly. Zuri was so happy, and this was one of the greatest moments of her life. Massimo was truly an amazing man, and even though her parents were not around to see this, she knew they were watching as her dream had finally come true.

The weekend had come to an end, and they were ecstatic to share the news with UQ. UQ embraced them with open arms as they entered back into the house and told him the good news. Zuri told UQ all about the engagement and the surprise that Massimo had waiting for her. It was one of the few times UQ was a regular grandfather—emotional and all. She was so used to him being a boss to her that it was moments like this that she cherished. After her parents were killed, she noticed that he took on a whole new role to ensure that she always had someone to go to and someone to trust—because family means everything.

Zuri was on cloud nine. The days seemed better and the nights with Massimo magical. She missed her parents daily but continued to embrace their culture by cooking and decorating UQ's house every now and again—UQ didn't mind. It reminded him of her grandmother and it made the house feel less like a place of business and more like a home.

A few weeks before the marriage, UQ called Massimo and Zuri into his office. "I need to talk to you both," he said but looked straight at Zuri. "I need to talk to you more as a grandparent and partially as your boss."

Zuri and Massimo nodded then sat down across from UQ.

"When we have female assassins join the organization, we ask them if they want to freeze their eggs in case anything happens to them. We found that some women still want their spouses to be able to consider and make the decision to have children. I want to ask you Zuri, I know this is very personal, but would you want to do this? I really do want to be a great-grandfather, and while I know I have not been the best father to your dad or grandfather to you, we have a chance to change the future, and you're the only one in the lineage, so I wanted us to talk about it."

Zuri sat back and thought about it. She knew this conversation was going to happen at some point. "Of course, I do, Grandpa. You're right, I am the only one left in the bloodline, and it is my choice—actually, it is my duty to do this. I want to be a mom and make Massimo a dad." She grabbed Massimo's hand and squeezed it. "I want to do this for all of us."

Massimo kissed her hand. "I will freeze as well." UQ and Zuri looked at him. "I want to be able to give Zuri a child in case I don't make it. The lifestyle we live is unpredictable."

UQ beamed. He grabbed some documents off of the desk and gave them both forms to sign, along with the contact information for the doctor who would do the freezing. "Thank you both for making me a happy, old man. I know I have not been the best representation of family, and I know you see me more as a boss than a grandparent, but I love you both—even though I do not show it as often as I should. You both mean the world to me."

Zuri stood to hug him. "I love you too."

Massimo came over and reached his hand out for UQ to shake. UQ pulled him in for a hug and said in Massimo's ear, "You're my family. I hope I made you feel as much."

"More than you know," Massimo whispered back.

Zuri and Massimo walked out of UQ's office feeling cheerful. They closed the door behind them, and Massimo immediately grabbed Zuri and hugged her. "I know we have to go get this done, but do you want to get started on making this baby?" Massimo asked her as he kissed her neck.

She smiled and nodded.

The next day, Zuri and Massimo headed to the doctor to get the procedures done. The night before, they discussed potentially just having a baby now. Zuri was on board because she wanted nothing more than to have a child, but she was unsure if UQ would even allow it. So, yesterday's news was exactly what she needed to hear. UQ also made it clear that when that time came, she would be excused to do as she pleases. She was elated that he wanted great-grandchildren, and even though they were on their way to get the procedures done, she was hopeful that she would be a mother sooner than later.

After the procedures, they headed home. Everything was signed, sealed, and delivered.

13

───────────

Finding Balance

They spent hours in the tech room at Massimo's safe house, sorting through the documents. They found an influx of information on Zuri from law school all the way to her job at the current firm. There were pictures of her out to lunch, dinner, and at bars. *I am absolutely stunning in these pictures.* Her complexion made it seem like she was wearing makeup, but she was not. Her skin was naturally radiant. In most of the pictures, she noticed that she always wore her hair in a bun, which at times, was messy but neat. In all the photos, she was in business attire and carrying a beautiful, expensive purse.

Zuri picked up a picture of herself from two years ago and stared at it. She discerned that she truly began to embrace legal fashion after she was on a track to become a partner. Her outfits looked more expensive, and she was starting to wear a lot of name-brand shoes and purses. Had it not been for this current debacle she found herself in, she would have had only three more years before she could buy into becoming a partner. Before this Paris trip, she was very excited. Now, she didn't know how to feel.

These pictures had Zuri's mind disheveled as she thought back on the timeline of her life. After she left that night and made the decision to start fresh, she decided it was time to get on the right side of the law. She disappeared to New York City—never looking back and only moving forward. She attended Yale Law and graduated in the top-ten percentile. The moment she graduated, she was hired as an associate attorney by the firm she worked for as a financial analyst. Then she passed the bar exam with a two eighty, and she had been thriving ever since.

Zuri realized quickly that she couldn't go down a rabbit hole of her life—it would cause chaos. Quickly, she moved the files that were specifically on her to one pile. The other pile was a file on her parents. It had documentation of conversations with the FBI, along with an explanation of who they were and what was needed. "Someone put out a hit on my parents," Zuri said as she dropped the papers in front of Massimo. "With all our resources, UQ was never able to find the killer. Now, we know why he could never find him. The Butcher was heavily protected by multiple governments, which made him practically untouchable." Zuri wiped the tears that started forming in her eyes. *What goes around comes around.* She could not help but think she was the reason her parents were dead. Had she not been in the business of killing people, her parents would not have suffered the same fate as those on the other side of her nozzle. Who knew how many people she and Massimo had killed up to that point?

She always knew there was a reason to kill people—finding ways to justify killing rapists, murderers, and pedophiles because UQ made them believe that it was the right and just thing to do. She agreed with UQ on some things—people who hurt other people should suffer for the trauma they caused. *But why my parents? They were innocent in all this. I should've been the one to die that day.* As she was deep in thought, rubbing the scar on her hand, she knew she couldn't change the past, but she was determined to change the future—even if that meant breaking the law for a few days and potentially sacrificing all that she had worked hard for.

Massimo left the tech room and came back with fruits and two glasses of wine, which were perfectly balanced on the center of the fruit platter. He gave Zuri a glass first, grabbed his glass next, and then proceeded to sit on the floor as he drank his wine slowly and watched her. Moments later, Zuri joined him on the floor and they ate in silence.

"Let's watch a movie," Massimo said as he took the platter and his glass of wine. "You need a distraction. I need a distraction. Let's get lost in another reality for some time."

Zuri smiled because this was exactly what she needed, and Massimo said it exactly at the right time.

Zuri woke up abruptly. They had fallen asleep in the bedroom during the movie, which was still playing in the background. Zuri's mind was racing, so she got up, leaving

Massimo asleep, and went back downstairs. She made a stop in the kitchen to grab some water and then headed downstairs to the tech room. She looked around at all the documents spread across the room.

The files from The Butcher had led them to figure out that whoever he was working for was powerful. He had governments on his side but did small contracts when he had a chance. From Zuri's perspective, The Butcher was responsible for her parents being killed and her being framed. He must have been tracking her since he killed her parents. This frustrated her because she had no one to interrogate to get more definitive answers.

If she had to analyze this logically, she would say that, with the series of events that occurred, there had to be a motive. *What was the motive? It had to be out of hate, so who still hates me?* She was back to the drawing board of the three people who would have disdain for her. However, Massimo was out of the question now; Alice was in Greece and Simon was in Africa. *Who lost the most because of me, Alice or Simon? Alice. Maybe Alice does have something to do with this.*

Zuri sat down and dug into Alice again, thinking she must have missed something. As she kept looking, she saw that Alice was no longer in Greece but had made her way to France. Zuri gasped. *Shit!* She continued to search for a specific location in France, hacking into some street cameras. *Bingo.* Zuri found visuals of Alice near the Eiffel Tower, time-stamped ten minutes before. *This can't be a coincidence.* Zuri knew this trip was too good to be true. Paris was supposed to be enchanting, and instead, it was opening up old wounds and making her re-live the very trauma she spent years running—and healing—from.

Massimo was still asleep when Zuri walked into the bedroom.

"Babe," she whispered as she rubbed his arm.

"Yes," he said in a groggy voice.

"Guess what I found out—Alice is in Paris. I knew it was her who set me up. We need to run surveillance and see where she is staying. It's time I do what I should have done years ago. End this once and for all."

Massimo partially sat up and looked at Zuri, confused. "I need another twenty minutes and then I want you to tell me everything."

Zuri kissed his cheek. Massimo laid back down and rolled over.

Twenty minutes later, he walked downstairs in sweatpants, still looking sleepy. Zuri was in the kitchen making herself a kale strawberry smoothie. He walked to the living room and plopped down on the couch.

"Come here, babe," he said as he laid on his back.

Zuri grabbed her smoothie and walked down the hall to the living room. She put her smoothie down on the table and lay partially on top of him, putting her head on his chest. Zuri's mind drifted off for a few seconds while she listened to his heartbeat. She remembered watching a movie where a character said that she and her husband had a unified heartbeat. Zuri always thought it was unlikely, but when she laid on Massimo, she felt it. She would never forget the night of their engagement, not only because it was a special night, but it was the first time she noticed their hearts beating in unison. At that moment, she knew they were meant to be.

Massimo rubbed her arm which brought her back to the present. Zuri snuggled in closer and listened. Their hearts were still beating together in unison after all these years. She smiled because she was in complete serenity.

"So, tell me what you found," he said as he played with her hair.

"You remember Alice, right? I killed her uncle when we first started going on missions for UQ. Well, her uncle was her only family, and she swore up and down that UQ and I were responsible for his death. Mostly, that I was responsible. I denied it for obvious reasons. Anyway, she couldn't let it go, and we fell out. *Well, that's a lie, but he doesn't need to know the whole truth.* Even though she never made a direct threat, I hacked her computer and read through the information she had, knowing she was going to try to get back at me for her uncle's death. Well, I saw it in her notes: **REVENGE**, written in bold large letters with a double underline. Back at my safe house, I did a search and saw that she was in Greece. When I did a search again on your computer, I found she is now in Paris. I dug into some security systems, and she was by the Eiffel Tower earlier today. I don't know how long she's been in Paris, but if she is here, I know it was her who set me up."

Massimo lifted his head to look at her. "Babe, you do understand in this line of work, we make a lot of enemies. What makes you so sure it was her?"

Zuri sat up. "We have a lot of enemies, definitely. But out of all those enemies, I only believed three of them ever hated me enough that they would have the motivation to do something to this extent—none of whom are from our line of work. You were initially on the list of three, but then you showed up, and I knew it wasn't you. The other two were Alice and Simon. Everyone else was low on the scale of revenge."

Massimo started laughing. "Not Simon from high school and college?"

"Yes, that Simon." She smirked because she knew that Massimo always hated him. When he finally left, Massimo was so happy. "He swore to me he was going to get back at us if it was the last thing he did. Granted, back then, he was young, angry, and naïve. Based on what I found, he is a Christian missionary in Africa."

"Well, isn't that nice?" Massimo said in a teasing voice.

Zuri looked at him. "You know when I left, I became a Christian—I still am. I know that, in this line of work, it seems hypocritical, but I believe in God. I believe in his power. He brought you back to me."

Massimo sat up fully which caused Zuri to change positions. "It's funny that you mention that because I kind of did the same thing. I changed the organization for the better. I'm no longer killing just to kill. Things are just different now, and I understand what you mean. I have to thank God because he kept us both alive this long and brought you back to me," Massimo said as he leaned in for a kiss.

14

————————————

Finding Clarity

It was dark outside, and they were on the road again, heading to Alice's last known location on the security cameras—the 7th arrondissement—close to the Eiffel Tower. They were strictly there to do reconnaissance, a surveillance and information gathering operation only.

They arrived near the Eiffel Tower, and Massimo drove around slowly while Zuri looked out the window, trying to see if she could spot Alice on the street. After several unsuccessful tries, Massimo decided they had a better chance of finding her on foot. Even though Zuri thought otherwise, Massimo went ahead and parked the car.

"C'mon, let's go for a walk. We know she's around here somewhere," Massimo said. He got out of the driver's side, and the warm night breeze blew into the car causing Zuri to feel comforted. Massimo opened her door and reached out his hand to help her out. They were wearing all black, and they looked like a normal couple—maybe on their honeymoon. It was the City of Love, after all.

They held hands as Massimo placed a Sony A7 IV camera around his neck. It was a great camera, and they knew they could get good photos from it. They walked through the grassy area near the Eiffel Tower. Massimo stopped every few feet to grab some pictures. Zuri posed for some of them and others Massimo took off guard.

They continued to walk until they got right next to the Eiffel Tower. It was packed and busy and beautiful. They kept walking when they spotted Alice. Zuri turned around with her back facing the direction of Alice while Massimo took pictures. From the looks of it, Alice was with her husband and another couple—all four of them were standing in a circle, talking, while they ate ice cream cones. Neither Alice nor the other three paid any attention to Zuri or Massimo. Zuri kept posing until Massimo said, "Let's go, bunny. Time to get ice cream."

Zuri skipped over to Massimo, grabbed his arm, and they walked back to the car. They got into the car—this time, Zuri was driving, and she drove to the other side of the Tower.

"They're on the move," Massimo said as he rolled down the window, pulled his camera to his eye, and started snapping pictures again. They followed Alice's group until they walked into the Pullman Paris Tour Eiffel Hotel.

Zuri looked at Massimo and said, "Let's wait thirty minutes to see if they come back out."

They did not.

Zuri decided to call the hotel and told the front desk that Alice Reese was just at her restaurant and left her room key, along with her credit card. The front desk said they would transfer the call to Alice.

The phone rang and a female answered, "Bonjour."

Zuri analyzed the voice.

"Hello? Bonjour? Is someone there?" the voice said again.

Zuri hung up the phone. "The voice . . . It wasn't Alice, but it sounded familiar. I just cannot place it," Zuri said as she racked her brain. "I need you to drive back to the safe house. I can't focus on driving right now. I have to figure out where I know that voice from."

Massimo stayed quiet as he exited the car to switch positions with her. With Zuri now in the passenger seat, she stared out the window, waiting for the memory to hit her. Abruptly, Zuri shouted, "My airplane neighbor!" which startled Massimo.

"The girl that was with Paul? *That* seat neighbor?"

"Yes. It was her. It just hit me. It was her, but how?"

Zuri was confused and started rambling her thoughts loud enough for Massimo to hear. "How did Sophia know Alice? What is their connection? We know how Sophia is connected to Paul . . . What the hell is going on? This is all connected, it has to be. I knew it. I knew it! This cannot be a coincidence. UQ always taught us that nothing in life is a coincidence. We need to go back and kill them."

Massimo turned to look at Zuri. "Babe, calm down. Let's dig into this before we move solely based on a theory."

"This is not a theory. This is me finally figuring it out," Zuri said. "When we get back to the house, let's do some research. I'm sure we are bound to find a connection between Alice and Sophia. I just know it. I feel it."

When they arrived at the safe house, Massimo parked the car, and they walked inside. Zuri wasted no time as she headed straight for the tech room. She started to do research on the woman, Sophia West, while Massimo compiled the data Zuri already had on Alice Reese. Two hours went by, and Zuri had finally matched the similarities between Sophia and Alice. "I got it. I figured it out. Take a look," she said, standing up and signaling for Massimo to review the typed-up annotated notes that showed the similarities within the files. "There was something familiar about Sophia that I couldn't put my finger on, but it's all finally coming together."

While Zuri paced back and forth waiting for his feedback, Massimo reviewed the extensive notes and detailed files.

Both individuals had no immediate family but were born on the same day—at the same hospital—by the same mother. Both of them were taken from their mother and brought to the United States from the Czech Republic under different identities.

Alice was sold to the highest bidder who cared for her like she was his own daughter. He was an older man who just wanted a family. Upon further research, Zuri found that his biological daughter was killed by a bacterial infection that got into her bloodstream at the age of five. This man bought Alice, raising her as if she was his daughter.

Her life was not terrible with him, but she was troubled. Alice grew up believing her caretaker was her uncle. She was too young to understand the circumstances of her situation. As a young girl, she wanted for nothing and got all that she asked for. As she grew older, she began to feel as though she was missing a piece of herself.

At the age of twelve, she discovered a hidden photograph of a woman and two babies. When she confronted her uncle about it, he let her know that she had a sister. Due to circumstances outside of his control, he had no idea where her sister was and was unable to reunite them. But he promised that if he found her sister, he would do just that.

The sister was Sophia. Sophia grew up the complete opposite. She was purchased by the highest bidder, who was a drunk couple that beat her every day. They had no business taking care of a child, but money can make all things possible. Sophia eventually ran away right before her tenth birthday. She spent months living on the street, then she ended up in a shelter and was eventually put into the foster care system. She was moved around from house to house because no one wanted her. She was damaged goods. Her sweet innocence was gone, and she was a broken girl. She grew up in the foster care system for eight years and then aged out.

It must have been fate that brought them together. Alice's uncle was able to locate Sophia and advocated for her to become a nanny for a family that he knew. After the initial interview, the family fell in love with her, and she was given room and board while she took care of their children, cooked, and cleaned.

One day, Alice and her uncle had tea at the house where Sophia was working. Her uncle introduced them—they were inseparable ever since.

A few years later, Alice's uncle was killed during an orchestrated robbery. This was one of the first solo kills Zuri did for UQ. She was wearing an all-black sweatsuit, had her silencer on the handgun, and knew the assignment—two shots to the head, point blank range, grab his wallet and his keys. The bullets were loaded into the magazine while she wore gloves to ensure she would leave no fingerprints on the shell casing. The gun was wiped down and the serial number was scratched off—the gun was untraceable.

Alice's uncle did the same thing every night; he was quite predictable. He would have dinner with Alice every evening, and on Monday, Tuesday, and Friday, he would then go over to a poker game where he gambled with some close friends. It was more of a night of socialization then gambling. The side door to the gambling spot was in an alley. This area was not very crime-ridden, but it was about to be.

Zuri knew the escape route; she practiced it over a dozen times. As she was walking to the gambling spot, she repeated the plan in her head. *Two shots, point blank range, grab his wallet and his keys. Walk past the body to the main street. Before you exit the alley, remove the silencer, holster the gun, take off your mask because it may have traces of his blood, take out your bun, shake your hair around to make it look full, make a left, and walk down three blocks before you get into a cab.* As Alice's uncle left the bar on a warm Monday night, Zuri was in the alley waiting for him. She pulled her mask down and walked out from behind a dumpster. His back was turned to her. "Hey, sir, do you have any change you can spare?"

Alice's uncle turned around, and Zuri immediately shot two bullets into his head. He fell down. She grabbed the wallet and the keys and walked past the body. She took the silencer off of the gun and placed it in her crossbody bag and then she holstered the gun behind her back. She took the mask off and put it in her bag right next to the silencer. She removed the scrunchie holding her bun, shook her hair, fluffed it with her hands, and turned onto the main street. Anyone who saw her would have assumed she just came from the house on the corner. She made a left and walked three blocks before getting into a cab. *Nice and easy.*

Massimo was astonished and impressed at what Zuri discovered. "What made you put two and two together?"

"It was her name. When I was doing research on Alice at my safe house, I started to dive into her background after I discovered she was in Greece. I was able to find information about her birth mother who she never spoke about, but I couldn't find the connection between her mother and her uncle. See, when Alice's uncle was killed, she finished college and moved away. Before she moved, though, I would see her on campus with this girl—it was Sophia. I always assumed it was a new friend she made, but it was actually her sister. I never met Sophia because Alice and I had already fallen out by that time. When we were boarding the plane, I thought she looked familiar, but I quickly pushed it out of my mind. When I got on the plane and found her seat was next to mine, she was such a nuisance, so I ignored her. I was wondering why she kept talking to me as if she knew me—it was because she did. When Sophia came back sweaty and messy, I figured it was because she had been with Paul, but what if she was in the back killing The Butcher, and she and Paul were in on it together?"

Standing there, Zuri drifted off for a brief moment, lost in thought. "That is why Marcy saw them coming out of the bathroom around the same time. We now know that the love triangle was false. It was probably information Paul planted for my benefit. He had to have known that I would find out some way. So, long story short, Marcy killed one male victim, we know Paul killed the one female victim, and now we know Paul and Sophia killed The Butcher—allegedly. She must have found out I was responsible for Alice's uncle's death and took her opportunity of revenge. What better way to destroy a lawyer than by having her break the law while in international airspace?"

Massimo stood up in disbelief and paced back and forth. "That makes sense, but it also sounds crazy to me, that she would go to such lengths."

"Yeah, they knew what they were doing when they found a guy like Paul. He was attractive, we had a lot of similarities, and I felt like I really knew him. The only reason I felt that is because Alice knew everything about me. She must have told him what to say and how to act," Zuri said while shaking her head. "I finally figured it out. We got them. We got them. I can clear my name. This can be done with." Zuri sighed heavily and sat down.

"I'm proud of you. I always admired your ability to focus, even when there's chaos around you. This entire ordeal has made me miss you and reminded me how good life was when you were there. Maybe we can work on this again," Massimo said confidently, gesturing between the two of them.

Zuri looked over at him.

"I think we can get it right this time. You're the one I always wanted to be with. You're the love of my life. You're my soulmate. You're my everything," Massimo said.

Zuri stood up, walked over to him, and kissed him. "Let's do it," she said.

Massimo grabbed her and held her tight. She forgot how great she felt when she was with him—untouchable, invincible, and on top of the world.

As he continued to hold her, her thoughts took a turn for the worse. *But how would the life I want to get back to factor in now that Massimo wants another chance with me?* She knew by agreeing to be with Massimo, she would have to move to the estate and maybe become a lawyer in Italy. She would have to start all over again. *He mentioned that the business had changed. What did he mean by that? Is this what I really want? Of course, it is. Of course, he is.*

Massimo let her go and looked into her eyes. "I know this is a lot. We just need to take it one step at a time. We can figure this out."

Zuri nodded, letting out a sigh of relief.

They decided to come up with a plan to turn Sophia and Alice into the police. While killing did not bother Zuri, she wanted to get out of that life. The only reason she was back into "assassination mode" was because of the current predicament but, if she turned Sophia and Alice in, there was still a chance. She could clear her name and get back to living her life.

This was the last piece of the puzzle, and it was imperative that they come up with a solution that was going to help fully clear her name. Step one, they decided, would be to get into Alice's and Sophia's hotel room to see if there was anything incriminating in the room. Then, similar to what they did with Marcy, they would wait and have a discussion with Alice and Sophia. The hope was that maybe Alice and Sophia would see reason and be able to let this go once and for all.

Before they went to the room, they had to separate Alice and Sophia from the men accompanying them. Zuri had an idea that could work. "All we need to do is call and offer the men a complimentary Paris Burlesque show and send a bottle of champagne to the room as a thank you for staying at the hotel," she said. "Simple but effective."

"What if the women want to go to the show?"

"Good point. I just can't think of another way to separate them. Dinner won't work. A party won't work. A spa will definitely not work, but if I remember correctly, Alice was never fond of the Burlesque scene. We had a Burlesque event in college, and she was not happy about it at all. She ended up not going. She felt it was too provocative, and it didn't help that a guy she liked at the time wanted to badly go. It made her angry. So, if she still feels that way, there's no way she'll accompany them when they go. And Sophia will stay with Alice—that's just what girls do."

Massimo contemplated what Zuri said. "What do we have to lose? Let's try it. Let me look up what they have available for shows tomorrow, and we can call their room in the morning."

"Let's do it," Zuri said.

15

The Chase

"Hi, this is Sherry calling from the front desk. We're pleased to let you know that we're giving you two complimentary tickets to a Burlesque show, and we'll be sending up a bottle of champagne as a thank you for staying with us. The tickets have been sent to your email, and the show starts at 6 p.m. with an expected arrival of 5 p.m."

"Wow, thank you so much. We really appreciate that, and we've truly enjoyed our stay at your lovely hotel," Alice said.

"Thank you for your kind words. It has been our pleasure. Do enjoy the show." Zuri hung up the phone.

A few minutes later, Alice's phone pinged with the notification of the two tickets.

With Phase I now complete, they moved on to Phase II. Zuri and Massimo geared up. They were not naïve. They believed a conversation could work, but there was already animosity there. They needed to go in prepared for any and every scenario. If Alice went through such grand lengths to get Zuri arrested, jailed, or killed, anything was possible. Zuri put on a thin bulletproof vest and then her hoodie. Zuri was dressed in a black Gucci sweatsuit, and Massimo was wearing a black Armani suit with a thin bulletproof vest underneath. They got into the car, locked and loaded. Then they drove to the hotel and waited patiently.

While they were waiting, Zuri pulled out a laptop she brought with her to track Sophia's, Alice's, and the accompanying men's movements. Before getting out of the car, they waited until they saw the men leaving the hotel, getting into a car, and the car pulling off toward the location of the Burlesque show. Upon their departure, Zuri shut the laptop and nodded at Massimo who was set to enter into the hotel first.

Massimo got out of the car and adjusted his suit. He took one look at his reflection using the car window and then headed into the hotel. The plan was for Massimo to sit at the bar and order a drink and a bottle of champagne. Based on the traffic of the hotel, Massimo would telephone Zuri so she could make her way inside. Once Zuri arrived in the staircase, she would alert Massimo. Then Massimo would head over to the staircase to meet her so they could walk to the sixth floor.

Zuri waited for Massimo's call. "Whiskey on the rocks is what he probably ordered," she whispered to herself while chuckling.

Her phone rang shortly after, and Massimo said, "It's time."

Zuri got out of the car, headed to the hotel, and walked through the front doors. She was not prepared for the chaos that was in the lobby. Everywhere was crowded—the bar, the restaurant, and the front desk. There had to be at least twenty people checking in. While she was annoyed that Massimo did not give her a heads up, she was also pleased that it was this busy because no one would notice as she slipped into the staircase.

While Zuri was in the staircase waiting for Massimo, she pulled out her gun and checked to make sure there was a bullet in the chamber, then she put the safety on. The goal was not to kill anyone but to scare them. She quickly put the gun back into the holster as she heard the stairwell door open. It was Massimo holding a bottle of champagne. "Ready?" she asked.

Massimo nodded.

Zuri pulled out and put on a pair of black gloves as they walked up to the sixth floor. Upon arrival, they waited a few seconds to catch their breath and then they stepped out of the staircase, making sure that no one was on the floor. They walked down the hall, and Massimo stood in front of the door to their room. Zuri was positioned to the side, where she would remain unseen if they used the peephole. She watched for any movement on the floor as Massimo knocked on the door and waited.

"Who is it?" a voice called out from behind the door.

Based on how close her voice was, Massimo knew Alice was looking through the peephole.

"Front desk asked me to deliver this complimentary bottle of champagne to your room," Massimo said holding the bottle closer to the peephole.

They could hear shuffling behind the door. A few seconds later, the door swung open, and Alice was standing there with a Cheshire smile plastered on her face, wearing nothing but a black slip. "Wow, I don't remember seeing you downstairs," Alice said as she took in Massimo's good looks. "You're very handsome."

"Thank you," Massimo said nodding and smiling back at Alice. Unbeknownst to Alice, the nod and smile was the signal for Zuri to enter the room. Zuri looked around the hallway one more time before she reached for her gun, which was holstered behind her back. With a one-hundred-dred-and-eighty-degree turn, Zuri appeared standing next to Massimo and raised her gun toward Alice. Frightened, Alice cupped her hands on her mouth and stared between Zuri and Massimo.

"Back up," Zuri demanded as they walked into the hotel room while Alice slowly walked backward with her hands raised. Massimo closed the door behind them, put the champagne on the nearest table, and drew his gun while searching for Sophia, who they suspected was in the room next door.

"Sit," Zuri instructed Alice who immediately obeyed.

Just as Massimo grabbed the adjourning doors, Sophia pushed through and walked in. Massimo backed up a few feet and kept his gun raised on Sophia. Sophia was so focused on her phone that she didn't realize what was happening. When she finally looked up, seeing Massimo's gun aimed at her, she screamed. Massimo quickly leaped in front of her and put his hand over her mouth, his gun still raised. "Shut up," Massimo said to her. "I'm going to move my hand, and if you scream again, I will knock you out cold." Sophia nodded frantically. Massimo removed his hand from her mouth and grabbed her phone. "Sit."

Sophia hustled over to the couch that Alice was sitting on and sat down beside her.

Alice started laughing which startled Zuri. "Well, well, well, you were always the smart one in the group—guess you figured it out, huh?" Zuri didn't break eye contact as Alice continued talking. "Long time, no see, Zuri. Time has been kind to you—you look amazing," Alice said with a smirk on her face.

"We were expecting you eventually," Sophia said as she looked over at Alice.

Zuri realized the scared demeanor that Sophia and Alice had was a façade. *So much for the element of surprise.* Zuri kept her poker face on. "Glad to hear. How about you get dressed so we can chat?" Zuri said to Alice. She gestured for Massimo to turn around. Alice stood up, grabbed her clothes, which were sitting on the table, and got dressed. "All good," Zuri said to Massimo who turned back around, smiling. Zuri knew exactly what Massimo was thinking—she always said his eyes were only for her.

"Pass me that bottle of champagne, doll," Alice said to Massimo.

Zuri walked over and grabbed the champagne, rolling her eyes in the process—she knew better than to hand Alice the bottle. Zuri opened the bottle, grabbed a glass, and poured some champagne in it. Spitefully, Zuri took a sip from the glass while she stared at Alice.

"I see you haven't changed much—hogging everything so no one else can have it," Alice said as she stood up and walked over to pour herself a glass. She took a sip as she walked back to where she was sitting. Alice gestured to Sophia as she sat down next to her. "Zuri, it's been a long time, so let me officially introduce you to my sister, Sophia. You may remember her from the plane ride."

Zuri nodded and said sarcastically, "Yes, I do. Great to see you again, Sophia."

"Enough with the formalities. What is it that you want?" Alice asked.

"I think the better question is, what do you two want from me?"

"Well for starters, I want you dead, but we can't always get what we wish for because here you are, standing in front of me. Secondly, I know you killed my uncle. We know it was you. So, the question is, do you want to die here, or do you want to die somewhere else?" Alice asked.

Zuri looked at Massimo and laughed. "If I killed your uncle without so much as a thought, what makes you think I won't kill you right where you sit?"

"You can't," Sophia said with a mischievous look on her face.

Massimo pointed his gun in her direction. "Sounds like a dead girl to me," he said as he clicked off the safety.

Zuri walked up to Sophia and put her gun to her forehead. Just as Zuri was about to pull the trigger, the door opened and the two men who had accompanied Alice and Sophia came in. Zuri quickly turned around.

"Babe, you aren't—"

Before one of the men could finish speaking, he noticed the predicament that they just entered into. With no time to flee, Massimo ran toward them and pulled them further inside the room. The door shut behind them. Zuri pointed her gun toward them, ready to shoot in case they made a sudden move.

With all the commotion going on, Zuri and Massimo had taken their eyes off of Sophia and Alice, both of whom had reached in between the couch cushions and pulled out a gun. Before Zuri knew what was happening, Alice was standing up, holding her gun to the back of Zuri's head. Alice cleared her throat to get everyone's attention. Massimo looked over to see what had just happened and saw Sophia had a gun pointed at him. Massimo lowered his gun.

"Drop it," Sophia said.

Massimo knelt slowly and placed the gun on the floor. One of the men grabbed it and walked over to Sophia.

"I told you, you can't kill us," Sophia said. "Now, you two are going to sit down and listen."

Massimo waited and watched as Zuri stood with her gun pointed toward the men, Alice's gun still pointing at the back of her head. The room fell silent and neither Alice nor Zuri made a move. "I'll take that," Alice finally said, reaching over Zuri's shoulder to grab her gun.

Disarm her or let her have it? Too many guns in play; the odds aren't great. Zuri let go and turned around to face Alice with her hands up.

"Sit," Alice commanded. "You too, Massimo," she said as she used her gun as a pointer to gesture to the couch.

Zuri and Massimo sat down.

"So, I will ask you again," Alice said as she playfully walked around the room, "do you want to die here or somewhere else?"

Zuri looked at Massimo and said, "I would at least like to die somewhere nice in Paris. You pick. Plus, it would be stupid to kill us in this hotel room—the extensive clean up alone—"

Alice chuckled. "Figures as much. You were always too good for anything normal, constantly needing to be extraordinary and extravagant. I'm so sick of you and your bullshit ways."

"No need to be angry," Zuri said. "Some people are meant to be extraordinary, and others are meant to be dull and normal—no offense."

Massimo snickered.

"Shut up! And get up! We are going for a little ride," Alice said.

Zuri and Massimo stood up, obeying Alice's command. The six of them started out of the room. Alice was holding on to Massimo; one of the men was holding on to Zuri, and Sophia was walking arm in arm with the other man. Sophia being the last to leave hung the 'Do Not Disturb' sign on the door. They all got into the elevator. Zuri was calm. *We have a better chance of disarming and killing them once we're in an open area.*

"So, who are these guys?" Zuri asked as the elevator slowly descended.

"Some men we hired. They knew my uncle back when he was gambling. Why? Did you actually think I would bring my husband on a mission to kill you? He loves me, but not that much."

Okay, so she is married. Good to know I was right.

"Speaking of my uncle, while I was never able to prove it, I know what you and your grandfather did. It's neither here nor there because I have you right where I want you. I knew I had you when I made sure Sophia was sitting next to you on the plane. I knew you wouldn't remember her so it was great to know how relaxed and unguarded you were," Alice said. "It was so easy to get close to you. Close enough to make sure that you slept the whole flight."

Just as Zuri was going to say something, the elevator dinged, and they were in the lobby. They walked together as if old friends and out the front door. The warm evening breeze hit Zuri's face, and she realized that more time than she had thought passed while they were up in the room. She looked around, checking her surroundings—there was no one nearby. They made a left, walking to the hotel parking area, and Alice signaled for them to get into a black SUV as she hopped in the driver's seat. They sat in silence as Alice drove toward the park around the Eiffel Tower. The area was suspiciously quiet, but Zuri couldn't focus on that because her mind was racing several miles an hour. *What did she mean when she said that Sophia was close enough to make sure I slept the whole flight?*

Alice stopped the car. "Get out," she said, looking back at Zuri and Massimo.

As they opened the door, they could hear the serenity of Paris' heart center. It was late and the area was quiet. They all got out of the car, and Zuri looked around, thinking this may just well be the last time she got to admire the beauty of the Eiffel Tower.

Alice walked around the side of the car to meet the rest of them, holding three handguns. Alice signaled to the two hired men who walked over slowly and grabbed the extra guns from her. *I don't remember her being this thorough and prepared when we were younger.* Massimo stood near the car, while all the other individuals spread out. Zuri grabbed their attention when she began speaking. "Before we go any further, I just have a clarifying question for you both," Zuri said as she slowly walked away from the car, Alice following close behind with the gun in her hand. "Alice, you mentioned me sleeping for the entire flight. Was that because of you, Sophia?"

Sophia turned to face Zuri, holstering her gun behind her back. "Yeah, it was easy. When I bumped into you, I gave you a nice dose of melatonin."

Zuri remembered that when she first boarded the plane and was walking to her seat, she was bumped by Sophia. Zuri ignored it because the plane was crowded—she didn't even consider it was intentional. Thinking back on it, she did feel very tired on the flight and only woke up to use the bathroom, but other than that, she did not remember anything but small moments of time. "Well played, Alice. Well played." Zuri looked up to the sky. *Not a bad way to die.* "Alice, I'll be honest with you, I did kill your uncle. Obviously, I didn't know who you were at the time, and the way we personally connected in high school and college made me feel guilty because I could see that you were still hurting over his death." Zuri looked at Alice, who was standing several feet away from the car with Sophia right by her side. The two guys were directly behind them, one holding a gun in his hand while the other put his hand on the grip of his holstered one. The men were waiting for Alice to make a move.

Zuri continued. "I didn't know much about who he was. I just did what I was told. Not sure if you know who he really was, but he was an evil man. He was known for trafficking girls and selling drugs. We know that is how you ended up with him. He *bought* you, and even though he gave you a good life, it was only because he did not have anyone else to love. He did right by you, though, and tried to make up for his past mistakes through you. Did you know he had a daughter who died? Anyway, that's old news. I know you changed his life for the better. I also know he meant the world to you, and for that, I'm sorry. When it's all said and done, we both lost something, but I will say that killing me will not make you feel any better. Trust me, I know." Zuri turned around, her back facing Alice and Sophia. Then she closed her eyes. *Death is imminent. Thank you, God, for it all, the good, the bad, the ugly.* "Do what you have to do," Zuri said as she took a deep breath and opened her eyes, staring at the Eiffel Tower one last time.

Alice walked from behind Zuri, gun raised, and turned to face Zuri. Zuri stared into Alice's eyes as Alice held her gun right to her forehead. "Since we are spilling secrets, let me fill you in on one you have no idea about." Alice laughed and pulled the slide back, a bullet loading into the chamber. She then put the gun back on Zuri's forehead with her finger on the trigger and the safety off. "Did you know that—"

Before she could finish her statement, Massimo, who had repositioned himself perpendicular to the entire group, grabbed his gun that was holstered on his ankle and shot Alice in the head. Her blood splattered over Zuri's face. Massimo then shot the two guys in the head, who were caught off guard, and before Sophia could unholster her gun, he shot her as well. As Alice's body slowly dropped to the floor, Zuri was experiencing an adrenaline rush. For some reason, her mind couldn't comprehend what had just happened. She stood there, frozen, realizing that Alice was dead—not her.

Massimo approached Zuri slowly when he noticed Zuri wasn't moving. "Baby, you're okay. It's okay, you're safe." Massimo grabbed Zuri's hand and then pulled her in for a hug.

Feeling his warm embrace, Zuri hugged him tightly as she rubbed the scar on her hand while she had her arms wrapped around him. *My past had finally caught up to me. I was okay to die and meet my maker, but apparently, God has other plans for me.*

Massimo released Zuri, who was still in shock. "Babe, I need you here with me," he said, staring at her. "We have a mess to clean up."

And with those words she snapped back to reality. "I'm good. Let's finish what we started."

Massimo and Zuri checked the pockets of each individual, pulling out their hotel key card, wallets, keys, and phones. They destroyed and discarded the cell phones but kept all the other items. They put the bodies in the SUV next. Zuri got in on the driver's side and drove toward her old safe house. They knew if they set the SUV on fire over there, no one would notice.

The car ride was quiet, but Zuri's head was not. She kept replaying what happened over and over again. Her relationship with Alice was dead years ago, so remorse was not a feeling she was currently experiencing. She was actually happy they were dead—one less person, or technically, two less people, who she didn't have to worry about. She knew no one would come looking for either one of them, at least not for a while. Zuri was just confused about what

Alice was about to reveal to her. *What was the big secret I didn't know?*

16

Caught Between a Rock and a Hard Place

Zuri woke up to Massimo holding her tightly as she laid on his chest. She forgot to set the alarm but after the night they had, they both needed to sleep in. She looked up at Massimo just as he opened his eyes. "Good morning beautiful."

Zuri smiled. "Good morning, handsome. What time is it?"

Massimo looked at his phone. "Just after eleven. I could get used to this again. I really do miss waking up to your beautiful face. We never did get to experience the married life. I pray that we do after all this is handled."

"I want nothing more than to wake up to you for the rest of my life," Zuri said as she leaned in for a kiss.

Massimo pulled Zuri in closer, kissing her deeply. He leaned back slightly and looked into her eyes. "I have a surprise for you. I know the timing isn't right, but I think it will help if we have just a few hours of retreat versus the constant stress we've been under."

Zuri smiled. "Tell me! Tell me! What is it?"

"Let's get ready and have some breakfast. Then, we'll head out."

Zuri got up and started jumping on the bed like a little kid. "I'm getting a surprise! Woohoo!" She fell back on the bed and rolled out of it. She ran to Massimo's side, gave him another kiss, and ran into the bathroom. "I need to soak, but I'll be quick," she yelled. *Today is going to be a great day.*

By the time Zuri walked out, breakfast was ready and waiting for her. She wore a beautiful black ensemble by M.M.LaFleur. Massimo was stunned when he saw her. He went up to her and pulled her in for a passionate kiss. "You're truly gorgeous."

"You're not so bad yourself," Zuri said as she dusted off Massimo's shoulder with her hand.

Massimo was wearing an all-black Amiri outfit. They were always in sync with the way they dressed, even after all these years.

After breakfast, Massimo pulled out a blindfold. "Now, it's time for your surprise," he said as he walked over to her.

She turned around so he could blindfold her. He grabbed her hand to help her out of the seat and led her to the other side of the safe house. Since Zuri couldn't see, it caused her other senses to heighten. She listened intently, trying to navigate the sounds around her. She heard a door open and Massimo let go of her hand. She felt Massimo stand behind her as he took a deep breath and said, "Are you ready?"

Zuri nodded with a big smile.

When Massimo took off the blindfold, Zuri was amazed at what she saw. Massimo had set up the room similar to the way he did for their engagement years ago. There were red rose petals everywhere on the floor; several dozen bouquets of flowers spread around the room, including orchids and a mix of blue, red, and white roses. Toward the back of the room was a large sign that said, "Will you be mine?"

Zuri turned around to face Massimo. There was a glimmer in his eyes that made her heart skip a beat. She hugged him, and he held her tightly.

Massimo released her and held her hands. "I know you've been going through hell, but I want you to know that I'm here for you, and I will support you. We'll get through this, and once we do, we'll be able to do all the things that we weren't able to do back then. I've spent too much time away from you, and I don't want to lose another moment with you. Even though the current circumstances are bad, I'm grateful because it brought me back to you." Massimo took a step back, got down on one knee, and proposed to Zuri. The ring was different than the ring he gave her the first time. This was a sapphire-centered square-cut ring with diamonds around the stone.

Even though Zuri didn't see this coming, she knew there was no one else in the world for her and that nothing would stop her from saying yes. "Yes!" Zuri said as Massimo slid the ring onto her finger. *Massimo is right—the circumstances are terrible, but the celebration of our love has provided a much-needed break from the chaos we have been dealing with.*

Reality hit the next day when Zuri walked into the computer room to see if the police investigation had gained any traction. After digging into the database, she was happy to report that the investigation had stalled. Massimo had been sitting beside her, but she realized she was so enthralled by the updates in the database that she hadn't seen him leave. Zuri headed upstairs to find him so she could update him on the good news. When she made it to the main floor, she saw him outside in the garden, tussling with his head of security. *That's not good.* She walked toward them and opened the garden door. "Baby, are you okay?"

"Fine. Please go back downstairs," Massimo said.

"Okay . . ." Zuri replied, confused on what the hell was happening. She wanted to say more, but she left it alone. She closed the door behind her and walked back downstairs—turning back a few times to see Massimo watching her. *What the hell was that?*

Zuri paced back and forth, trying not to stress about the encounter. *Ehh. That's the life of a boss. His head of security must've royally messed up.* Zuri made a note to ask him about that later. *I have my own crap to worry about.* She quickly sat down, putting the minor altercation out of her mind, and continued her research into planning their next steps.

About twenty minutes later, when she was about to head back upstairs to check on Massimo, a notification from the dark web popped up on the screen titled, "$500K BOUNTY: ZUR." Zuri clicked on it, and sure enough, there was a half-a-million-dollar bounty on her head. As she read further, the post stated that whoever found Zuri should turn her into the police—alive or dead—whichever they preferred.

Just as Zuri was about to yell for Massimo, Massimo walked into the tech room. "Look!" Zuri yelled to Massimo while pointing at the screen.

He saw the message on the screen and became furious. "I
will get this taken care of right now," he said as he grabbed his cellphone from his back pocket.

"Wait, I think it's time I turn myself in. I'm one of the best damn lawyers in the U.S. I can defend myself, prove my innocence, and I can do it sooner than this bounty will be fulfilled. If I turn myself in, which is all they want, we can control the narrative. While I do that, I need you to take care of this and have it called off. I imagine that the person who posted this is someone who was either close to The Butcher or part of one of the organizations that is searching for me. This has to be someone who is connected to both sides."

"I cannot and will not let you do that. Hear me out. I know you're stubborn, and I know you'll do what you want, but you need to understand that we can change the narrative without you ever having to turn yourself in. I've been thinking, we got rid of Sophia, Alice, and those men, which means we have a perfect opportunity to pin the murders on them. We know you didn't do the murders, and based on the conversations we had with Sophia and Alice, this was all a set up to frame you. They are responsible for those murders, not you. We need to go back to their hotel room and see if we can find evidence that will link them back to the murder. If not, then we plant it and get the hell out of there."

Zuri sat there, thinking. "That's not a bad idea. Not a bad idea at all . . . Let's do it. This way, my name will be clear, the bounty will be clear, and we can get out from under this bullshit. I will check the hotel database and see if the rooms are still reserved. If so, let's get over there. It will give us an opportunity to check, plan, and strategize," she said as she started typing away.

"I'll get some things packed for the trip and figure out an entrance and exit strategy," Massimo said as he left the room.

Zuri got to work planning what would hopefully be the final stage of this chaotic episode. Zuri was clear-headed but angry. In all her years as an assassin, she never had a bounty on her head. *It's times like these that I miss UQ because he would have tracked the person down and made sure they never saw the light of day again.* She laughed to herself. Zuri realized that she wouldn't be the person she was today if it wasn't for UQ. Regardless of all the bad UQ did, a part of her still loved him for who he was to her when she needed him. He taught her—

"Time to go," Massimo said, annihilating Zuri's thought process.

Zuri turned around and nodded. *Oh well. Time to focus on the present. The past is dead and gone, just like Alice, Sophia—and UQ.*

They headed out of Massimo's safe house just before dark. The plan was to walk in through the front door of the hotel, looking like a normal couple staying there. Before they left, Zuri was able to find out that there was a big event happening at the hotel, which meant the lobby would be packed—just like last time.

They arrived at the hotel in the midst of the chaos. Parking alone was horrendous. As they got out of the car and approached the front of the hotel, it was mayhem. They walked in showing security a room key that they took from Sophia's pocket. The security guard let them in, and they headed for the elevator hand in hand. *Phase I complete.*

They were relaxed and calm as they got into the elevator with several people. After a few stops, they finally arrived on the sixth floor. The elevator dinged, and the doors opened. They got out and walked to Sophia's room. They were relieved to see the 'Do Not Disturb' sign was still hanging on the door, which meant the room would look the same way it did when they left it a few days ago. They keyed into the room and saw a light on. *Phase II complete.* As soon as the door closed behind them, they began their search. Zuri signaled Massimo to start searching one side of the room while she did the other. They looked everywhere—in between the couch cushions, under the rugs, in and underneath the clothing drawers—pulling the entire room apart. After twenty minutes, Massimo called out, "I found something."

Zuri walked over to him and saw a USB drive in his hand. "Bingo," she said.

They kept searching for another ten minutes but came up short. Besides the USB drive, there was nothing else incriminating. Zuri took one final look around. The place was trashed, but in the grand scheme of things, it didn't matter because they got what they were looking for.

"Let's go," Massimo said as he reached for Zuri's hand.

They left the room, and Zuri felt a sense of accomplishment as they headed for the elevator. The elevator arrived, and they rode it back down to the crowded lobby. *Phase III complete.*

The lobby was even more chaotic than it had been when they first entered. They made it through the front door, and Zuri noticed two things as the lobby door opened—the sound of a helicopter approaching and the feeling of a midsummer's breeze.

"Babe, we—" Zuri's sentence was cut short as cop cars rounded the corners of the hotel street, sirens blaring. Her heart started to race as police officers stepped out of their cars with their guns drawn and pointed at Zuri and Massimo. To make matters worse, the helicopter that she had heard was right above them now, shining a bright light down on them.

"Hands up!"

"Get down!"

"Do it now!"

She could hear the voices of several police officers shouting commands at her. *Damn it.* Time slowed in her mind as she looked from left to right. With her hands slowly raised, Zuri noticed that the moon was sitting perfectly round in the sky. As she knelt to her knees, hands still raised, Zuri looked around and noticed that there were not just police officers on the scene but a few detectives and MI6 agents with firearms pointed at her.

Her thoughts were scattered when she felt a push on her back that sent her flying forward. She could hear the handcuffs being drawn and then felt the cold metal on her wrists as the officer brought her hands behind her back, one at a time. Two officers hoisted her up, and as she stood, a smile escaped her lips. *UQ would be proud to see me go out with a bang.* As they walked her to a police car, she could hear Massimo yelling, "Don't say anything. I'll get you a lawyer."

Zuri snapped out of the daze she was in. As an officer put her into the back of a police car, she held her head high, looked back, and yelled, "I am a lawyer!" As the car pulled off, Zuri could see Massimo talking to two officers. Zuri had never been in the back of a police car, and she detested the fact that she was—the scent of donuts, sweat, and throw-up was less than desirable.

They arrived at the police station, and there was a media frenzy awaiting her arrival. *My very own perp walk.* She couldn't imagine what the headlines would be. In sync, the officers got out of the car, and one officer opened her door as the other helped Zuri out. The camera flashes were bright and hurt her eyes, so she looked down as they walked into the police station. *Now, I know why all perps look down. Always thought it was guilt—but no—it's because they are being blinded.*

The officers escorted her to an interrogation room, un-cuffed her, and sat her down in a cold metal chair. They walked out, leaving Zuri all alone as she rubbed the area of her wrists where the handcuffs used to be. She looked around the room and noticed that the room looked like all the interrogation rooms she saw on TV—dim lights, no real windows, a crappy metal table, and crappy metal chairs.

She waited for what felt like hours. Finally, two detectives walked in. One was a woman, a Parisian native it seemed, with a white blouse and gray slacks. The second was a man who looked to be part of MI6. He was wearing a black suit with a navy-blue shirt, no tie. Zuri looked at them, observing and watching. She was watching for their tells that would be hard for the average person to notice.

The woman sat down in front of Zuri, and the man stood to the left of them. *They sent the woman in first hoping to make this personal.* Zuri met the eyes of the female, and both stared without a word being said.

"Zuri Dawson, we've been looking for you for some time now," the male detective said as he threw her folder down on the metal table.

Zuri didn't flinch nor did she break her gaze from the female detective. *A good old-fashioned stare down.* Zuri slowly moved her eyes to the male detective and then to the folder. She grabbed the folder, but before she could open it, the female detective snatched the folder from her hands. Zuri smirked and leaned back in the chair, watching as the female detective scratched her eyebrow before she spoke.

"Zuri, we want to talk to you about the flight coming into Paris. We have reason to believe that you have prevalent information on who did what and why."

Zuri held her position, not moving a muscle.

The male detective jumped in, "What did you see? Did you see any suspicious activity? We know about the other two individuals. The one who was clearly guilty of a murder and the other who killed in self-defense. Then we have the third suspect—you—who we believe is guilty of the final murder."

"The murder of a diplomat, at that," the female detective stated rather quickly.

Zuri only looked back and forth between the detectives. *They need answers to questions that they obviously don't have.* She leaned forward enough to fold her hands on the table and then she crossed her right leg over her left and smugly said, "Sounds like jack shit to me."

The detectives just stared at her, until finally, the female detective broke the silence, "Let me explain something to you; we have witnesses and evidence that puts you by the stall at the approximate time of death. We have someone who recorded you walking to the bathroom at the same time the diplomat was there. We have enough evidence to keep you in jail for the rest of your life. And let me not get started—"

Zuri cut the female detective off by putting one finger in the air. "That type of lie must work on less educated individuals. See, I'm a lawyer, so let me explain something to you. First, I know for a fact that no one was recording me while I was walking to the bathroom. That's just creepy. Second, let's say this magical recording doesn't exist. We all know eyewitness testimony is not reliable—one person sees this, another sees that. Who knows what they really saw on a dark plane. If you're trying to fool me, try again. I know the laws in Paris, so let's cut the bull." Zuri leaned back, keeping a smirk on her face. *I'm the best in the business—this is the shit I live for.*

"We have one last question for you," the male detective said. "That guy you were with, we can't seem to find who he is or where he is. Apparently, shortly after arresting you, he disappeared. Can you give us his information so we can contact him?"

Zuri lifted her middle finger as she smiled. *But where did Massimo go?*

17

Everything Has Its Time

It had been eight months since Zuri was arrested in front of the Pullman Paris Tour Eiffel Hotel. It was a waiting game at this point. Zuri hoped that the pressure from her lawyer—her Parisian friend who helped Marcy—along with Massimo's status, could get her out of there, but it was highly unlikely. She was in unfamiliar territory.

Zuri was neither tried nor convicted of the murder of the diplomat. She was so confused how she got here considering she was one of the best lawyers in the damn business. *Technically though, I'm one of the best corporate lawyers in the business—which, I finally have to admit to myself, is not helpful in this situation.* This was not America either, and the laws were drastically different.

The investigating magistrate was working on Zuri's case and due to the severity of the crime, she was denied bail and put in pre-trial detention. Zuri knew she had made a fool of the Parisian police, FBI, and MI6 considering how long it took them to find her. It came at a cost because she was sure that the magistrate was going to make an example out of her. Additionally, there was negative media attention surrounding the case, and Zuri knew Paris was trying to save face at this point—at least, that is what her lawyer had mentioned to her. The lawyer had done his best to help Zuri, but the process was slow. Massimo had tried to help as well, but again, the process was slow.

A few days after her arrest, the lawyer pulled strings for Massimo to see Zuri. Massimo conveyed three pieces of information to her. First, he dispelled the lies the detectives told her about him being missing. He had cooperated as best he could, without drawing too much attention to himself. Second, he let her know that the USB drive they found was heavily encrypted with coding that he had only seen once on a mission in Central Europe. He had his entire tech team working to break into the drive. Third, he was able to get the bounty on Zuri's head removed.

Every visit from Massimo since then had sounded like a broken record. Each time he showed up, Zuri made sure to ask about the USB drive, but he could only tell her the same thing. *Every time we get closer, another firewall blocks our access.* So, every day for the last eight months, Zuri paced her prison cell.

Some days, she accepted that this was her fate—her karma—for all the people she had killed. She knew this day would inevitably come. Other days, she was defeated and was waiting for a miracle that she knew she didn't deserve. Zuri realized very early on that prison had a way of making people look inward at who they were and who they were destined to become before their lives changed for the worse. In addition to the self-reflection, Zuri also had adapted to the physicalities of prison life.

The prison conditions were horrendous, and she knew this was the last place she wanted to be, especially because France had previously been reprehended by the European Court of Human Rights due to the poor, inhumane detention conditions. Zuri was unable to get acclimated in prison because she refused to talk to anyone and got into several fights with other inmates within her first few days there. Being surrounded by other females made Zuri miss her space, her privacy, and her sanity, but more importantly, she missed her freedom.

At this juncture, she realized that God should've allowed Paul or Alice to shoot her dead. She had accepted that death was her inevitable demise. She couldn't understand why God would spare her life just for her to rot away in prison. Zuri acknowledged that maybe, death was too easy of a punishment for the life she lived. She believed there was only so much sinning and killing one could do before God became agitated. His punishment, His wrath, His judgment had been declared on her. Zuri conceded that she would endure her misfortune and persevere.

"Dawson!" one of the guards yelled, breaking Zuri's concentration. "You have a visitor."

Zuri was handcuffed and escorted to a room where Massimo and her lawyer were sitting. The guard took the handcuffs off as Zuri sat across from Massimo and her lawyer. "What's going on?"

"We did it," Massimo said before her lawyer could get a word in. "We got into the USB."

The lawyer started laughing and glanced at Massimo just before he looked at Zuri. "You will be released shortly," the lawyer said to her.

She looked at both of them dumbfounded. "I'm confused. How did this happen?"

"One of my associates found a pre-recorded video file from Sophia. She and Alice had planned the attack for years. There were also files and video recordings of both of them walking through each step of the plot and plan. We checked for authenticity—nothing was altered. We showed the evidence to the investigating judge and the prosecution. The judge reviewed the files and made the decision to vacate the charge and release you. You're free to go," Massimo said with a huge smile on his face.

Her lawyer jumped in. "I have some paperwork to complete, but you should be out by the end of the day."

Zuri couldn't believe what she was hearing. She was finally going to be out of this place. She grabbed Massimo's hand and squeezed it tightly and then she shook her lawyer's hand. "I cannot thank you enough. It hasn't been easy, but I wouldn't have wanted anyone else representing me," she said.

The lawyer nodded at Zuri with a grin on his face. "Thank Massimo. If it wasn't for him getting into that USB, I don't know how much help I would've been."

"It was a team effort," Massimo said, patting the lawyer on his back.

Zuri got up, shook the lawyer's hand one more time, and then signaled for the guard. The guard came over and handcuffed Zuri to take her back to her cell.

"I'll see you soon, baby," Massimo said just as she was walking away with the guard.

Zuri took a deep breath as she stepped out of the prison—finally free. Eight months of her life were gone, and while not a big deal to some, she felt as though she had already lost too much time. It was cloudy out, and the cold air sent a shiver down her spine. Zuri saw Massimo, and he ran to her, picking her up, swinging her around, and giving her a kiss. She missed those lips and didn't want to let him go. Yes, she missed her freedom, but she missed her freedom with Massimo even more. She hated not being able to kiss him, touch him, or hold him these last few months.

"Let's get you out of here," he said as he picked her up and carried her to the car.

Massimo put her down as they neared the vehicle and opened the passenger's side of a red two-door 1987 Ferrari 275 GTB4. In the passenger's seat was Zuri's Michael Kors double-breasted princess coat with fur cuffs. Massimo grabbed it and helped her put it on. Warm and cozy, Zuri got in, sat back, and prepared to enjoy the ride. "Where are we going?" Zuri asked as Massimo sped down the road.

"First things first, we need to get you a warm bath and some sleep in a nice bed. Tonight is a night for you to enjoy your freedom and rest. We are headed to the 16th arrondissement."

Zuri nodded and let the air from her partially rolled down window soothe her soul.

Three hours later, they arrived at a building Zuri had never seen before. Massimo turned off the car and got out first. He ran around the back of the car so he could open Zuri's door for her. He helped her out and led the way into an amazingly stunning apartment.

As Massimo opened the door and led Zuri in, her mouth dropped at the luxurious place before her eyes. The apartment consisted of high ceilings and beautiful beige walls with gold accents around it. The place was fully furnished with colorful artwork and black furniture. As she walked around, she saw a door leading to a pool and a garden, as well as a dining room, kitchen, bedroom, study, and fitness room. The floors were gorgeously marbled.

"Come, babe," Massimo said.

Zuri ran down the hall so she could follow him up to the second floor where there were four bedrooms, including the main suite. The main suite consisted of a king-sized bed and two nightstands and was connected to a private bathroom. Massimo led her into the main suite and then into the private bathroom. He walked over to the bathtub and started running the water for her. Zuri sat down on one of the chairs, exhausted.

Zuri's mind was blank—her body was sore, and her soul was tired. These last few months had drained her to the point of no return. She felt defeated, even though the fight for freedom was finally over.

"Z, I know you're tired. I'm not sure if you want me to leave you be or keep you company, but whatever you need, I'm here. There is also a wine cellar downstairs, so I can grab you a bottle of Cabernet Sauvignon while you get into the tub."

"Wine would be perfect." She winked, if only to let him know she was appreciating his effort.

Massimo walked over to where she was sitting, kissed her forehead, and then walked out of the room.

Zuri got into the tub to soak. Truthfully, she wanted to drown herself. She wasn't sure what prison had done to her—she felt trapped in her mind. She no longer felt like herself and wanted to stop the pain. She couldn't fathom how people spent years in prison because eight months had completely broken her. Just as she was going to slide her head under the water, Massimo walked in with her wine.

"Baby, are you okay?" he asked, walking over to her and handing her a glass.

Tears started to well up in Zuri's eyes, causing Massimo to kneel by the side of the tub and grab her hand, interlacing his fingers in between hers.

"I feel lost. I feel lost, and I'm tired—emotionally, mentally, and physically. These last few months took a toll on me, and I don't know how to pull myself out of this."

Massimo let go of Zuri's hand to grab a wooden stool that was near the chair Zuri was previously sitting on and pulled it closer to the tub so he could sit with her. He took her hands in his again and kissed the top of them. "Z, it's okay to feel this way. You were just released from prison. You don't have to be strong. I'll be strong for you. These last few months were hell on you, and I know how hard that lifestyle can be. It will take time, but you will start to feel like yourself again. I know you will. Just take it day by day. Right now, I think you're overwhelmed. It's been a long day, and a lot has happened. Let's get you to bed, and maybe you will start to feel better after a long night of sleep."

Zuri quietly stood up in the tub, ready to get out. Massimo grabbed a towel and wrapped it around her. Once she was fully out of the tub, Massimo held her tightly. It only took a few seconds before Zuri was sobbing into his chest. He rubbed her back and said, "It will be alright, Z. It'll be alright."

She stopped crying long enough to dry off, and Massimo helped her put a robe on. They walked out of the bathroom and into the bedroom. Massimo pulled the covers back for Zuri to get into bed and then he cuddled alongside her, under the covers. As they spooned, Massimo could feel her quickened heartbeat as well as the tears landing on his arm where her head lay. He lay there, holding her until she fell asleep.

It was evening when Zuri woke up. She was so confused on where she was that she began to panic. She quickly turned around to see that Massimo was sitting on the bed beside her. A wave of calmness fell over her. "I had no idea where I was for a second."

"I had a feeling you might wake up confused. You slept through the night and all of today. It's now time for dinner, which I have prepared for you downstairs."

Zuri turned to face the clock—6:07 p.m. She had slept for almost twenty hours. She laid her head back on the pillow, rubbing her eyes and staring at the ceiling while Massimo watched her. Five minutes later, she turned to face him. "Kiss me, baby," she said in a playful voice.

Massimo transitioned over to her side of the bed and kissed her.

She pulled his face in for a few more kisses. "I want us to get married today. I want to be yours forever. I want to have a baby," she said.

Massimo pulled back. Even though he was smiling, Zuri could see the confusion in his eyes. "Babe, what's going on? You know that I want all these things as well, but you just got out of prison and haven't even had time to adjust. Are you sure you want to jump into things? Maybe take some time to get back to yourself."

"I thought about it, and I already lost the life I built. The case was international. I know I no longer have a job—the firm dropped me the minute news spread about my arrest. I'm sure the Bar Association is ready to take away my license even though I'm innocent, and honestly, I'm happy about it. I just want to be yours and live the life we always dreamed of—a life of success, happiness, and love. I don't want to go back to the life I built. I want to build a new life—with you."

Massimo kissed her lips and said, "How about this, go take a shower and get ready. Take some time to think this over and let's revisit this conversation later."

"Promise?"

"Promise."

Zuri got out of bed, hopped in the shower, and got dressed in a black Dior hoodie and black leggings. She wanted to keep it simple today. Even though she felt better than she did before she went to sleep, she knew she was not one hundred percent. She could accept that it would take time to get adjusted, but she also knew she would never get back to the person she once was. Therefore, it was time for her to embrace the new Zuri.

She looked at herself in the bathroom mirror and noticed the dark circles around her eyes. She looked different—tired. She wiped the tears that were falling down her face. *Weakness is what I see. But even though my enemies won the battle to frame me, they are all dead—I won the war.* Zuri laughed to herself as the words crossed her mind. She turned her back to the mirror and looked around. Zuri was in love with this bathroom.

The bathroom had extra-large marbled tiled floors with a beige-pink color throughout the bathroom. The tub and shower combo, along with the bathroom cabinets, all matched perfectly. There were two large mirrors and a beautiful window that the sun was coming through.

Zuri looked toward the window and then looked at herself in the mirror one last time. She took a deep breath and headed for the door.

18

The Ceremony

It had been several weeks since Zuri was released from prison, and she was feeling better each day. With Massimo by her side, being a constant support and sounding board for her, she really was accepting this new Zuri.

Zuri thought of herself as a caterpillar; prison was her pupa or chrysalis stage where she was cocooning, locked away, and waiting. After she was molded within the cocoon, prison, she was released from her old self. Her freedom was her final transition into a beautiful butterfly. Through the tears, anger, bitterness, and pity she had blossomed into something new and captivating. She decided to take each day as it came—making a vow to herself to look at herself in the mirror every morning, repeating the lines, "I am a butterfly. Bold and Beautiful. I've shed my cocoon and will no longer let it weigh me down. I am profound."

This morning was no different. After Zuri took her shower, she wiped the fogged-up mirror so she could look at herself. "I am a butterfly. Bold and Beautiful. I've shed my cocoon and will no longer let it weigh me down. I am profound." Zuri smiled at herself as she got dressed, wearing a beautiful turquoise-blue sundress that she bought from a little boutique in Paris. She was excited for another day of freedom, and hopefully, a romantic day with Massimo. She looked at herself in the mirror one last time—taking a breath in to accept the positivity and letting that same breath out to release the negativity. She smiled and headed for the door.

When Zuri opened the door, Massimo was standing in front with a bouquet of white roses and two rings. "Let's do it, baby. You're my light. You're everything I wanted in this life and more. Without you, my life lacks meaning. Your presence creates a lightness in my soul. You're my rock as I am yours. You're my safety and my truth. You're my best friend and my fiancé. You're everything I have to have, and there is no one like you."

Zuri smiled as a tear ran down her face.

"These are for you, baby," he said as he gave her the roses. "Let's go get married."

Zuri grabbed them, and Massimo pulled her in for a deep kiss, which completely mesmerized her. Releasing the lip lock, Massimo grabbed her hand, and led her out of the bedroom and down the stairs.

"If we're going to get married, I have one request," he said.

"What is it?"

"Let's go to Italy. I want us to be around old family and friends."

Zuri thought about this for a moment. It had been years since she was at the family house in Italy—decades even. She was ecstatic because deep down, she missed Italy. She missed the food, the culture, and the language, which she used to be fluent in. "Let's go."

Zuri realized that there was no more running. She knew by accepting his engagement proposal, and now this wedding proposal, she was stepping into a new life with Massimo. If these last few weeks had taught her anything, it was that she could not run from fate. Yes, she may have tried to leave this life behind, and yes, she was able to for a little while, but when it was all said and done, it was this life that gave her hope for the future. UQ used to say there is no freedom for an assassin, but she and Massimo proved him wrong—they were free. *UQ was wrong. You can live by the sword and die by the sword, but you can also survive the sword, and that is the biggest challenge of them all.*

"I cannot run from who I was born to be anymore. Let's go back to the house and run this organization the way UQ would have wanted us to—as husband and wife."

Massimo smiled and grabbed two duffle bags that were on the floor at the bottom of the stairs. "I packed a bag for both of us, and I have a private plane waiting for us at the airport. Let's go be the power couple we were meant to be."

Zuri grabbed her bag and skipped to the door. *This is what was meant to be.*

They arrived in Italy and were escorted to the family house by Massimo's security team. Zuri marveled at the length of time she had been away from Italy and the estate. She never thought she would see it again, *ever.*

The Italy estate was gorgeous. Thinking back on it, Zuri always dreamed of getting married to Massimo there and starting a family, if not the safe house in Paris. The estate was secluded and surrounded by an immense number of trees and forestry. The mansion sat on nine acres of land and had eight bedrooms, seven bathrooms, and an Olympic-sized in-ground pool.

The car pulled them in front of the estate, and one of the security guards opened her door, reaching his hand out so he could help Zuri out of the car. "Welcome home, Signora Dawson! We missed you," the guard said when he saw who she was. "Good to see you again Signore Mariano."

Massimo nodded to the security guard and then walked over to Zuri and grabbed her hand. "Welcome home, baby."

"Race you to the doors like old times? Winner chooses dinner?" she asked.

"You're on. Ready?" He got into his running stance.

"Set," she said, getting into hers.

"Go!" they both yelled and bolted toward the front door. It was about a quarter mile from the car, and Massimo made it to the door first.

"You haven't beat me since we were little kids," Zuri said.

"Winner gets to pick dinner! Don't worry, I'll make sure it's something special," he laughed. They both were picky eaters so whoever won always had to eat something the other hated. It was the best revenge. Massimo would lose to Zuri ninety percent of the time when they were younger, and Zuri took delight in watching him suffer at the dinner table.

They walked into the house, and at the front door, they were greeted by several security guards on the premises.

Zuri continued walking deeper into the house and was amazed at all the beautiful changes Massimo made. "This place looks amazing. You did a good job with updating it while not taking away from the history of the house—it's perfect."

He hugged her from behind, his arms around her waist. He spoke softly into her ear, "You want my honest truth?"

"Shoot," she replied, wrapping her arms around his.

"Call me a hopeless romantic, but I was getting this house ready for us to live in. I knew that there was a chance I would die before that happened, but I had a sliver of hope that you would come back to me." He turned her around to face him and held her hands. "Cheers to the sliver," he said as he laid one kiss on the top of each hand. "Come, let me show you something." Massimo held onto Zuri's left hand and led her toward the living room.

When they got in there, Zuri noticed several chairs in the room and several people who were standing around, talking amongst themselves. Zuri quickly recognized one of her old trainers, two of the teachers who homeschooled her, and two of UQ's most trusted men—who were now two of Massimo's most trusted men. Once they saw Zuri, they all shouted her name in unison and collectively walked toward her and Massimo.

After a few minutes of conversation and hugs, Zuri's old trainer handed her a bouquet of flowers. The talking stopped and a podium was rolled out by a Pastor. Zuri looked over at Massimo, who was across the room. Zuri realized that this wasn't just a reunion but a wedding—their wedding.

Massimo walked within a few feet of Zuri. "Mar, if you'll have me, I want us to get married here and now, and before you say—"

Before Massimo could finish his sentence, Zuri jumped in and giggled as she said, customizing the famous line from the movie Jerry Maguire, "You had me at Mar." Zuri couldn't pinpoint the last time Massimo called her by the nickname Mar. She thought back to the time he formed that nickname for her. He spent all afternoon trying to come up with a nickname that was unique to him, and when he finally settled on Mar, she loved it. This nickname held so much emotion and power in it that it caused her heart to skip a beat when she heard it for the first time in decades.

Zuri walked closer to Massimo, closing the gap between them, and wrapped her arm around his as they made their way down to the altar. The Pastor nodded to the people in the area, signaling for them to sit. Zuri and Massimo faced each other and held hands as the Paster began the ceremony, blessing Zuri and Massimo as well as their marriage. Shortly after, the Pastor gestured for them to give their vows, and though they didn't prepare any, they spoke from the heart and made several people in the audience cry.

The Pastor asked for someone to bring the rings. One of Massimo's trusted men reached into his inner suit jacket pocket and pulled out a blue Tiffany ring box. He stood up and walked over to Massimo, smiling with approval as he handed Massimo the box. Massimo let go of Zuri's hands as he grabbed the box and opened it. Inside were two wedding bands, a sapphire stone platinum wedding band for Zuri and a plain platinum wedding band for Massimo. He took out both wedding bands and gave Zuri his and then put the box in his pocket. The Pastor continued on as they both recited traditional marriage vows, each putting a ring on the others' finger at the conclusion. "I now present to you, Mr. and Mrs. Don Massimo Mariano. You may kiss your bride."

Everyone cheered as Massimo grabbed Zuri in close and kissed her passionately. In between kisses, Massimo said, "Here is to the beginning of forever."

It was late when everyone finally left after a day filled with catching up with old friends, eating, drinking, and of course, the wedding. Zuri was happy to have Massimo all to herself after everyone left.

"Mrs. Mariano, would you like me to carry you over the threshold into our bedroom?"

"Yes, please," Zuri said.

Massimo picked her up, one arm holding the back of her legs and the other on her back as she wrapped her arms around his neck. He walked up the stairs and pushed the door open, revealing the main bedroom, which was lit with candles, rose petals on the bed, and wine being chilled in an ice bucket.

Zuri gasped and smiled, taking in the beautiful romantic setup Massimo had created for their wedding night. He gently placed her on the bed and proceeded to lay on top of her. She stared into his eyes and played with his hair before she said to him, "I love you—you know that, right?"

"Yes, I know. I love you too." He leaned in for a kiss, and they spent the night for the first time in their lives as husband and wife.

19

The Ultimate Betrayal

It had been a few weeks since the wedding, and the married couple couldn't be happier. Zuri was in heaven as she lay by the pool, relaxing. She loved being Massimo's wife, and Massimo loved being her husband. It all felt surreal to Zuri—she took it step by step, day by day—accepting this new life she had wished for and watching it blossom before her eyes.

Motherhood was on her mind when she thought about the life she had wished for. She believed that motherhood was the next step in their journey. She had yet to mention it to Massimo because he had been focused on getting caught up with the business, which she knew was her fault. Massimo had spent so much time focusing on getting Zuri free, that the syndicate took a few hits, and Massimo had a few problems that needed to be addressed immediately.

"Mar," Massimo called as he walked through the back door and headed toward Zuri by the pool.

Zuri turned around to see her sexy husband dressed in a blue pinstripe suit with a black tie and black shoes.

"I need to ride into town. I have a few urgent meetings and need to take care of some things. I'll fill you in when I get back." Massimo got to the chair Zuri was sitting in and leaned down to kiss her.

"Sure, babe. I'll make sure dinner is ready for you when you get back."

"Sounds like a plan. If I'm running late, I'll let you know. Have the chef prepare whatever you're in the mood for. And please make sure you do something besides sit by the pool—maybe go for a walk or for a swim."

"Yes, babe," Zuri said in an annoyed voice. She hated that people were reporting back to Massimo what she was doing during the day. She had a strong inkling it was the maid, who Massimo called when Zuri didn't answer the phone. She did have to admit that even though she was feeling like herself, every time Massimo left the house, she found herself saddened and slightly depressed. She wasn't sure what was going on, but she had grown dependent on him—she felt like she couldn't live without him.

As he walked away and got into the car, Zuri couldn't help but think about how alone she already felt. The car pulled off, and the maid came through the back door with a glass of sparkling water. "Here you go, Signora," she said.

"Thank you, Luna," Zuri replied, grabbing the glass from her.

Luna retreated, and Zuri put the glass down on the table next to her. It was a warm sunny day, and there was a calm wind blowing. *I'm going to go for a walk today. No time like the present to push myself out of this funk.* Zuri grabbed the water and headed back into the house to change her clothes. She put on a pair of leggings and a t-shirt so she could walk around the estate. She made sure she carried her gun with her at all times because it was the only thing that made her feel safe when Massimo wasn't around. She holstered it behind her back and walked downstairs to the kitchen. Zuri chugged the water Luna had brought her, put the glass in the kitchen sink, and then headed out the side door.

Zuri wasn't sure how long she had been walking, but she knew it had been at least over an hour because when she turned back, the estate was far away. As she continued walking, she noticed a structure a few feet to the left, surrounded by trees. *That's weird. I know this estate like the back of my hand. Maybe this is one of Massimo's new additions?* As she got closer, she realized that the house was off the gravel path, and she had to walk in the grass to access it. She got closer and saw it was a quaint, little house. Zuri walked to the front door and tried the door handle—it was open. Slowly, she walked into the house and called out, "Hello?" There was no answer. Zuri checked her surroundings one more time before she fully stepped into the house, closing the door behind her.

The single-story house was cozy and smelled of cinnamon. As Zuri looked around, she noticed that the entire house was painted with white walls and had exquisite cream furniture. It looked like a staged house in a home décor magazine. The house consisted of two bedrooms and two bathrooms. Each bedroom had a king-sized bed with two nightstands and a lamp on each nightstand; one bedroom had a writing desk and a bookshelf, while the other had an armoire wardrobe closet. Each bathroom had a single sink with marble floors; the first bathroom had a shower and the second bathroom had a bathtub. The kitchen had an island with updated appliances.

The house looked fairly new and barely lived in. She walked into the living room and saw a few pictures sitting on the side tables next to the TV. She walked over to one of the tables. It was Massimo and a little girl. *Who is that with Massimo?* Zuri grabbed another picture, which looked like the same little girl but a few years older. Zuri had a bad feeling. *Why the hell does this little girl look like me?* She put the picture down and reached for her phone so she could call Massimo and ask him what was going on.

Just as she was about to call him, she heard a noise. It was faint but loud enough that she noticed it. Zuri put her phone back in her pocket and walked toward the noise. It was coming from the bedroom that had the bookcase. Zuri put her ear to the wall and heard the noise again—this time, it was louder. Zuri felt around the walls to see if there was a hidden door somewhere, but she couldn't find one. After thoroughly looking, she decided that she should move the bookcase, thinking maybe there was something behind it. Zuri mustered up the strength and pushed the bookcase over to find a hidden door.

Zuri opened the door and saw that there were stairs that led down. *What the hell? Maybe his safe room? But he never mentioned it to me.* She continued looking down the stairs, contemplating if she should go down or just walk away. She chose the former. The staircase was dark, and Zuri had to use the flashlight on her phone just to make her way down. At the bottom, she found a light switch and returned her phone back to her pocket.

The walls were metal, cold, and insulated. She could tell because these were the walls she used in the shed that led to her safe house. Zuri heard the noise again and pulled out her gun, pulling the slide back so she could have a bullet ready and waiting in the chamber. Slowly, she ventured down hallway with the gun pointed straight ahead.

The hallway contained two doors, one to the left and one straight ahead. Zuri headed to the door on the left. She kept her gun raised as she opened the door. She felt around on the left side of the wall for a light switch and then flicked the lights on. Zuri was surprised to find two screens mounted on the wall and paperwork scattered all over a long rectangular metal desk. The room was empty besides that. Zuri checked the hallway to make sure she wasn't followed and then she fully entered the room, quietly closing the door behind her. She holstered her gun and walked up to the desk. There was a keyboard and mouse underneath the papers, so she moved the papers over and shook the mouse. Immediately, both screens turned on, and Zuri gasped as the content appeared. *What the hell?*

On one screen, there were multiple pictures of her over the last seven years, and the other screen had a list of her movements in the last seven years. *No way Massimo was tracking me all this time.* She knew he might have been—but the level of detail was borderline obsessive. As she looked through the pictures, she started to pinpoint where they were taken—in her first apartment, in her current house, fresh out of the shower, and even some of her at work. She had no idea what she was looking at, but it was alarming. She minimized the first collage of herself, and another collage popped up.

"Wait, no!" she yelled, slapping her hand on the table. Zuri rubbed the scar on her hand before she pulled out her gun and held it in her right hand at her side as she started pacing back and forth. On the screen were pictures of everyone involved in the airplane murders—Alice Reese, Sophia West, Paul Black, The Butcher, Sherry Moore, and Marcy Evelien. Zuri's face was in the center of these pictures. *I cannot believe this.* In anger, Zuri slammed the gun on the table, leaving it there, and pushed all the documents to the ground. "He planned all this! He literally planned all this."

She took a deep breath and noticed something among the documents that she threw on the floor. She grabbed a document that was stapled and saw that it held a detailed account of the plan—who was supposed to do what, when, and where. As she flipped through the stapled packet, she saw personal information on every individual; where they lived, what family they had, and how much he paid them. She threw the paper down and grabbed another one, which contained messages between Sophia and Massimo—showing that Massimo confirmed he had the seating arrangements altered so Sophia would sit next to Zuri. *Massimo knew who Paul and Alice were. Massimo planned everything—the people who died, the suspected murderers, all of it was a lie.* "Damn it!" she yelled.

Zuri walked around the room as her heart was beating faster and faster. She grabbed the gun in her hand. Lividity was running through her veins as she yelled, "I'm going to kill him!" Zuri slammed open the door and walked out of the room with her gun held up. The hallway was still clear and quiet. She needed to find Massimo—but before that, she needed to see what was behind the door at the end of the hallway.

Swiftly, she walked toward the door and opened it slowly. The room was pitch black. Zuri reached alongside the wall, feeling for a light switch but couldn't locate it. She pulled her phone out of her back pocket and turned the flashlight on. She quietly closed the door behind her, unsure of where she was. She shone the flashlight around but then something in her gut told her not to move. Zuri placed her back against the door and took a few deep breaths. Just as she was preparing to move, a light turned on.

"Hey, baby," Massimo said. "Fancy seeing you here."

Zuri's eyes adjusted to the light. She quickly turned off her phone's flashlight and put it in her pocket using her left hand while still holding on to the gun in her right. She looked around, trying to figure out where she was. It looked like a cave—electrical wires were running above, and in the far-left corner was a random metal desk, similar to the one she saw in the previous room. On the desk sat a few documents, stacked neatly, and there was a black office chair in front of the desk. Massimo was standing behind the office chair, watching Zuri.

"You son of a bitch. How could you?" Zuri asked as she took a few steps toward him.

"Don't be dramatic. It's really not what you think," he said to her, smirking.

Zuri finally figured it out. She played back all the moments since Massimo came into the picture. *This was all a setup. The finding and rescuing me. Killing Paul.*

Cherishing me. Loving me. Was any of it real? No. How could I be so stupid? How did I allow myself to be fooled by him? Zuri realized that the reason they were able to move from safe house to safe house, staying under the radar in France and continuing to identify numerous suspects who may have caused those crimes, was all because Massimo set it up. He knew everything they were going to do before they did it. She realized that, all along, she was being played by the one person she trusted in the world because of a decision she made years ago—a decision that stopped a reckless man from bringing any more pain into her life.

Zuri looked up at Massimo. "It was you." Tears ran down her face as she processed everything that happened. "It was all you . . . from the beginning."

Massimo looked at her and smiled. "It's really not what you think. I did this to get you back here so you could be the mother I always knew you could be. I know you think I am evil and manipulative, but truthfully, you wouldn't have come back any other way. You're too stubborn. I knew love alone wouldn't work, so I added some conflict but—"

"Wait! What do you mean be a mother? A mother to that little girl I saw you in the picture with upstairs? Who is she? You expect me to raise a daughter that is not mine? Are you insane?"

"Oh, baby," Massimo said. "She is your daughter. I could never have a child with anyone else."

Flabbergasted, Zuri felt her knees go weak. She steadied herself by slowly backing up until she felt the wall behind her.

"Long story short, do you remember the paperwork UQ had us sign to freeze your eggs and my sperm? Well, when you left over ten years ago, I waited three years for you to come back, but you never did. At that point, I knew you weren't coming back ever again. I grew impatient, and I decided it was time to have the baby we always wanted and talked about. I had the doctor we saw overlook your permission, and I had a surrogate carry our daughter to term. Both the doctor and surrogate are dead—just in case you get any ideas about pursuing legal actions toward them. Anyway, you have a daughter. Congratulations." He grabbed a picture from the top of the stacked pile of papers and held it up toward Zuri. "This is your daughter. She's amazing. I promised her I would bring you back to her, and here you are. I did this so we could be a family again. I know that whatever feelings you have toward me, it will be outweighed by the love you want to show our daughter. This was the final surprise I had for you, but I wanted you to get settled in before I broke the news because I needed you to be in a more . . . understanding state of mind. Who knew that the one day I suggested a walk, you would actually take it."

Zuri's tears had yet to cease. She knew Massimo was conniving, but this was a different level of manipulation. He was sick and needed help. Zuri lifted the gun and pointed it at him.

Slowly, Massimo walked toward Zuri. "You're not going to shoot me. I'm the love of your life, remember? And we have a child who needs the both of us."

Zuri stood there, replaying how it would feel to shoot him over and over again in her mind. *Maybe as good as it felt shooting UQ.* "How old is she?" Zuri asked, gun still raised.

"She is seven, about to turn eight, and baby, she's brilliant, intelligent, and beautiful, just like her mom." Massimo smiled as he finally reached where Zuri was standing.

Zuri thought she was dreaming. "Are you serious? My daughter is almost eight years old, and you kept her from me? Does she know who I actually am?"

"She knows everything about how amazing you are. She knew that I was going to bring you back into our lives no matter what, and now, babe . . . Now, we can be one happy family," he said, reaching out to grab her hand.

Zuri smacked his hand away and shoved the gun into Massimo's chest, pushing him backward. Zuri felt an anger surge in her that she never felt before—it was borderline rage. "We will *never* be a happy family because only one of us is going to make it out of this cave alive," Zuri said as she released the safety lever on her gun.

"You aren't who you used to be, and I'm not who I used to be. I love you, Zuri, but I love our daughter even more. She will not grow up in a life of chaos and turmoil like we did."

His words didn't matter to her anymore, so she stopped listening to him. *Do I take the easy route and shoot him or beat the shit out of him?* Zuri knew that she would not allow herself to take the easy route. She slowly lowered the gun, never taking her eyes off Massimo. She knelt and slid the gun to the other side of the room as a smile formed on his face. Zuri stood up and stared, waiting for Massimo to make the first move. They both knew that when the guns go down, the fists go up.

Massimo put his hands up and took a step forward, releasing a right punch. Zuri leaned to dodge the punch, and Massimo quickly snapped his hand back. *Someone's moving slow.* They kept staring at each other, trying to gauge what the other was thinking. The sight of Massimo now made Zuri's rage multiply.

Zuri charged at him, closing the gap between them. She punched him in the face twice then proceeded to kick him. When she kicked him, he grabbed her leg and threw her backward. She lost her footing but managed to keep herself from falling. In the quick second she took to adjust her stance, Massimo ran toward her, picked her up by her throat, and threw her backward, causing her to fall on the floor and land hard on her back. Her adrenaline was rushing so she didn't feel the pain as much as she should have. Zuri quickly rolled on her side and did a swing kick at his legs. He fell, and his back hit the floor, causing him to groan. Zuri pushed herself up and quickly crawled on top of Massimo, releasing blow after blow. Massimo managed to grab her left arm and kneed her at the same time, throwing her off of him. *He's not fighting back. He's deflecting. Why?*

This angered Zuri even more. She stood up, and Massimo followed suit. Zuri walked over to him as she held her fighting stance. Massimo followed her actions, and once they were within a foot of each other, they fought continuously, trading several different punches and kicks, neither of them faltering.

After five minutes of fighting, Zuri noticed a change in Massimo's eyes. She wasn't sure why she noticed it, but it was as if the life left his body and his eyes were soulless. Massimo moved closer to her and double-punched her in the stomach. *Cheap shot.* She keeled over, flabbergasted because Massimo had never done that to her before. She stood up, trying to recover, but was not prepared for the roundhouse kick Massimo delivered to her shoulder. Zuri felt her body give out as she fell to the ground, landing hard then rolling over from the force of the kick. "This is done," he said as he walked over to her.

Massimo grabbed Zuri by her neck, lifted her up, and slammed her back into the wall. The wrath she was feeling was reflected in Massimo's eyes. Massimo banged Zuri's body against the wall a few times and then dropped her, causing her to tumble to the floor, defeated. Massimo didn't stop there. He kicked her, punched her, and watched as she balled up, defenseless. In all her years, no one had ever been able to beat her like this, and she knew at that moment, the ones you love are the ones who are the most dangerous to your well-being.

"Stop!" Zuri shouted.

Massimo ignored her screams and delivered blow after blow. Zuri could feel the life leaving her body. Massimo stopped just before she was about to lose consciousness. Zuri had blood running down her face. Her body was annihilated. The anger, the rage, the love . . . it was all gone.

Massimo walked over to the gun Zuri had thrown across the room and grabbed it. He walked back over to her and pointed the gun at her. "Get up, now!"

She crawled closer to the wall and used it as an anchor to help her get to her feet. *I should've shot him. If only I had known that he was stronger and faster than I once remembered. I should've known.* Zuri could hear Massimo moving closer to her, and when she finally felt steady, she looked up to see the barrel of the gun directly in front of her eyes. "Massimo, please, I surrender."

Massimo slowly lowered the gun and then started pacing back and forth.

"The night you left, I hated you more than I hated my parents. They abandoned me, but you, you're the one who knew me better than I knew myself, and you took something so dear to me. You broke my heart more than they did. I gave you everything. I gave you every part of my being. I loved you more than I loved myself. You took away the only family I ever knew. You took him and then you left me to pick up the broken pieces. So, I did."

As Zuri continued to hold herself up, she could feel that her body and spirit were broken. She was destroyed, and Massimo would finally get the revenge he always wanted. *This is it.* Zuri's vision blurred as the blood from a gash on her head traveled down her face and into her eyes. She knew that this was the end of the line.

"One last surprise for you, babe," Massimo said, causing Zuri to lift up her head.

In the shadows, Zuri saw a figure walking toward her. Massimo turned to face the figure, and Zuri squinted, rubbing the blood out of her eyes to get a better view. Her eyes widened. "How could this be?" She was in disbelief. "Grandpa—"

Part II

Prologue

Has your mind ever played a trick on you? Making you see something that's not there? Making you look for something that you could have sworn you put down in one location, only to find it somewhere completely different? All you can do is wonder how it got there. That's how you should look at this story—think of it as your mind playing tricks on you.

What if I told you everything you just read was only part of the perception of an alternate reality, a reality that was only one side of the story—but not the whole story? You have to understand that dissociative identity disorder, better known as multiple personality disorder, causes a person to have two or more separate identities. What does that mean? It means that Zuri is only one of three identities. What you read prior to this was Zuri's account of events amidst some delusions and amnesia.

What you're about to read now is the reality of what Massimo experienced with Zuri, who Zuri truly was, what other identities Zuri had, and what actually happened to her. Keep an open mind as the stories converge in some areas and diverge in others.

Who am I you may be asking?

My name is Amara Paula Mariano. I'm the daughter of Zuri and Massimo Mariano. Dawson was my mother's maiden name. I was born into the largest crime syndicate to be known in Italy. My great-grandfather, UQ, was an honorable but ruthless man. He fought hard to ensure that we upheld the family name. I never did get to meet him, which was my mother's fault, but I'll get to that later.

Speaking of grandparents, I also never got to meet my father's parents. His mom wasn't in his life, and his father was a drunk. My mother's parents were the complete opposite—they were amazing. I spent so many years hearing stories from my dad, telling me how my mother's mom was the best cook in the world, and my mother's dad was the most loving man you'd ever meet. Outside of their awesomeness, Grandma was an international liaison, and Grandpa was an account manager for a financial company. I spoke to them a few times on the phone and through FaceTime.

The love they had for each other reigned supreme above all. Their love was a Godly love, a spiritual love, a royal love. I never did get to meet them face to face—and who is to blame for that? You'll find out very soon.

I do want to let you in on a secret. Between me and you, what you read prior to this, a majority of it was a warped perception, which includes some events that never actually happened in reality. That is why I'm here to clear up a few things and tell you the real story—from the other side.

20

History

It's only right to start this chapter with the history of how my parents came to be. The beginning of two individuals, Massimo and Hope Sarah Amara Mariano, my dad and birth mom, had a love for each other that was the source of truth.

We begin with my dad, Massimo. See, Massimo's life changed one cold winter evening in New York City. UQ owned a lot of property in NYC and spent quite a bit of time there when he was not in Italy. Massimo was the son of a close friend of UQ—whose name is irrelevant. All you need to know is that my paternal grandfather was a useless drunk. He didn't care about Massimo, and he would beat him every night after downing a bottle of Phidian's Rum. UQ tried to step in and help Massimo's father, but the bottle was a stronger influence.

UQ couldn't stomach the beatings Massimo was receiving, and after he saw Massimo with an eye that was swollen shut, he decided to take Massimo in until his father finished rehab and got well. Six months later, Massimo's father drank himself to death. UQ took this opportunity to adopt Massimo at the tender age of seven. He worked hard to get Massimo into a better mental space by first moving Massimo to Italy. With psychotherapy, Massimo began to heal and develop a confidence that he lacked before. UQ also made sure Massimo was homeschooled and learned how to play the piano and several sports.

UQ grew to love Massimo like he was his own. As a father figure, he wished for two things for his "son"—leadership and fatherhood. UQ knew that Massimo was the perfect successor, and the empire would be handed to him when the time was right. UQ also knew that Massimo would be an exceptional father himself one day. When Massimo did become a father, I was told it was one of the few times he cried. I couldn't have asked for a better dad. The love I felt growing up surpassed anything I could ever comprehend. Now that I am older, I completely understand that my father is a unique, loving, God-fearing man.

While I was growing up, Massimo raised me in a similar manner to the way UQ raised him. He made sure that we traveled a lot so that I could see and experience different parts of the world. I also had an incredibly strict schooling routine. At the age of ten, I was reading *Atlas Shrugged*, one of my mom's favorite books. My dad believed you can tell a lot about a book by reviewing the author's life. Then once you understood the author's life, you could grasp the book at a different level. So, with every book I read, Massimo made certain that we would have in-depth conversations about who the author was, the type of life the author led, and the subliminal messages behind the words.

By the age of fifteen, I had visited every continent, was fluent in four different languages, and could play Chopin's Etude Op. 10 No. 4 on the piano. Needless to say, I inherited my father's brilliance.

Now, we move on to my birth mom, Hope Sarah Amara Mariano, better known to you as Zuri. Hope's life changed on multiple occasions, starting with the car accident when she was a child that left her with a broken hand and leg as well as severe brain swelling. It took Hope months to recover from this, and her parents were not sure if she would ever be the same again. Although she did recover, Hope developed a limp from the accident, which caused her to become insecure in a way she had never known before.

This new insecurity became a problem for Hope—emotionally, mentally, and socially. On Hope's first week of starting fifth grade, she was made fun of by other children due to her limp. The bullying caused Hope to refuse to go back to school. Even though her parents tried for weeks to get her to go back, they failed. This challenge put a strain on her parents because my grandma's job required her to be in other countries for months on end, and my grandpa was not the homeschooling type. Regardless, they managed to homeschool Hope until it became too much. That is when they asked for help.

Hope's parents asked UQ if he could take Hope for the summer in Italy. As my mom would tell it—her perception—UQ kidnapped her, but that was not the case. She went out to Italy, *voluntarily*, that summer at the age of nine. That summer, Hope learned how to swim, how to read increasingly hard novels, and how to speak Italian. UQ ensured that both Hope and Massimo took up martial arts. They practiced three times a day for the entire summer. Between Karate and Tae Kwon Do, TKD, Hope and Massimo were fighting machines.

With all the TKD and Karate, Hope was able to recorrect her limp, which made her happier than ever. Before the summer was over, UQ begged Hope's parents to come visit and see the progress Hope had made. They refused to visit, considering UQ's line of work, but agreed that Hope's progress was greater than anyone could have ever imagined, including the doctors.

Hope's parents loved her dearly and only wanted her to grow and excel in life. While she was away for the summer, her parents were constantly talking to her and video chatting. They saw how she was thriving like never before and always seemed so happy on their calls, maturing quite nicely during her time away. They realized that Italy was better for her than NYC. They knew that NYC was a hard place to raise a child, and they knew that they made the right decision to ask UQ to have her for the summer months. They allowed Hope to spend the entire next year with UQ in Italy.

While they didn't agree with the lifestyle UQ chose, they believed family meant everything. Her parents had one stipulation for UQ. He was given clear instructions to keep both Hope and Massimo away from the day-to-day of the syndicate. UQ listened and agreed—up until it was no longer beneficial for him.

One year turned into two and then into four. Hope ended up spending a huge part of her childhood in Italy. The mansion that they lived in consisted of eight bedrooms, seven bathrooms, and an Olympic-sized in-ground pool. The mansion also had a game room, which had a pool table and multiple game consoles. UQ's office had a massive bookshelf, a spa, a movie theater, and a gym. He built multiple smaller houses on the land for the help and paved numerous trails for hiking, biking, and walking. The house was majestic—is majestic. It is where I currently live, but I digress.

When Hope and Massimo turned fourteen, their training changed. While UQ promised to keep Hope and Massimo out of the syndicate life when they were younger, he never agreed to keep them out of the life forever. They were at the age where it was time to start working for the syndicate. In UQ's mind, a teenager had the mental capacity to understand and learn at a far greater pace. When he made the final decision to begin training them for life in the syndicate, he increased their training, making it more intense and teaching both teens how to shoot firearms.

The focus wasn't only on being able to shoot handguns, which required close contact, but UQ was more concerned with them becoming snipers. It worked in his favor as well—they were young enough to get out of areas quickly without being caught. After one year of training, the teens were put out in the field—unbeknownst to Zuri's parents.

The first mark was an older gentleman who they were given limited information on. A few days before they were supposed to go on the mission, UQ gave them clear instructions on what had to be done and what would happen if it was not completed. He told them to be prepared for a knock that would come in the middle of the night.

One night, that knock came. A bodyguard was sent for them and told them to get ready. Hope and Massimo exited their rooms at the same time, wearing all black. "This is it," they whispered to each other as they headed down the stairs to the side door.

By the door were two bags, one containing an AXSR rifle and the other containing two handguns, a change of clothes, binoculars, and two-way radios. They headed out, got into a running car, and were dropped off in front of a high-rise building. They entered through the loading dock, took the elevator to the top floor, and then the stairs to the roof. Hope set up the rifle while Massimo searched the area with the binoculars. "We have ten minutes until he comes down. Instructions say we take him out the minute he steps outside the door. Quick and easy."

They knew nothing of who they were killing except what UQ wanted them to know. Time seemed to move slowly on that roof as they waited in silence. Hope always counted her breaths moments before she was going to shoot so she could slow it down and keep her mind focused. One breath. One shot.

After the success of that mark, UQ sent Hope and Massimo on numerous missions together. They would get woken up in the middle of the night by a bodyguard, walk down the stairs, and grab the bags before they headed out to the car using the side door. They were always dropped off at a building where they would set up the rifle on the roof. One would do surveillance, and the other would snipe. They alternated depending on the day, but they were both great at what they did. This went on for years.

This lifestyle left them numb to the world around them, but the emotions grew strong between the two of them. They had a dirty murderous little secret that few people knew. Regardless, they found serenity in the whole process. Between Hope and Massimo, moments before they were getting ready to take out a mark, there was a stillness they felt being with each other—a simple stare. It was indescribable and gave validation that they were in this together. Their love story developed on rooftops after a few years of constantly working with each other. But the start of their love story began on the estate—with a kiss.

Massimo remembered the first time he kissed Hope. They were in the movie theater watching *Love and Basketball*, Hope's favorite movie. During the final scene where Q says, "Double or nothing," Massimo turned to Hope, gently grabbed her chin, and kissed her softly. From that moment on, they were even more inseparable—if that was even possible.

UQ picked up on this closeness. He had a feeling this would happen, so he made sure to have the birds and bees talk with both of them—separately—when they both turned thirteen. Hope also heard the talk from her parents—at thirteen—because that is when she got her first period. Even though Hope and Massimo lived under the same roof, they were innocent. Their minds were focused on murder and making out, nothing more and nothing less. UQ made it this way by reminding them to stay focused on the task at hand and instilling fear in them, so they never messed up—in the field or at home.

Their romance and killing sprees went on for quite some time, around three years to be exact. UQ was able to rely on both of them when he needed to, and they relied on each other. It was a well-oiled machine, a disturbing and psychotic one to some, but well-oiled and normal to them.

At the age of seventeen, Massimo and Hope both wanted to move back to the United States and attend college, but things didn't go as planned. Hope ended up attending senior year of high school as well as completing four years at UNC-Chapel Hill while Massimo stayed behind in Italy. UQ knew Hope didn't understand loyalty, but Massimo did, and he was bound to UQ for life.

Knowing what I know now, I believe UQ was nervous to have Massimo end up back in NYC after all the work they did to heal him from his past trauma. UQ may have feared Massimo would not strive in the U.S., but he would never admit it. From Massimo's perspective, he believed he had an empire to run, and with UQ's age, it was time to focus on that. He didn't have time to focus on dreams of college the way Hope did.

During Hope's four years at college, she ended up dating Simon but realized early on that their relationship was unrealistic. Her love for Massimo was so deep and pure that she could not fathom being with anyone else—no matter how hard she tried. From what I hear, Simon knew it too, but they tried to make it work. At a point, Massimo thought that this was Hope's way of trying to see if she could be without him and love someone other than him—but it would never happen.

Massimo told me about the time Simon ran out of the room and never spoke to Hope again, saying he played a huge part in their demise. He had called Hope one evening but when she didn't answer, he left a voicemail, singing to her. Apparently, Simon was the one to listen to the voicemail, and when he heard the song, he was infuriated and broke up with Hope that night.

I'll be your knight in shining armor
if you'll be my serenity.
A fire lit on a candle, for whenever you can't see.
A piece of a puzzle that's always been missing—
been missing.
I'll be the one standing there with a hanky
whenever you're crying,
Standing there telling you to keep on trying.
Just thought that I should let you know—
just thought that I should let you know.

Ironically, that song has become our family anthem. Massimo sang it to me numerous times since I was a baby. He sang it to soothe me. He told me the loves of his life,

Hope and I, were entitled to this song he wrote, and it has brought me so much comfort over the years, even as I tell you this story.

Had it not been for this song, Hope would have never come back to Massimo, and I would have never grown into the strong, courageous woman I am today.

After Simon left Hope, Massimo decided it was time to make her his again. So, he waited for Hope to graduate, giving her time to heal from Simon, before he put his master plan into action and in the meantime, he made sure he was intertwined in every part of her life.

A few days after graduation, on a warm summer evening, Massimo sent Hope an encrypted text message that said, "Forever mine. Forever yours."

Hope sat up in her bed and paused the TV show she was watching to read the message. She smiled and called him. "What does that mean?" she said, chuckling.

"Go to the front door. There is a box waiting for you. Be ready by midnight. You can dress casually for now, but make sure you bring the box with you. There will be a car waiting outside to transport you to your next destination. We are taking a mini trip—I have a few graduation surprises for you." Massimo hung up the phone, giving Hope no time to ask further questions.

Hope looked at the phone and was slightly confused—but excited. If there was one thing she knew, Massimo was a romantic in every sense of the word. She got out of bed and ran downstairs. She opened the front door to find a large white box with a huge red bow on it. She grabbed the box and ran back upstairs. She put the box on her bed and stared at it for a moment before unraveling the bow. Under a few layers of red tissue paper was a beautiful Alexander McQueen mock neck long halter gown in a beautiful gray navy-blue color. She pulled the dress out and put it up to her body as she turned to look at herself in the mirror that was placed in the corner of her bedroom. She always wanted this dress—it was her dream dress. She looked back into the box and saw a pair of black hot chick sling Christian Louboutin's. She squealed loudly, causing her mom to run upstairs and knock on the door.

Hope showed her mom the gown as well as the shoes and told her what Massimo said. Her mom was so excited for her, and they spent time gossiping while Hope was getting ready for this big surprise. Hope made sure she grabbed the set of diamond earrings and necklace that she received as a graduation present from her mom.

At exactly midnight, the doorbell rang, and Hope left her room wearing an ASOS light grey tracksuit; a matching sweatshirt and sweatpants ensemble. She had her hair up in a messy bun. Hope's mom followed her down the stairs and kissed her goodbye. Then Hope headed out the door and got into the car.

The car ride to the Westchester County Private Airport took about an hour with some light traffic. The car door opened and Massimo was standing there in jeans and a cream-colored hoodie. She loved how sexy he looked even when he was dressed casually. Massimo helped her out of the car, and she hugged him. "I missed you," she said.

"I missed you more."

The driver grabbed her bags and loaded them onto the plane.

"Where are we going?" she asked, smiling.

"It is a surprise!" he said, kissing her forehead and leading her onto the plane.

Nine hours later, in the early afternoon, they landed in Venice, Italy. The warmth from the sun felt amazing on their skin as they got off the plane. A few yards ahead, there was a limo that was waiting for them.

"Ciao e Benvenuto a Venice, Mr. and Mrs. Mariano."

Hope looked at Massimo and wanted to correct the driver but decided against it because she liked the sound of that—Mrs. Mariano. Anytime they traveled together, people always thought they were married, which Hope enjoyed. They got into the limo, and Hope admired the exquisite form of transportation.

The limo took them to a beautiful luxury villa in Via Terraglio, Venice. The property had three levels; the ground floor had a guest room, laundry room, bathroom, a bright living room with large windows, an expansive garden, and a porch, along with an oversized study containing a floor-to-ceiling bookshelf. The upper level had three large bedrooms with suite bathrooms, a closet, and two splendid terraces overlooking a park. There was also a gym, a cellar, and a pool.

Hope's jaw dropped when she saw the property and walked the grounds. Massimo came up behind her and kissed the back of her neck. "I love you so much," he said.

She turned around and kissed him. "I love you even more."

That night, Hope wore her McQueen dress and Christian Louboutin's that Massimo had given to her. Massimo was dressed in an all-black custom-made Alexander McQueen suit. He looked handsome, and she looked beautiful.

After they finished getting ready, Massimo led Hope downstairs and outside to the secluded private garden where a meal was waiting for them—cooked by a hired chef. Massimo pulled the chair for Hope to sit down and then he followed suit. They ate a five-course Italian meal with a 2008 bottle of Domaine Leroy Musigny Grand Cru. The meal was amazing, and dessert was Hope's favorite—strawberry shortcake cheesecake.

After dinner and dessert, Massimo walked over to a record player and put one on. As the music played, Massimo pulled Hope close to him, and they danced. "You're so beautiful, Mar. I wanted to make your college graduation special for you."

"You definitely did. This has been truly amazing."

"You ready for your final surprise?" he asked.

Hope's face lit up. Massimo grabbed her hand and led her upstairs to the large open space where there were candles lit and rose petals everywhere. Straight ahead was a sign that said, "Will you marry me?" Tears filled Hope's eyes, and she looked back at Massimo.

He was on one knee with a five-carat blue diamond pear-shaped engagement ring. "I have known you for so many years, and we basically grew up together. I know you better than anyone, and you know me better than I know myself. I'm so in love with you, and I cannot imagine spending another day not being by your side. You have made me see the world in a different light. Will you marry me?"

"Yes," Hope said.

Massimo grabbed the ring out of the box and put the ring on her finger. He got up and kissed her deeply. She couldn't stop crying. She looked at her hand and was in disbelief that she was finally going to be Mrs. Mariano.

The next morning, they called UQ and her parents to let them know the good news. Then they spent the next few days exploring Italy, including making a stop at the Trevi Fountain to throw a penny in and make a wish. They both wished for the same two things—first, a strong marriage built on the principles of love and respect, and second, parenthood.

A few months later, they had the wedding, and two hundred guests arrived at the Legacy Castle in New Jersey. Hope was wearing a Pronovias Luise sleeveless Mikado princess-cut wedding dress, and Massimo was wearing a custom Alexander Amosu three-piece tuxedo. UQ spared no expense on the wedding, making it everything the lovely couple imagined and more.

That night, I was conceived.

21

A New Life

After the wedding, Hope and Massimo made the decision to stay on the estate with UQ because there was more than enough room in the main house for all of them. Even with the news of the pregnancy, UQ insisted that they stay at the family house.

During the time Hope was pregnant with me, she was unable to work in the field, so UQ kept her on the surveillance side. She became really good at computer hacking and learned the ins and outs of breaking into different government systems and websites. Even though Hope and Massimo weren't physically on assignments together, they still worked well as a team, like clockwork. Hope did all the research, gathering information on the marks, while Massimo carried out the deed—doing all the killing.

About seven months into the pregnancy, Hope started to experience a lot of difficulties. She was dealing with severe depression and even tried to kill herself on multiple occasions. It was not until 'the event' happened that Massimo had to get Hope admitted into a mental hospital for the remainder of the pregnancy. She was also kept on suicide watch, and it was difficult because no one understood what was happening.

Massimo told me the story once, in a moment of sadness, but he refuses to tell it again. He has tried to block out the pregnancy, but some days, I catch him staring at me with a look of sadness in his eyes. He does not blame me for anything, but sometimes, I think he sees my mother's pain when he looks at me. So, here's the story about 'the event.'

It was a regular day, and Hope had finished putting together the paperwork for the mark Massimo was going to snipe. Massimo walked into the room, grabbed the papers, and then kissed Hope before he headed out the door. Hope went into the living room—like she did every time—waiting for Massimo to come home. Hope sat down, turned on the TV, and ended up dozing off a short while later.

After Massimo took care of the mark for the night, he was exhausted. He entered the house through the side door, turned the hallway light on, and heard the TV playing. He walked into the living room to see Hope fast asleep on the couch. He always left her there because, since the pregnancy, she hated being woken up out of her sleep. Therefore, Massimo grabbed a blanket and put it over her. Then he walked upstairs to change and shower. Usually, by the time he got out of the shower, Hope would be awake and ready to get into bed. But this night, when he returned back downstairs, the TV and hallway lights were off. All he could hear were shallow breaths. "Babe, are you okay?" he asked as he reached for the light.

The light came on, and Hope was sitting there with blade cuts all over her forearms. It looked like she was attacked by an animal. She sat still with her hands on her thighs. The blood ran down her arms and legs and onto the floor. Massimo ran to her and yelled for help.

UQ ran downstairs, and their most trusted security guard ran inside. UQ stopped dead in his tracks after he saw what was happening. As he ran toward Hope and Massimo, he yelled for the security guard to grab some towels from the kitchen. Once the security guard came back with the towels, all three men picked Hope up and loaded her into the backseat of the SUV. Massimo sat in the back with Hope, keeping pressure on her forearms as the blood soaked through. He kept talking to Hope, but she just stared at him with blank eyes the entire ride. They finally made it to the hospital just as Hope passed out.

After 'the event,' Hope was not allowed to leave the hospital. There was a major shift in her demeanor, and for the final two months of her pregnancy, no one could get Hope to talk. UQ and Massimo believed that Hope's inability to kill caused her mental distress, which scared them tremendously.

Massimo visited Hope every day, making sure to hold her, sing to her, and update her on the movements of the syndicate—all the while, watching for any change in her behavior. Through it all, Hope sat there with a blank stare, trapped in her own mind.

Two months later, several amazing things happened. During labor, Hope started acting like herself. Once her contractions started, it was as if the pain snapped her out of her mental distress. She asked the nurses to call Massimo, who was in the cafeteria grabbing her food. Upon Massimo being notified, he quickly made his way upstairs to see a completely different persona in Hope. In between the contractions, Hope was talking and laughing. No one knew for sure what happened, but they believe I brought her back to life—literally. Several hours later, I was born, a healthy baby girl, seven pounds, eight ounces. Massimo cut the umbilical cord, and Hope held me with the biggest smile on her face.

They named me Amara Paula Mariano. They came up with the name Amara because it had several meanings such as *grace* in African culture and *everlasting* in Latin. They came up with the middle name Paula because it was Hope's grandmother's middle name.

The first year of my life was a breeze. Hope's mental state was back to normal, and their marriage was back on track. Hope and Massimo had around-the-clock care for me, giving Hope the ability to get back to work. Hope was in the field where she belonged and loved every minute of it. She was able to rise up the ranks in the organization while Massimo was leading directly under UQ.

One night, Hope suddenly awoke and was unable to fall back asleep. She heard Massimo's light snores, confirming he was still sound asleep. She quietly rolled out of bed and headed to the bathroom. For some reason, Hope did not feel like herself, but she chalked it up to being tired. She had been working nonstop since the doctor cleared her to go back to the field.

As Hope was heading back into the bed, she heard a noise. It was UQ's house, so she was used to people coming and going at all times of the night. But this night, Hope decided to check out the noise. She walked soundlessly down the hall until she heard voices. It was coming from the meeting room that was located near the staircase that led downstairs. She sat on the stairs and listened.

UQ started raising his voice, "Never come back into this house and talk about this again. She is doing fine, and I do not care what the doctors are saying. My granddaughter will not be burdened by this. She does not know, and can never know. However, Massimo needs to know as soon as possible. This is alarming. I can't explain it. It makes no sense. At this time, there is no room for emotion. We need to be strategic. She'll never understand or forgive herself."

The room went silent, and Hope looked up, waiting for someone to exit the meeting room, but there was no movement. Hope was confused, so she slowly got up and walked toward the meeting room, putting her ear to the door. She lightly knocked and then entered the room to see no one there. Hope laughed to herself because she realized that she must've dozed off on the stairs and dreamt about the conversation. Closing the door behind her, she walked back to her bedroom, got into bed, and fell right back to sleep.

That night was the beginning of a journey that pains my heart like no other. As I explain to you what happens next, stay focused on the little details—they matter.

A few weeks later, Hope was checked back into suicide watch by Massimo. Massimo could have sworn that he saw Hope intentionally burning her fingertips when she was cooking him breakfast. She claimed it was an accident, but he watched her do it. They kept her in the hospital for a few weeks, and it seemed as though she was getting better—until that one rainy night in August.

It was 3:00 a.m. when Massimo got a call from the nurses at the hospital. Hope had escaped. No one knew how or when. Security cameras did not even pick up her leaving, but the entire hospital staff was looking for her. Massimo got out of bed and paced back and forth, hoping that Hope would come back home.

Hope arrived on the estate an hour later. Massimo did not realize until he heard her voice coming from UQ's study. Massimo slowly opened the study door to see Hope holding UQ at gunpoint. "Mar—what are you doing?"

"I hate him! After all he has done to me—to us—putting us in this life—he needs to pay. He is scum. He is filth. I hate him for killing my daughter and my parents. I hate him for killing me inside. I hate him for making me crazy. I cannot remember anything. Cannot think clearly. It's his fault. He locked me up in the psych ward with those maniacs. He held me hostage so he could control Amara's life. He killed her. He killed my parents, so, now, I need to kill him." Hope pulled the trigger.

UQ grabbed his chest and fell backward into the bookshelf, slowly collapsing to the floor.

Massimo called out to UQ, but there was no answer.

Hope put the gun in her holster and just stood there, eyes blank. Finally, with tears down her eyes, she said, "I had to do it."

Massimo ran across the room, startling her. She quickly moved away from them as Massimo went to check UQ for a pulse. There was a weak pulse; UQ was barely breathing. Hope could see the anger forming in Massimo's eyes and the pain he was feeling—she felt both emotions too. Massimo turned around and grabbed Hope. He slammed her against the wall. "What did you do?!" he shouted as tears ran down his face.

She tried to get out of the hold he had her in, but she couldn't. Hope headbutted him, and he stumbled back. He ran toward her again and swung at her, causing her to duck down. She followed up with a punch to his stomach. Massimo stepped back, losing his balance, and fell to the floor. He wiped his tears and stood up. He got into his fighting stance, and so did she. He punched her, and she kicked him. This fight went on for what felt like forever. They had fought and trained before as per UQ's wishes, so this was a normal thing, but it felt more emotional this time around.

Five minutes later, Hope stepped back and said, "I'm done."

Massimo put his hands up to show he was done too.

She turned to look at UQ crouched on the ground. Suddenly, Hope started screaming at the top of her lungs, "UQ! No!"

Massimo was so surprised that he ran up to Hope and grabbed her from behind. He held her in a bear hug, trying to calm her down. She pushed backward and slammed his back into the wall, but he refused to let go. Still holding on, he allowed his back to slide down the wall until they were seated on the ground. She continued sobbing in his arms. He couldn't comprehend what was happening. Hope had just killed UQ but then reacted as if she was seeing him for the first time.

After several minutes, Hope calmed down, and she told Massimo she was okay. He let her go and immediately, Hope got up and wiped the remaining tears left on her face. Massimo stood as well and started walking out the door so he could grab the security team. Right before he made his way around the corner, Hope grabbed her gun out of the holster and shot Massimo in the leg. "You never loved me. You used me to make yourself feel better. I hate you too."

Massimo's first instinct was to protect me. He realized if Hope could shoot UQ, pretend she didn't, and then shoot him, she may have no issue taking my life either. Massimo gathered himself and limped quickly to the bedroom where I was sleeping. He locked the door, grabbed me, and pushed an alarm signaling security.

Hope escaped from the house that day, never to be seen again.

22

The Trauma

I know this seems like a lot, but hang in there just a little longer as I take you back further—back to the very beginning. In order for you to understand what happened and how we got here, I need to take you back through Hope's entire life.

Hope was born a beautiful baby girl at the New York Presbyterian Hospital located in NYC. She was raised by two loving, caring parents who worked hard to ensure she received everything she ever needed. She was spoiled but structured. Up until the age of eight years old, she lived a perfect life. Then the car accident happened.

I mentioned the car accident earlier, but the severity of it was more profound than anyone could have imagined. The brain swelling from the impact led to a shift in her brain, which is how we got here. The doctors didn't know it at the time, but the car accident triggered a disorder. After she underwent months of recovery, she developed a limp, which left doctors perplexed—it was a physical symptom that they couldn't explain. Some say the limp was intentional, but they couldn't prove it. The limp is why she got pulled out of school with the supposed bullying she was encountering. Her parents took her at her word and never questioned her—but they should have.

At the age of nine, she was showing signs of extreme mood shifts, but no one could quite understand if she was just growing up or acting out. Eventually, her parents couldn't handle her behavior, and they were struggling with homeschooling her, so they reached out to UQ, who gladly agreed to take Hope for the summer. They gave her the option to go, and she agreed.

When she arrived in Italy, UQ noticed what her parents were talking about. One moment, she would be happy and loving. The next, she was angry and aggressive. UQ decided that Tae Kwon Do and Karate could help stabilize her mood and give her an outlet. It worked for some time—she was thriving in the environment. As the summer was coming to an end, her parents decided it was best for Hope to stay in Italy with UQ, so she did.

A few years went by, and everyone chalked up her behavior as a child to be what it was—childish behavior. That lasted until she turned fourteen and two situations occurred causing UQ to be concerned. First, she became increasingly violent. She tried to break the neck of one of the bodyguards for fun. No one could explain this, so UQ decided it was time for her and Massimo's training to be more rigorous. Their training increased in intensity and time, and they both became proficient in handling firearms, more specifically, assault rifles. UQ felt the more he pushed her into the lifestyle and tried to channel her emotions, the more it would *hopefully* shift her mind and energy away from this destructive, out-of-control behavior. There was an additional benefit because he used her and Massimo to help him take care of some syndicate business as well.

Second, she started experiencing random fainting spells on the trails. Massimo usually found her and would have to carry her to her bed and wait until she woke up. This lasted for two years, but it only happened once a year. There was more to these fainting spells that she experienced. There was a man who had his thumb on the pulse of her life. A man who shall remain nameless. At fourteen, this man came into her life but only to hurt and harm her. She never told anyone, but it happened on three separate occasions as she jogged through the estate. The man was waiting for her near the unoccupied maid's quarters. He had been watching her, sweating her, wanting her each time she jogged her way through the path. And one day, he took her.

She was jogging her normal path, and he startled her, causing her to lose her footing and fall down. The man jumped on top of her and pinned her to the ground. She noticed a scar on his neck because it was distinguished and different. While on the ground, the man happened to enjoy the fight that she put up, the power struggle. She was able to fully fight him off and escape but never told anyone what happened—not even Massimo.

A few weeks later, unbeknownst to her other personality, Hope switched paths and was taking a stroll when she was shot by a tranquilizer dart. She felt it and pulled it out of the side of her neck. At first, she thought it was Massimo playing a trick on her. She looked around and called out to him, but there was no movement or call back. She approximated the direction the dart came from and headed over there.

The man was waiting for her. She tried fighting him off but started to feel a grogginess. He told her to relax because he was not trying to hurt her. She passed out, and when she woke up, the man was on top of her, taking her virginity. She felt his body weighing on hers, taking her from innocent to immoral, but she couldn't move.

That night, she woke up in her bed, tucked under the blanket with Massimo sitting next to her. No one knew what happened to her, but when they found her, she was passed out on the trail with a slight head injury. Everyone assumed she had fallen. Eventually, she began to assume she had fallen as well, and life went on.

When she was put in the field at the age of fifteen, she was thriving. Little did they know that while most people killed because they had to, Hope killed because she *needed* to. It was her drug, it was exhilarating to her. She enjoyed taking people's lives, a true God complex. She shared her thoughts with Massimo, saying how she felt like a God and how she enjoyed watching the life leave someone's body and the thrill she felt from watching that first drip of blood escape. When Massimo saw the look in her eyes, it scared him.

Massimo had a hard time resonating with Hope's addiction to killing because, for him and UQ, this was for a higher purpose—purging the world of evil people. What they did was a responsibility, not a game. So, Massimo began to report back to UQ some of the things she would tell him. In their discussions, they realized that there was a chance Hope would go rogue, so they devised a plan to ensure everything was done as a team—this is why she and Massimo started working marks together. But even then, she still snuck out of the house for long jogs on the path. So, a year later, it happened again with this man. This man came back to her, to take what he thought was his. He found her on the path, attacked her, and raped her. She could never recount what caused her fainting spells, and her other personality never shared.

Regardless, like clockwork, she woke up, tucked into bed with Massimo sitting by her side. Because so much time had passed between her fainting spells, UQ was unsure what to think about it. He entered her room, approached her—like a grandfather, not a boss—and asked her if she knew what happened.

She sat up and first looked at Massimo then at UQ and said, "I had a date with the devil." Upon seeing their change of facial expression, a smirk broke out on her face. She then proceeded to lay back down, falling right to sleep. It was at this point UQ knew that she was unwell. There was a fear inside of him that he may have created a monster. Therefore, he decided it was time for her to start seeing a psychiatrist.

UQ employed the same psychiatrist Massimo had used years earlier. Psychotherapy lasted a year and a half, during which she had another fainting spell and she was diagnosed with dissociative identity disorder, better known as multiple personality disorder. After her diagnosis, UQ, her parents, and the psychiatrist agreed that she should go back to NYC and try to assimilate into the real world. They wanted her to meet people her own age and do activities that regular people did. When they brought it up to her through a mini-intervention she gladly agreed to go back to the U.S. and be with her parents. She hated that Massimo stayed behind, but UQ was trying to ensure that she had some separation from this life.

With one year of high school and four years of college, she adapted to the lifestyle of being normal, but there was nothing normal about her. Even though she went to school, tried to date, and explored different avenues, she struggled.

During those five years, she lost chunks of time and memory because what one personality experienced, the other personality lacked. She never disclosed it to anyone because she thought nothing of it, but deep down, there was one personality who knew what was going on. Regardless, she found that the struggle didn't last much longer because once she graduated and Massimo proposed, she felt as though she finally understood her purpose. She was meant to be a killer, a wife, and a mom. Plain and simple.

23

Lost and then Found

Now that you understand Mom's history, we can move forward. After she disappeared that horrid night, Dad worked hard to raise me on his own. He spent countless hours with me and worked to ensure that I grew up without knowing too much about the chaos Mom caused. Every now and again, he would let something slip or tell me a story that had just enough details so I wouldn't ask too many questions. The older I got, the more comfortable he was explaining Mom to me.

That treacherous night, UQ was put in the ICU after an eight-hour surgery to repair the damage the bullet did. He survived but was never the same. Dad was hospitalized for a few days after surgery to remove the bullet that was lodged in his thigh. Once he was able to stand, he left the hospital. He hired a physical therapist who rehabbed him back to health on the estate. I grew up for years believing my mom was in the U.S. saving the world because that's what Dad told me, but the truth is, for years, Dad could not find her.

When she fled, they searched for months—he had a team of people looking for her—but she didn't emerge anywhere. After a while, Dad assumed she was dead. It was not until I was about eleven that Dad found her. She appeared suddenly on their radar after a story was put in the ABA Journal about her amazing breakthrough work as an international lawyer. I will never forget the day he received the call. I didn't hear what was said on the other line, but Dad got up and ran as fast as he could into his office. He closed the door, and I ran to listen. "Where is she? Send me the pictures right now. Right now!" he yelled.

I moved away from the door because I hated when Dad yelled, but I know now that he had found her. They had a picture of her in the Journal, and surveillance video showed that she was living back in NYC. After that article and the surveillance video, Dad lost her again. He believed she was intentionally hiding from all the cameras, and in the rare moments when a surveillance camera caught her, the video would disappear in a matter of hours. Dad knew she was fighting hard to stay off the radar, but at least now he knew that she was safe.

I knocked on the door shortly after I heard him yelling, but he didn't hear me. I walked in and saw tears running down his face. He was mesmerized by how beautiful and how well she seemed to be doing. He wiped his tears, closed the laptop, and told me to come over. He hugged me tighter than he had ever done before and told me we were going to get ice cream.

After that day, I lost Dad to Mom for several months. Every morning, he would wake up and sit in his office and then go downstairs to the war room—the room where he discussed syndicate business that I wasn't allowed to know about—until it was time for dinner. The dinner table was the only place I saw him. Every now and then, I would ask Dad to take me outside for us to play basketball or swim together, but he would always say, "Not now."

It was a lonely couple of months for me in that house. Thankfully, I had the maids and a few friends from the swim club, but I missed my dad. What I know now is Dad would spend hours hacking cameras and watching Mom go out with her friends, go home, go to work, and any- where else in between. Eventually, he stopped eating at dinner and would only come upstairs to take a break. After I took my last bite, he would head right back downstairs to his war room. Dad found out that Mom recreated her- self—she went to law school, became a big-shot lawyer, and was doing well.

All that obsessive surveillance came to a halt the day I was injured. I was riding my bike on one of the trails with a maid, and I hit a rock, causing me to fly forward and off the bike. I ended up spraining my wrist while also getting scrapes on my knees and elbows. It was not a huge issue, not more than a normal bike injury.

The maid ran inside to call Dad, and when he saw me dusting off the dirt on my knees, he ran right to me, picked me up, and brought me into the house. He quickly reached out to the on-call nurse, and she came over to the house to check me over. She put a small wrap on my wrist and then cleaned and bandaged my cuts. After she left, Dad spent that entire day with me, and whatever hold Mom had on him, dissipated. He stopped obsessively watching her all day and started spending time with me again. When I would come back from school, he would be there waiting for me. For hours, we would talk about my day, read together, and go for long swims. Dad was an amazing swimmer and ensured I was as well. I was able to join the elite competitive swim team at my school, and every day, Dad would train with me so I could be the best of the best.

A couple of weeks after my accident, I woke up in the middle of the night and saw the light on in his office. This was the first time I realized he was still watching her—he just stopped doing it during the time I was awake. I began to notice the toll losing sleep over Mom was taking on him, and it worried me because I couldn't understand what was going on at the time. All I wanted was for him to start feeling better.

I took it upon myself to try to get Dad out of whatever funk he was in. So, one day, I asked Dad to take me on a trip to Disney World because I knew Disney World was magical, and maybe some of that magic would make him feel better. We spent a whole week there during my summer vacation, and it was marvelous. I believe that magic did rub off on him because, after that trip, he was different. But like most good things, it was transient.

It was about a year after Mom was found on a sunny, beautiful day when Dad and I had just finished our afternoon swim. We were about to sit down in the movie theater when Dad received a call from his security guy. When Dad hung up the phone, he told me to stay in the theater. He ran out of the theater and to the living room. I peeked my head out of the theater just as Dad grabbed the remote and turned to what sounded like a news station.

"—three individuals who were found dead in the back restrooms on Flight RD4379 going from JFK, NYC, to CDG, Paris. We are looking to locate all individuals that were seated on this plane. Police are going to start interviewing the pilots and flight attendants to see what they know. If you know anyone who was on this flight or have any information, please call our emergency line 112 or 17." The coverage cut out to some video footage of the flight and the three bodies being rolled into ambulances—the scene looked chaotic. "We are looking for this individual who is said to be the main suspect of these heinous crimes."

Zuri Sierra Dawson's face was plastered on the screen. The news reporter stated that Zuri was a prestigious lawyer from NYC, known for her amazing negotiation skills and high deal closure rate. She had a completely different name, but Dad was certain it was Mom. "If anyone knows or sees this individual, she is armed and dangerous. Do not approach her, but contact us immediately."

Dad looked mortified. "Sebastian!" He yelled for his head of security.

Sebastian came running into the house. "Yes, sir?"

"Get the jet ready and fueled, I need to be in Paris by tonight. Get me the location of the safe house. Get me her last known. Get the nanny to come stay here." Dad ran upstairs and started packing a bag. He put some essentials into a black duffle bag. He ran into his office and shut the door. A few minutes later, he emerged in a black ensemble—a sweatsuit it seemed. Dad never wore a sweatsuit, so imagine my surprise seeing him in one. His duffle bag was bulky, and I later found out that it contained his bulletproof vest, a few firearms, and some clothing.

As he was coming down the stairs, he spotted me peeking to see what he was doing. "Come here," he said as he arrived at the bottom of the stairs, dropping his duffle bag on the floor.

I followed Dad to the living room. I sat on the couch, and he knelt in front of me. Then he grabbed my hands in his and began to sing to me.

I'll be your knight in shining armor
if you'll be my serenity.
A fire lit on a candle, for whenever you can't see.
A piece of a puzzle that's always been missing—
been missing.
I'll be the one standing there with a hanky
whenever you're crying,
Standing there telling you to keep on trying.
Just thought that I should let you know—
just thought that I should let you know.

"Sweetie, I have to take a trip, but I will be back as soon as I can. Please listen to your elders, especially your nanny and the security team. I promise I'll be back as soon as possible. Be a good girl, and stay focused. I'll call you every chance I get." He kissed me on the forehead, hugged me tight, grabbed his bag from the bottom of the stairs, and walked out the door. I didn't see Dad for a few weeks after that.

When I was old enough, I heard the story of everything that happened. Here is my dad's perspective.

24

Iron Sharpens Iron

As I got on the plane, I was scared, angry, sad, and felt a dozen other different emotions all at once. I lost her that day—the day she shot me and UQ and then fled. I thought she would never come back to me. I had accepted that fate and moved on. I had to be a father. As a dad, I wanted the best for Amara.

Amara blossomed into a beautiful young lady. She has my oval-shaped eyes and her mom's naturally flawless eyebrows. She didn't inherit my heterochromia, but she has perfect hazel eyes. We have the same complexion, and she also has my chin. She did inherit most of her mother's traits, especially her slightly wider nose, oval face, and forehead. I always joked when she was younger that she had a five-head instead of a four-head.

I did my best to keep her sheltered from this life, but sometimes, my human nature got the best of me, and I failed her once or twice—like any parent does. My failure and neglect happened when I spent weeks obsessing over Hope. I got so wrapped up in Hope's world that I became inattentive to my world and neglected the only person who deserved my attention, who required my attention. Amara forgave me like all young daughters do, but I knew I needed to forgive myself.

Outside of those instances, I've worked tirelessly to be the person Amara could come to for anything, someone who she could lean on in her time of need. And I succeeded. I'm a single father running a syndicate and doing everything I need to sustain and ensure the success of the family name.

The plane ride seemed so long, and I fought the urge to yell or even punch something. Then I received an alert that someone hacked the estate cameras. The hack was brief—in and out—and untraceable. That's when I knew it was her. I had been looking for her for quite some time. I thought she was dead, but now reading the news story for the seventh time, I cannot figure out if this is better or worse. I don't know what I am walking into. I can only pray that she remembers me and the life we built. She seems to have built a whole new life outside of Amara and me. My mind has been racing with thoughts. *Does she remember me? Does she remember UQ? Does she remember Amara?*

The plane landed in La Campagne à Paris. I had the coordinates to the safe house that we built while she was still part of the organization. She worked so hard on the safe house, but we never got to visit it together. We had plans, but plans never worked out when it came to Hope, or should I say, Zuri. It seems that she changed her name when she left our life behind. Since she is no longer my Hope, I'll call her Zuri.

Six of my bodyguards and I arrived at the safe house after the sun had set and the moon was rising in the sky. I knew where all the cameras were on the property, and I intentionally tripped the system as I walked closer to the door. I knew she was watching and would get a motion-detected alert. I heard her footsteps as she slowly approached us and then I heard her gun go off—she sent a warning shot into the night sky.

"If I shoot again, I'm taking all of you with me," she shouted. "Ask yourselves, are you prepared to die tonight and meet your maker?"

"That's cute, but not if I shoot first," I yelled back.

I heard Zuri stop dead in her tracks. She knew it was me. I heard her whisper my name. I walked out of the shadows and straight toward her, turning on my flashlight and pointing in her direction. I lowered my weapon so she could see that I was not a threat to her, but she kept her gun raised. Once I was within a few feet of her, I said, "I come in peace." It was like seeing a ghost—it had been ten years since I saw her in person. "I know you were tracking me. Listen, so much has gone unsaid, but I want you to know I love you regardless of what happened. I thought you would come back to me, but you never did. You just disappeared," I said to her.

She lowered her gun, holstered it, and then took a few steps toward me and hugged me. I was so happy to see her and didn't realize I could feel this way again. Ironically, in her presence, I felt safe. My heart and body had yearned for her touch. I noticed that she tried not to show her relief and happiness, but I could read her like a book. We let go of each other, and she grabbed my hand, leading me toward the shed. "Come inside," she said.

I spoke to my team through the earpiece and told them to stay alert. They called back to me, acknowledging the command and confirming their presence. "Alpha Red, copy. Beta Blue, copy. Gamma Green, copy. Delta Denim, copy. Epsilon Emerald, copy. Zeta Zucchini, copy."

I could see her turn around and count six men on my security team.

We walked into the shed, and while on the elevator down, I noticed her rubbing the scar on her hand. She always did this when she felt vulnerable or scared—it was her tell.

Once off the elevator and down the stairs, she unholstered her gun and placed it on the kitchen island and then she headed to one of the guest rooms and started talking. "It's okay. It's someone I know. Paul, this is Massimo. Massimo, this is Paul."

I walked in behind her, curious to see who Paul was. I looked around, but there was no one there. I looked around again and then started walking to the tech room. I could see the confusion on her face as she followed me. She kept looking back as if someone was there. I got into the tech room, and she stood in the doorway, waiting to see what I was doing. At this moment, fear crept into my body. She was still unwell, but I knew this was not the time to try to talk to her about her condition, and I also knew I had to be on high alert because last time when she was in this phase, she tried to kill me.

I plugged in a USB drive and downloaded a program onto her computer. As the program continued downloading, I took off my bulletproof vest and put it on the table. I felt safe knowing she was not carrying a gun. I quickly located an empty chair to sit in by the desk as the program reached ninety-nine percent. Several files of information I had compiled began popping up on the screens, showing the details of the investigation and how the police were narrowing down who killed the three individuals. She seemed shocked by all the information she saw. She slowly walked from the doorway toward the screens.

"I came to get you out of here. When I saw your face on the news, I knew this was not good. I knew you would come to this safe house—it was the closest one." I turned my chair around to face her and then told her to sit down next to me. I grabbed her hand and continued. "I have another safe house a few miles away. Let's go there and figure out our next steps."

She gave me a confused look. "What do you mean?"

"When you first got the houses built over a decade ago, UQ made me set up safe houses next to yours. He said it would give us a better chance at survival if either of us were ever compromised. All my safe houses are within ten miles of yours. Plus, if I could find you, I'm sure that it'll only be a matter of time before someone else finds you."

After considering what I said, she nodded in agreement. We made a plan to leave for the other house in the morning.

She quickly got up and said, "I'll tell Paul the change in plans, and we can leave in the morning,"

I watched as she walked down the hallway. I stood up to see what she was going to do next. She knocked on the guest room door, which was ajar, and started talking. "We're going to have to relocate in the morning. Massimo and I had a discussion, and he brought up a few great points that I agree with. Get yourself gathered tonight because we will not be returning to this house. And trust me when I say, we will get through this. You don't have to go. We're not going to bring you against your will. You can always go back to the city and pretend this trip didn't happen. I'm sure a conversation with the cops can lead to you clearing your name. Regardless, I'm going to need you to make a decision right now."

After she finished talking, she walked back toward me. When she was a few inches away, she reached out and grabbed my hand—pulling me closer to her. She whispered, "C'mon. It's time for bed."

I nodded and closed the door to the tech room and then I followed her upstairs. She changed into pajamas and grabbed me my old sweatpants and t-shirt. I was surprised to see that she kept these clothes, and once I put them on, I could smell her scent on them—roses. She always smelled faintly of roses.

We headed to bed, and I drifted to sleep holding her closer than she could bear. I missed this, but I knew that there was something wrong. This wasn't going to last. I began reminiscing about our days growing up. When she first started training with UQ, she was careless, reckless, and definitely not in tune with her emotions—she was sloppy. Then she blossomed into someone who was controlled, calculated, and calm. Now, I didn't know what to expect.

Was she going to be reckless like her teenage self? Or controlled like adult Hope used to be? Or was I going to meet the other person—the one who loved to kill just for the hell of it? Only time would tell.

I was awoken by three back-to-back gunshots—*bang, bang, bang*. I quickly jumped out of bed and grabbed my handgun, which was holstered to my pants, on the floor by the bed. I turned around to check the bed and saw Zuri was not in the room. The fear I felt the night before crept back up into my stomach.

I exited the room quietly, and I heard movement downstairs. I headed toward the noise, cautiously checking my surroundings. *Bang, bang, bang, bang.* I didn't have a clear view of who was shooting, but I kept moving.

"Who the hell are you?" I heard her yell.

A magazine dropped to the floor and someone reloaded. *Who was she talking to?* As my eyes adjusted, I saw her stand up from behind the kitchen counter and shoot one round straight ahead. She jumped over the counter and shot two bullets into the floor. There was no one there but her. All the bullets I heard were coming from her gun.

At this point, I knew—I needed to get her help and fast before she hurt herself or me. I grabbed her by the arm, took the gun, and told her to pack her bags. She ran down the hall into the tech room, oblivious to what I said to her. I followed her to see her frantically deleting files. I grabbed her again and stared into her eyes. "Go upstairs and pack a bag," I told her again.

She nodded and then ran down the hallway and upstairs. I grabbed the USB drive and placed the gun on the desk. I took a deep breath, starting to feel the stress of her disorder again. I knew this wasn't the time for me to start thinking, though, so I quickly snapped out of my thoughts and headed toward the kitchen to call my security team. I told them to secure the perimeter as I saw her coming down the stairs with a Louis Vuitton duffle bag.

She nodded to me, and I ran upstairs to get dressed. After I was done, I walked downstairs and grabbed her duffle bag, which was sitting at the bottom of the steps. She led the way as we headed up the stairs to the elevator. We rode the elevator in silence, and I noticed her rubbing the scar on her hand again—it made my heart sink into my chest because there was nothing that I could do for her at that moment.

As we headed out of the shed, the warmth of the sun was the comfort I needed. I whistled for my team to come out. As they headed toward me, I dropped the bag near her feet and walked over to meet my team. I looked at them, and they could see the worry in my eyes. "She's unstable, and we have to be very careful. You all know what happened ten years ago, and we cannot have a repeat. I need you guys to stay close and unseen. I don't want her knowing that you're here. We are going to walk to the other safe house—it will give me time to talk to her and figure out her mindset. Remember, close but unseen."

My team nodded.

I walked away and headed to Zuri, who was staring into the sky. I came up behind her and put my hands around her waist. She jumped but then relaxed when she realized it was me. "Let's go," I whispered into her ear.

We arrived at my safe house, and I could see she was mesmerized when she saw it. It was an above-ground, beautiful two-story house with a basement, equipped with bulletproof glass as windows. Outside, it had a terrace and a backyard. Once inside, there were four bedrooms and two bathrooms—the living room sitting to the right of the house and the kitchen all the way down the hall to the left. There were two staircases—one staircase went from the kitchen to the second floor, and the other went from the living room to the basement.

"Custom made, just like yours. It was a hassle having the right people come to create this masterpiece, but you know nothing is impossible for people like us," I told her as she continued walking around, admiring what I had done with the place. In my earpiece, I heard my security team checking in. They had just arrived at the safe house. I knew I had to get her upstairs so I could strategize with the team. "Come with me. Bedrooms are upstairs, and I have a computer up there, so you can take it easy."

I grabbed her bag and then led her upstairs and into the main bedroom. I could see the exhaustion on her face as she collapsed on the couch. After a few seconds, she pointed to the laptop that was sitting on the wooden desk—I grabbed it for her. I knew this would occupy her for a while, so I took this as my opportunity to go communicate with my team. "I'll be right back. Need to coordinate with my security team," I said as I kissed her forehead. I walked out of the room, closing the door behind me, and then headed back downstairs. I went to the driveway, where my team was waiting.

"She's stable for now, but I need you all on high alert—especially at night. Doctors used to say that anything could trigger her. Let's keep the noise to a minimum and keep watch. I don't want any surprises for these next few days. If I need you, I will signal for you through the two-way radio."

My team acknowledged the instructions and then split up to their respective positions. I slowly walked back to the house, trying to figure out how to make this transition for her as smooth as possible. There were so many thoughts running through my mind as I ascended the stairs. A part of me wanted to turn around and go straight back to Italy—leaving her to her own vices. Another part of me wanted to put a bullet in her head to end this nightmare. But truthfully, I just wanted to hold her, to lay with the love of my life—my soulmate.

I entered the room to see her putting the laptop to the side. She looked even more exhausted than she had a few minutes before. I knelt in front of her and stared into her eyes, hoping to find Hope there, but all I could see was confusion.

"Let me take your mind off of the chaos . . ." I said to her.

25

Unbalanced Equilibrium

We spent the next forty-eight hours rekindling. I was constantly reminded of what I loved about her and how genuine that love was. I felt complete again—being able to touch her, hold her, kiss her, make love to her—it was everything. Her body was the pinnacle of my mind, but her mind was the dread of my soul.

I looked in the bathroom mirror one last time before I went back into the bedroom. "Z, is everything okay?"

"All good. We just need to figure out our next move," she replied as she got out of bed and walked toward me wearing my white button-down collar shirt. "Let me get dressed," she said as she playfully tugged on my black sweatpants. She then kissed my cheek and headed for the closet.

I nodded and watched her walk away as if walking down a runway, and she turned back, catching me staring. I smiled, and it caused her to giggle. She went into the closet and got dressed.

I quickly grabbed my phone on the nightstand and checked the security cameras—same as the last three times I checked them: clear except for my security team. I took a deep breath and then grabbed my black t-shirt.

She emerged from the closet wearing a pair of black leggings and a black t-shirt with Burberry written across the front—it made me smile. I stood up and kissed her and then I grabbed her hand and led her downstairs to the basement. In the basement is where I had my team set up weapons and computers. "Go ahead," I told her as we got to the door.

She put her thumb on the doorknob and looked at me, surprised. It seemed like she thought there was a thumb scanner—but there wasn't. I watched as she opened the door and the lights automatically turned on. I didn't say or react to her obvious delusions because I knew I had to make her feel safe. It was always the one thing that kept her mind calm.

"You're my true love, Mar. Your safety means the world to me—never forget that."

She looked back at me and didn't say anything but proceeded into the room. Amazed by all the weapons, she headed over to a glass case that had smaller firearms and bulletproof vests. She grabbed a vest and started fitting it to her body. I was not sure what she was getting ready for, but it seemed like war. I went along with it and started helping her get her vest on since she was struggling. She then grabbed a vest and gave it to me. I put it on reluctantly. Next, she walked over to the firearms and took four pieces along with additional magazines for each. One gun was on her hip—her favorite; the S&P Shield. She put another one on the front of her vest, a Glock 17, one on her thigh, a Sig Sauer P210, one on her ankle, a Kahr P380, and one on her back, a Beretta APX. She was geared and ready to go.

Her phone began to ping, she grabbed it and yelled, "Someone breached the perimeter! They're here!"

"*Not again*," I whispered to myself.

"Seven people are out there," she said. "We should have brought your security with us."

I realized she saw a visual from the night when I arrived—it was me and my six bodyguards that she was looking at. There was a look in her eye—it was the same look she would get when we were being sent on a mission to snipe someone. It was a look of satisfaction, the hunger she needed to feed so she could be fulfilled, the hunger to kill. Before I could respond back, a devilish smile slowly formed on her face, and she grabbed her S&P and held it in front of her. I quickly grabbed three firearms just in case I had to defend myself against whoever she had just switched to.

"Get behind me babe," she commanded. I stood behind her and she signaled for me to put my left hand on her right shoulder. I realized that she wanted us to move the way we did in trainings with UQ. I followed her lead. *Is she having a flashback? What is she seeing in her mind?* "Let's move," she said.

I quickly sent my team a static signal, telling them to stand down. Then I tapped her shoulder, and we started walking to clear the house.

"Clear," she whispered as we continued. "Clear," she said again a moment later.

All of a sudden, I felt her body tense up. I obviously couldn't see what she was seeing, but I dropped my arm and took several steps back. I raised my gun and had it aimed at the back of her head—just in case.

Still facing forward, she pulled the trigger, putting holes in the walls, stairs, and furniture. After she fired eleven rounds, dropping the S&P after she fired all the bullets and grabbing the Glock to fire the last few rounds, she turned around, and I saw a whole different expression on her face—she had nourished that hunger.

That night, she was going on and on about how we just killed eight people and weren't any closer to finding out who killed those three individuals on the plane. She was manic. I had to take her upstairs to the bedroom so she could calm down. After a few minutes, her demeanor changed, and she transitioned from being a euphoric killer to a perturbed pessimist.

I ran her a bath and helped her into the tub so she could relax. I checked in on her often to ensure she did not try to kill herself like she did years ago. My phone rang during one of my check-ins, and I stepped out of the bathroom to take the call. It was my head of security telling me to come downstairs.

I went downstairs and saw the damage she had caused. My team saw it too and looked at me with shock and disbelief. I could only return a defeated expression. "I know. She's getting worse. I'll figure something out . . . Just clean this up as best as you can. I'm about to put her to bed. She'll sleep through the night. Did you grab it for me?"

The head of my security handed me a bottle of sleeping pills. I grabbed the bottle and went to the kitchen before he could say anything. In the kitchen, I found an unopened bottle of Château Latour, Pauillac, a wine glass, and a wine opener. After I opened the bottle, I poured a glass of wine for her and put three sleeping pills in it. Then I walked back upstairs carrying both the glass and the bottle as my team cleaned up.

I entered the bathroom to see her peacefully lying in the tub. "You okay, Mar? These last seventy-two hours have been rough," I said as I went over and gave her a kiss.

"You can say that again," she said rubbing the scar on her hand.

"Take all the time you need. You deserve some relaxation. Here, I brought you a glass of wine. It's your favorite."

She smiled like a Cheshire cat and reached out to grab the glass. I watched as she chugged half the glass and laid her head back. She dozed off a few minutes later. I carried her out of the tub, dried her off, dressed her, and tucked her into bed.

This was the norm several years ago since we couldn't get her to take the pills her doctor prescribed. Even though it could have side effects, UQ, the doctor, and I agreed that if she wasn't going to take them voluntarily, we would have to manipulate her into taking them. Wine was the only thing that worked because when mixed in, she couldn't taste the pills.

Years ago, she would go three to four days without sleeping and that was when her delusions and personality switching were at their worst. It was a scary situation to experience, even for someone like me who doesn't get scared easily. It also made me feel helpless watching her walk around like a zombie, ready to kill anything that got in her way. That's how I felt at that moment—her delusions, those fictitious murders—this was the beginning of a spiral, a nightmare—one I wish I could wake up from. But until then, I would continue to drug her each night for her own good.

26

Visions Beyond Me

She was in and out of sleep for the next thirty-six hours. It was much-needed considering she barely slept since the night that I arrived. When I woke up that morning, I went down to the tech room to find her already there, looking through random files. I saw the manifesto from the flight, which had three names circled—the dead individuals. Then I noticed she circled three other random names. *I'll have to look into who those people are at a later time.*

On the screen, I saw that she was investigating the various flight attendants too. I could hear her whispering to herself, running through different thoughts and scenarios. She didn't even realize I was standing right next to her, and if she did, she didn't acknowledge me.

As I watched her and listened to her voice, thoughts of the night she vanished flooded my memory. *She shot UQ. She shot me. Who is this woman sitting in front of me? Who was she that night?* Then came thoughts of who she had become. *I can't fathom what time may have done to her. I can't fathom what life may have done to her.* I was jolted out of my thoughts when she began speaking in her normal tone.

"I remember seeing Marcy Evelien crying on the flight and another flight attendant was comforting her. This was shortly after I went to the restroom, around three. At that time, three of the bathrooms were already occupied. I am assuming that this means the murder happened between midnight and 3 a.m. During that time, I was pretty much sleeping because you know I love my sleep! The only constants on the flight were Paul—who is now dead—and Sophia, the girl in the seat next to me."

I stood there listening.

"Sophia was all hot and sweaty at one point and then she came back wearing a fresh set of clothes—maybe she was involved in one of the murders . . . or all of them. She obviously is not a suspect in the investigation that the police are currently working on, just based on the files they have in their database. Let's take this one step at a time, though. First, let's find this flight attendant, Marcy. Then we can worry about Sophia."

I grabbed a chair and sat down behind her as I watched her frantically dig for information on where Marcy, this flight attendant, would be staying. She came across the name of Marcy's aunt who lived in the 5th arrondissement near the Pantheon but could not find Marcy anywhere.

Obligation—the thought flooded my mind as I realized that I couldn't sit back and watch her suffer in her current predicament. I moved my chair beside her and told her to let me take a look. I began to dig for information on who Marcy was. From my prior investigation, Marcy had not been tracked down by officers yet. This meant she had to have checked in under a different name, so I broadened my search for aliases and potential property deeds that she may have had. Still, I found nothing.

After about an hour of searching, I came across a news article about a brutal beating and rape that took place years ago. It was a young girl named Rachel Antoinette Myers. There were similar attributes between her and Marcy, but I was unsure. "There's only one way to find out," I said to myself as I put the last name Myers into my hotel search in the 5th arrondissement. There were two hotels with individuals that had that last name. I printed the short list of hotels and handed it to Zuri so she could look.

She grabbed the list and put it down on the table. "I need your help with something first," she said to me.

"Sure, anything."

"I think it's time for a new haircut," she said as she tugged on her hair. She then got up, kissed me, and headed upstairs.

I followed her upstairs to the main bathroom and helped her cut her hair into a bob. Then I left her alone to finish styling her hair and get dressed while I prepared myself for this journey. There were several things that needed to be done before we arrived at those hotels. I first needed to prepare my security team and then I needed to find which hotel this Myers lady was staying in so I could speak to Myers and the hotel staff before we arrived.

I left the bedroom, closing the door quietly behind me. I called my head of security to meet me in the backyard.

I let him know my plan and had him call both hotels to find Myers. He reported back within a few minutes that Myers was staying at Hôtel des Grands Hommes, near the Pantheon and then he handed me the phone.

I spoke to Myers and the hotel manager and explained to them what needed to happen. They agreed to play along for a sum of money. With both parties on board, I just had to get Zuri in and out before she did any damage.

I got dressed in a navy-blue Louis Vuitton suit, accompanied by a black dress shirt and black Velasca Giacalustra Oxford leather shoes. As I stood outside the front door waiting for her, she opened it and emerged wearing a black pantsuit with white Louis Vuitton pumps and a white Louis Vuitton handbag. Her hair was dyed a dark red, and she was unrecognizable with makeup, shades, and a new hair color and haircut. *I don't recognize my wife—the mother of my child—I don't know who she is or who she has become.*

"Damn, babe. If we didn't have somewhere to be—"

I cut her off before she could finish, "But we do."

She playfully rolled her eyes at me and then turned to head to the car. She stopped abruptly when she saw the beautiful white BMW M5 that I had sitting in the driveway. She looked back at me, and for the first time in a long time, I saw Hope in her eyes. I escorted her into the car, and we headed to the Hôtel des Grands Hommes. During the drive, she called both hotels to see where Myers was staying—unbeknownst to her, I already knew where we were going.

"Got it, babe. Hôtel des Grands Hommes." I nodded in acknowledgment and had her put it in the GPS.

We arrived at the hotel, and I got out of the car first so that I could open the door for her. I put my hand out, which she grabbed, and helped her out of the car. We walked into the Hôtel des Grands Hommes, and she greeted the man at the front desk and started explaining to him that she was surprising Rachel Myers. "She's our sister," she told the attendant.

I nodded at the attendant, and he winked at me.

"Today is her birthday, and we told her we would not be able to make it, but here we are. We would like to surprise her in her room, so please don't tell her we've arrived." Before the man could answer, she pulled out a passport with a fake name—Zuri Myers.

I was astonished at first because I was trying to figure out at what point she had time to make a fake passport, but then I remembered who I was dealing with—my wife and her several personalities.

"What a nice surprise," the attendant said, bringing me back to reality. "Let me get you a room key. We also had a complimentary bottle of wine we were going to bring up as a thank-you since she is staying with us for an extended period. Would you like to take it up?" he asked.

"Yes, please," she smiled. "We just flew in from London. This is going to be such a great surprise. We haven't seen each other in several years."

The man handed her the key and the wine, and in return, she handed the man five hundred euros and smiled—again, I was flabbergasted. I made a note to remember this and try to figure out where she was finding all these additional resources. We got on the elevator and went up to the sixth floor. We found Marcy's room, and playing along, I let her know there was a camera at the end of the hallway. She nodded and keyed into the room.

When we got in, Zuri was horrified. "This place is a mess. It looks as if Rachel or Marcy or whatever her name was, was in a hurry to go somewhere." She began searching the room. I had no idea what she was looking for, but she was determined to find it.

Keeping up appearances, I helped her look around. I went into the closet and discovered a safe. I proceeded to open it and found that it was completely empty. "Good girl," I said to myself, realizing that Marcy was thorough in removing her items from the safe.

Zuri must have heard me because she turned around, appalled at the sight before her. She pushed past me and knelt down to get a better look into the safe. "There is $30,000 here and a diamond ring that costs about $200,000. What was she doing with this amount of money and this ring?"

Frustrated, I looked at her as she kept talking.

"Something is not right. She is a flight attendant . . ." she said. She stood up and walked toward the desk, grabbing a stack of miscellaneous papers. Some of it was in French, which she knew how to read, but the rest were in English. There were pamphlets for various menus and shows in the area. "We found motive," she said. She pulled out her phone took pictures of the supposed files and then kept reading. She held up a picture of a man on one of the pamphlets and asked me, "Have you heard of this guy before?"

I looked at his picture, and I told her I may have seen him before. She looked back at me as if she didn't believe me.

"Try again. Why are you lying to me?" she said.

As I was about to answer, she side-stepped and looked at the door. The events from here on out petrified me. What she saw, I never did. She signaled for me to get behind the door, and she sat on the bed. She suddenly put up her hands and said, "Calm down. We're not here to hurt you. We just want to know what's going on." She dropped the pamphlets on the floor as she remained seated. "This guy was found dead on our flight. I'm assuming you killed him. My question is, why?" She paused for two minutes, I'm guessing as she 'listened' to a response. Then she said, "What did they mean by that?" Five minutes later she said, "Wait, I heard about this guy. They called him "The Fire Rapist" and I remember when they found the DNA evidence. The authorities were finally relieved to have caught the guy even if he was only charged for one girl." I made a mental note to look up this "Fire Rapist" to see if he was a real person.

After ten more minutes of no movement, she stood up, took off her blazer and shoes, and hugged the air. "I'm sorry for what you went through. We'll help you." She turned around and grabbed a random duffle bag as well as the papers she had dropped on the floor earlier.

The conversation continued, "How many people know about the assault?" A few moments went by then her demeanor changed. Whatever response she heard after the assault question triggered something inside of her. A fragility grew over her, and I saw it—the beauty, confidence—Hope was back. "I know how you feel. I was assaulted before. It happened when I was fourteen."

Horrified, I took a few steps toward Zuri. *What the hell is she talking about?*

She put up her hand to stop me and then looked in my direction. A tear rolled down her face. I waited for her to continue.

"My grandfather owned an estate in Italy. There were these trails—walking, biking, and running trails—where I would go to have some solitude. And one day, I was attacked. This man came out of nowhere and startled me. I tripped and fell down, and he took that as an opportunity to jump on top of me and hold me down." She took a deep breath as the tears continued falling. "There was a scar on his neck," she said as she used her hand to show where the scar was. "I fought him off and made it back to the estate safely."

I released the breath I was holding. It was weird because the guy she mentioned sounded familiar, but I just brushed it off because I knew she was having delusions. I was ready to go to her and get her out of this room but then she started talking again.

"But he tried again."

I felt paralyzed as I watched Hope tell someone—me—what happened to her at fourteen; that night we found her on the trail, unconscious.

"He succeeded that time. He took my virginity. I don't know how I got there, but I woke up with him on top of me, violating me. Then I woke up in my bed to see my one true love sitting next to me. And I honestly thought it was all a bad dream, so I decided not to tell him." She turned to face me and mouthed the words, "I'm sorry."

Everything in me wanted to murder this man. I knew when we left that hotel room, I would make it my top priority to find him. I would have my team search everywhere for him, and when we found him, I would torture and kill him. He would die a slow and painful death for what he did to my baby girl. Who the hell would have the nerve to come onto the family estate and attack the granddaughter of the most powerful man in Italy—the most powerful man in Europe? Indignation filled my body as I grabbed my phone out of my pocket. Just as I was dialing my head of security, she started talking again. This time, her voice was different.

"These men, all they do is take, take, take, and have nothing to give."

I turned to face her and noticed that a darkness had grown over her. She looked over at me, and I couldn't put my finger on what her facial expression was, but I remembered it from that night—the night she shot me. It was an expression of pure evil. I slowly put my phone back in my pocket and retreated slightly from where she was standing. I reached my hand behind my back and placed it on the gun that was holstered there. I stood still as she continued.

"I was born from an experience, a gateway of my creation, a breakthrough for the weak. What was absent in one, was developed in me. Oh, that night, penetrated by darkness. Fifteen was a golden year, a year of an awakening so profound that even I have to congratulate myself on the win. Oh, that estate—I was never alone because the man was always lurking. Like a snake in the night, he would slither silently to me, seeking me. At first, I couldn't see him because he would hide from me, too shy to show me who he really was. Then one day, he came to me to conquer and dominate me. A bond so deep that no mere mortal could break it. A date with the devil."

Holy shit. I remembered that night we found her on the path again, and when UQ asked what happened, she said she had a date with the devil. Endless streams of thoughts flooded my mind. I couldn't comprehend what was happening. For the first time, I felt sick to my stomach as I watched the love of my life tell me she had sex with the devil. I needed to get out of there and fast. See, when she said it at the young age of fifteen, we knew something was wrong. But hearing her say it now, being able to comprehend the meaning behind it, I regret coming to find her. I regret trying to help her, to change her, to heal her.

"Mar?" I called out to her.

She didn't answer. I couldn't get her back into reality. She was gone, forever lost in this other personality. She had that blank stare in her eyes, the same one she had when she was pregnant with Amara. The stare that left me with nothing but pain. I had just spent the last few hours watching my wife, the love of my life, have a conversation, strategize, and plan with no one in the room but me. It was time I did what I should've done that night that she shot UQ and me. A tear dropped down my face as I unholstered my gun and pulled it out from behind me, holding it at my side. "Mar, I'm sorry," I said as I slowly raised the gun in front of me.

"Marcy, you should turn yourself in and let them know what happened. Tell them that he recognized you and was trying to finish what he started. He pushed you into the restroom and tried to kill you. You were able to get the knife out of his hands, and you stabbed him. You will be okay," she said as she hugged the air again. "Massimo and I have worked with this attorney before. He will help you and keep you safe. I trust him."

I lowered my gun, realizing Zuri was back. Her facial expression was worried but focused. Her demeanor was calm but strategic.

"Babe, let's go. Let's leave her to rest," she said as she grabbed the duffle bag with the pamphlets and headed toward me.

I holstered my gun and followed Zuri out of the room. We got on the elevator in silence. I couldn't say anything to her because she was unrecognizable to me. My skin crawled being next to her but then she grabbed my hand and kissed my lips with a softness that made me realize that I still loved her. I kissed her forehead in return, dreading the fact that her evil personality could be triggered at any moment.

27

Weeping Will Endure for a Night

We headed back to the house, and I put on some music to break the silence in the car. She started rubbing the scar on her hand, and for some reason, I felt the need to comfort her. I reached for her arm and said, "Don't worry, babe. We will get through this." But even I had a hard time believing me.

She grabbed my hand and kissed it. "I know, babe. We always do."

When we arrived at the house, I looked over at her before getting out of the car. She looked exhausted. As we were headed inside, she asked me to run her another bath, so I did.

While she was soaking, I went to the kitchen and poured myself a drink—bourbon on the rocks. After three glasses, I mustered up the strength to go check on her. When I walked in, she was lying in the bed, and the first thing I noticed were the tears falling down her face. I climbed into the bed and held her.

"You make me feel safe," she told me.

I kissed her forehead and said, "I will never let anyone hurt you again—I swear it. Now, get some rest. I have a few calls to make and then I'll join you." I tucked her into bed and waited until she fell asleep. Once I could hear her lightly snoring, I headed out of the bedroom and went down to the tech room. I closed the door behind me and sat down to video chat Amara. We spoke for almost thirty minutes before I heard the nanny call her for dinner. "I love you," I told her. "I love you so much." Tears began forming in my eyes.

"I love you too," she responded.

I smiled at her one last time and hung up the phone, allowing the tears to fall down my face. I sat there, crying, for the next ten minutes. The pain of watching the love of your life lose herself is something no man can bear. I couldn't tell you the anger I felt—at myself, her parents, God. "How could you do this to me, God? What did we do to deserve this? I've tried to live my life on the straight and narrow since she left. Please, just bring her back to me. I need my wife back. Our daughter needs her mother. Please, God, have mercy on me," I prayed.

That night, I couldn't sleep, so I stayed up and reviewed all the files Zuri had pulled the day before. I looked at the notes she took, unable to read any of them. It reminded me of the hieroglyphics that were written by the Mayans and Aztecs. Needless to say, it was not English or French.

I started breakfast around 8:30 a.m.—pancakes. When we were younger, we would always have a competition to see who could flip the pancake out of the pan with the most stealth; she always won. I took this moment as an opportunity to try and relive my youth. I grabbed the handle and took a step back from the stove, holding the pan with the pancake ready for flipping. With as much stealth as I could muster, I threw the pancake in the air but ended up hitting the pan against the stove, the pancake landing on the floor. I laughed to myself, and it felt good because it was the first time in weeks that I felt whimsical.

That moment quickly died when I saw Zuri round the corner with her gun pointed at me. She lowered the gun and said, "You scared me, dummy. What are you doing?"

"Trying to make you breakfast, beautiful. I dropped the pancake on the floor while trying to flip it. Then the frying pan smacked against the stove. It burnt me but I'm fine. I definitely am a better cook than I was when we were together, but flipping pancakes is the one area I haven't mastered."

She giggled and put her gun on the kitchen counter. "Thanks, baby. I cannot wait to taste what you put together." She kissed me on the cheek and walked down the hall into the living room. I could hear her turn the TV on as it blasted from the other room. She was flipping through channels, trying to find something to watch. Eventually, she landed on the news, and I could hear reports on the protests. It was just about to change to the meteorologist's report when I heard a report say breaking news. "Breaking news, detectives, MI6, and the FBI are working diligently to find the individual who they suspect was involved in the flight murders. We turn it over to Lieutenant Grey, who is leading the search."

"Good morning. As of last night, we still have no information on the whereabouts of Zuri Sierra Dawson. We have a few passengers telling the police what they know about her, but we have nothing concrete or solid as of yet. We ask everyone to please stay on high alert and call us if you see this woman. We did identify two of the three victims. One victim was a European diplomat, who was traveling back home after working at the United Nations, which was the main purpose of his trip. The second victim's name was Sherry Moore, a schoolteacher and mother of two. The last victim has not been identified as of yet. The FBI and MI6 are launching a joint task force to look into this further. Again, if anyone has any information on Zuri Dawson, please give us a call. Back to you, Alexandre—"

The TV muted and then I heard her yell for me.

I put her breakfast plate down and ran to her. "What's going on?"

"Why did the police just find Paul's body on the street? You did this?" she asked as she pointed to the screen. "You took his body and did this?"

I looked at the screen and saw her face and name at the bottom, with news reporters still talking. *Paul was the guy she introduced me to the first night—I'm assuming the one she 'shot dead' by putting two bullets into the kitchen floor.*

She continued to intently stare at me. When I didn't answer, she asked, "Who was he to you? The day you arrived, you didn't acknowledge him. There was something going on there. Be honest with me. How did you know him?"

I pulled up a chair and sat in front of her. I couldn't do this anymore. I grabbed her hands. "Baby, you're not well. We need to get out of here so I can take care of you. We need to go back to Italy. Paul, he isn't real. Do you understand what I'm saying to you?" I knew it was now or never. I had to put a stop to these delusions and hallucinations once and for all.

"Darling, I feel fine, and you're taking great care of me. We have work to do before we go back to Italy. I understand that you want us to run away, and that will work out perfectly, but only once I clear my name. What I don't understand is why you won't tell me who Paul was to you. He is real—real dead. Don't you remember I shot him?"

"Can you give me a second? I'm getting a call," I said as I got up, taking my phone out of my back pocket. I hid the screen from her so she couldn't see I wasn't really getting a call, but I had to get out of there. I headed toward the kitchen.

I looked to see her sitting back and continuing to watch me—study me. I talked on the phone as if to my head of security. Eventually, she looked away once I was out of earshot. I put the phone down and stared at it as it lay on the kitchen counter. *How do I maneuver this? How do I break this? Do I lean into her delusions and hallucinations—these fantasies—or do I try to show her proof of reality? I don't know how to handle a situation like this because our realities are not the same.*

I looked up to see her walking toward me—she had tears falling down her face again. She began talking. "I am so sorry. I'm so sorry, babe. I had no idea," she said to me. She moved in closer to hug me.

Confused, I waited to hear what else she had to say.

She wiped the tears from her face and continued. "I am sorry I was not there for you. Please forgive me," she pleaded.

"Forgive you for what?"

"Forgive me for not being there for you. I had no idea the pain Paul caused you and losing your mom after finding her after so many years...I should've been there for you."

I decided to play along because what else was I supposed to do? "It is not on you," I said as tears continued to fall down her face. Although I was only going along with the Paul thing, I still took this time to get some things off my chest—things I've wanted to say to her for years. "I've forgiven you for everything. I love you, and I haven't been the same since you left. Seeing you the other night, it made me so happy. Everything about you makes me happy. You complete me. I just wish I was enough to complete you," I said as I leaned in to kiss her.

She kissed me back with a passion that I felt in my soul—Hope. I accepted this moment of serenity and like teenagers, we made out in the kitchen.

28

Sorrow Is Better
than Laughter

For the first time in days, I was able to fall asleep next to her. There was a calmness that fell over me from experiencing Hope yesterday. It made me realize that with all the chaos and trauma, she's still in there. I wanted to live in this tranquility forever but then I heard her get out of bed and head into the bathroom. I lay there as I heard the shower going—I wasn't ready to let this moment go. I just wanted to hold onto it for a little while longer.

A few minutes later, she emerged from the bathroom wearing a sweatsuit. She left the bedroom quietly so as not to wake me as I pretended to be asleep. I figured she was on her way to the tech room.

I pushed myself to get out of bed and get ready for another unpredictable day. Showered and dressed, I checked in with my head of security, who had nothing to report, then video-called Amara to see how she was doing.

"I'm fine, Dad. How's it going over there? You look tired," she said to me.

"All good, baby girl. I'm getting closer to being on my way home. Hopefully soon!"

"Alright, Dad, sounds good. Be safe. I'm heading to school now. Call me later, gotta go. Bye, Dad. Love you."

"I love you too," I said to the phone, knowing she was already on her way out the door. I laughed to myself, imagining her running out of the house and forgetting her swimming duffle bag like she did every morning. Once she got to the car, she would remember and run back to grab it.

It's going to be a good day I told myself as I headed out of the bedroom and down the stairs to check on Zuri. When I walked into the tech room, she had her head in her hands. She got up swiftly and punched the wall. "Who would frame me to this extent? People will be looking for me at every turn," I heard her say to herself.

"You okay?" I asked, annoyed at how short-lived my happiness was around her.

"Yeah, just frustrated. I am usually able to narrow down suspects and motives. For some reason, I don't understand. This guy was a European diplomat. Whoever did this knew that I would get additional time for killing a diplomat. They knew what they were doing. This is smart. It's strategic. It's diabolical. They also knew that he was tied to the U.S. government, which means he was connected. Why him? Why me?"

"Let me take a look. You might be missing something because you're too emotionally involved. Go eat something, and I will try my best to figure it out," I said to her as I grabbed her arm softly.

She rolled her eyes at me and moved her arm away from my grasp. "Who wouldn't be emotional at a time like this? Your entire life, snatched from you in the blink of an eye. If we don't find the killer soon, my life will be over." She stormed out of the room and went upstairs.

I sat down and reviewed her theories. This time, it was well thought out and methodical. I was impressed with the level of detail and research she conducted. A tinge of happiness floated back in me but quickly dissipated when I realized that she was trying to answer the "why him" question—that only one of her other personalities knew the answer to. It seemed to me that Zuri was blameless in all of this, and I knew Hope wasn't capable of this type of destruction. Hope was sweet and loving—she always understood our purpose for killing those we were tasked to kill; it was for the greater good.

This meant that her evil personality was the driving force in these murders—as long as it was only the three personalities living inside of her. *Not a problem for today.* The evil one, whoever she was, I wished I could remove her from the others and just send her to jail. Sadly, they were a package deal, which meant the whole package would have to go. *Again, not a problem for today. Focus on the now.*

I cleared my mind and pulled any additional information I could, filling in any gaps in her research into Ethan Sparrow the EU diplomat aka The Butcher. I moved some files around on the screen and noticed a picture there—a picture of the diplomat. I brought it to the front of the screen, examining his face, and saw a distinguishing scar on his neck. Then it hit me like a ton of bricks—I knew this man. He would stop by the house once a year to visit UQ. I caught a glimpse of him one time when Zuri was having her fainting spells on the running trails. He had walked past me in the hallway as he was headed up to UQ's office. I remember him because of the deep scar he had on his neck. It wasn't until I actually saw the scar in the picture on the screen that I was able to put it together.

When Zuri was having her hallucination, 'talking to Marcy,' she said the guy she was assaulted by had a scar on his neck. It was the scar—the goddamn scar—and this was the guy. It had to be him—the man who hurt my baby girl and caused the birth of something evil inside of her. I stood up, grabbed the chair I was sitting in, and threw it against the wall. Then I screamed, allowing all the emotions that had been boiling up inside of me to be released.

There was an anger inside of me, and for the first time, I was happy that Zuri and Hope had an evil side. Grateful that the bastard got what was coming to him. I could feel my anger rising again so I left the tech room and headed upstairs to the kitchen where I poured myself a scotch on the rocks. I swallowed it with one gulp and then I poured another. I grabbed my drink and headed upstairs to the bedroom to check on her.

It had been about two hours since she had gone upstairs, and when I looked in on her, she was fast asleep. She looked like an angel lying there, peaceful. I let her rest knowing that it was much needed, even though everything inside of me just wanted to hold her.

As I went back downstairs to the living room, I considered taking a nap on the couch. She was so draining to be around, and the more I discovered about her and this situation, the more I realized that I needed as much rest as possible to deal with it. I sat on the couch and stared at the black TV screen. *What to watch?* I grabbed the remote, remembering I had the security team put in a Fire Stick. My go-to entertainment was horror, but I needed something a bit lighter and calmer. I grabbed the remote and put on *The Office.* This was Hope's favorite show when we were growing up. UQ let her stream the episodes, and sometimes, we would spend hours—on the weekends—watching and laughing at the humor the show delivered.

I sat back on the couch and watched as Michael stood in Ryan's business class and spoke about the paper business. My stomach growled not too long after, alerting me to the fact that I had yet to eat anything. I got up and headed to the kitchen. I decided to cook some food, and once I got going, I didn't want to stop. I made a spread that consisted of bacon, pancakes, eggs, toast, hash browns, corned beef hash, and Hope's all-time favorite, mimosas. I could only hope that Zuri liked the same foods. Right when I finished pouring a mimosa, I heard her descending the stairs. She looked at me and smiled. I knew the key to her heart was food—no words needed to be exchanged.

She grabbed a mimosa and her already prepared plate then briskly walked into the living room. She saw *The Office* playing and became giddy. "Yay! Thank you, babe," she said to me smiling ear-to-ear. She sat cross-legged on the couch and ate.

I made myself a plate and joined her, enjoying the silence between us and the bursts of laughter we shared while watching the show.

After eating and four mimosas in, all of which she drank, she snuggled up on the couch and began to relax. I gave her a gentle kiss on her forehead and then climbed onto the sofa behind her, cuddling up next to her as she fell asleep again. I decided to fight for these moments of serenity because I had missed them for so long.

It was around 6:00 p.m. when she jumped out of her sleep. It startled me and caused me to hold her tightly. I could feel her heart racing—she was breathless and had sweat dripping down her brow. "Hey, it's okay. It was only a dream," I said to her as I rubbed her back.

She grabbed me tightly in a way that said she didn't want to let go.

We were back on the road again, heading to Versailles. Versailles was less than an hour from where our safe house was. We were going to Versailles because The Butcher had a home and bunker there. I was skeptical at first, but the information didn't lie. Upon further research, I was able to find a vast amount of information on him that pointed us to this location. The information also showed that this man had many enemies. In my line of work, I knew this trip could be a problem, but in hindsight, his having enemies worked in our favor. If we could prove that he was killed by someone other than Zuri, it would show reasonable doubt, and that is all we needed to ensure she didn't face the death penalty.

When we arrived at his house—windows down—it was so quiet you could hear a pin drop. It didn't look like anyone had been home in months. The grass was high and unkept, the yard was trashed, and there were no vehicles in the driveway. We got out of the car, and both of us unholstered our guns. We moved slowly toward the house, searching to see if anyone was around, and when there was no movement or sounds, she walked up to the front door and tried the handle. The door was unlocked, so she pushed the door open and raised her gun in front of her. I signaled to her that I was going around back. She nodded and then continued into the house. When I got to the back door, it was unlocked as well. I walked inside and cleared the back end of the house. Silence.

After clearing my end of the house, I began looking for Zuri. The house was ominous, and a dark feeling floated into my body. After five minutes of searching, I found her in the kitchen, poking around in the cabinets. She had a sinister look on her face as she turned to face me, and it sent a shiver down my spine—the evil one was back.

"I'm going to look around," she said to me before I could ask her what she was doing.

I followed suit, keeping my gun in hand. I strolled around, unfazed by the destruction that lay before us—it was left by someone who was looking into the diplomat or into his former life as The Butcher. I walked down the stairs, toward an ajar door that looked like it led to a bunker. I pushed the door open with my gun raised. Once the door was fully open, automatic lights turned on. There were monitors and papers everywhere, but the real image that caught my attention was Zuri's face on one of the monitors. I yelled out to her, "Hey, you got to see this!"

She walked toward my voice and down the stairs. At the sight of her face on the screen, she stopped dead in her tracks before running to the computer. She grabbed the computer mouse and started scrolling through several documents and files. I had no idea what she was looking for, but I took it upon myself to review some of the papers that had been thrown on the floor.

I continued to explore the papers, moving the irrelevant ones out of the way and picking up the ones that held some significance to me, her, or the family name. Amongst the documents, I saw a picture of her father and UQ. When I picked the photo up and turned it around, my heart stopped. This was a picture that UQ had given to Zuri years ago. I knew it was the same picture because, on the back, there was an inscription that said, *May you never forget that we are mortal men, trying to live like creatures of success. Though we may fail you—remember we are a product of our environment, and we did the best we could, with the knowledge we attained over the years. — UQ.*

For a few seconds, I stared at the inscription and didn't move. This picture was near and dear to her growing up, and even when she left the house, that picture had disappeared with her. I was confused, and my thoughts were racing as I could feel her staring at me. *When did she come here? Was she and The Butcher sleeping together? Is this her home?* The only explanation is that she had been there before, and if that was the case, then she may have known who The Butcher was before she killed him—or at least before one of her personalities did.

She nonchalantly got up from the computer, acting as if she was looking through some papers, but from the corner of my eye, I could see her moving closer to me. I felt apprehensive and unsure of how to proceed. I held my gun tighter. *The evil one is back. I always feel a darkness come over the room when she arrives.*

She reached for a paper on the floor, held it up, and asked, "Did you know?"

Before I turned to fully face her, I put the picture in my pants pocket. Then I walked over to see what she was talking about, my gun still in my hand as I realized that devilish smirk on her face. I grabbed the papers and started reading. UQ's name was on the top of the page. The document was dated fifteen years earlier. It seemed as though UQ hired this diplomat to kill a few people because there was a payment receipt of $1.5 million wired to the diplomat's account. "Holy crap! I had no idea. UQ stayed away from people like this, but I also know he had a dark side. This must have been one hell of a job for him to reach out to The Butcher." I added the document to the stack of other papers I had gathered.

We both continued to look through the papers on the floor when I saw another picture peeking out from below some papers. She saw it too. She walked over to the papers, cleared them away, and grabbed the photo. From where I stood, I could see it was a picture of her parents. In an instant, she started to tear up. I couldn't understand why at that moment, but it became clear the next day.

I could see her demeanor change as she wiped the tears from her face. She looked at the picture one last time and then kissed it and put the picture in her pocket. Suddenly, there was a faint but distinguished beeping sound that I could hear coming from upstairs. We looked at each other with horror because we knew that beeping sound anywhere—an explosive device. She grabbed as many files and papers as she could, me doing the same, and we ran through the bunker door, up the stairs, and out the back. We kept running until there was a loud explosion behind us. The blast sent us flying forward a few feet, papers going everywhere. My ears were ringing as I rolled over and looked at the house.

"Someone was trying to destroy the information in that house," I said as I caught my breath.

"Yeah, seems like The Butcher was a busy man. At least these files can point us in the direction of who hired him, and hopefully, give us some information on how my parents and I are involved."

We got up, dusted ourselves off, and worked together to gather the papers that were scattered from the blast. Avoiding the burning house, we walked around to the front as I could only hope the car was in one piece. Thankfully, it was.

"I think we finally have a substantial lead in figuring out why me," she said as I pulled off.

I lay next to Zuri as she was asleep, my mind racing, re-playing the events in my head. *How would a bomb activate itself without a trigger? There was no one in the house except her and I. The area was deserted.* I thought back and focused on the two times that I felt uneasy in that house with her—times when I believed her evil side was present. The first time was when I saw her poking around in the kitchen cabinets, and the second time was when I picked up that picture and read the inscription left by UQ.

At that moment, with the picture, she noticed that I had come to the realization that she had been in that house before. It felt too convenient—to methodically planted. *Did she want me to find it and connect her to it?* I didn't know, but something inside me couldn't shake the feeling that this trip—maybe unconsciously to Zuri—was a plot of destruction for her evil side. If she had been in that house before, which I suspected she had, then there were prob-ably more clues that could have linked to her presence there. Considering we only searched the bunker before the house blew up, destroying all the evidence, I'll never truly know. *The explosive device.*

The device was planted on the first floor because as we ran out the back, I could hear it getting louder and louder. I lay there going back to the first instance, the time I couldn't hear or see her, when I couldn't find her. The thought crossed my mind, but I couldn't bring myself to believe it because there was no way—*did my wife just try to kill us?*

29

The Grief of Wisdom

I spent hours in the tech room sorting through the documents and carefully putting them into two distinct piles. The first pile was her timeline beginning after she shot UQ and me. I found an influx of information on her attending law school, and there were also pictures of her out to lunch, dinner, and bars. In all the pictures, she was in business attire. The second pile was a file on her parents. It had documentation of conversations with the FBI, along with an explanation of who they were and their assignments. I wanted to dive deeper into the second pile because I knew her parents well, and this was not them.

I began examining the second pile of documents when she entered the room. I could see the exhaustion in her eyes as she sat down and yawned. I made a note to cut back on the number of sleeping pills I was giving her because I may have overdone it last night.

As I was looking over at her, I felt disgust rise within me. I didn't want her in the room with me after my revelation last night, but I couldn't send her away without raising suspicion. She noticed that I had two piles of documents, and without saying a word, she grabbed the first pile and looked through the files briskly. Then she took her time on the second stack, studying the information in front of her.

"Someone put out a hit on my parents. With all the resources UQ had, he was never able to find the killer. Now, we know why he could never find him. The Butcher was heavily protected by multiple governments, which made him practically untouchable."

I was in utter disbelief—surprised that after all this, she could still shock me. *Her parents were alive. I spoke to them a few weeks ago.*

The tears began falling down her face again. I was getting so sick of her crying all the time. She wiped the tears from her eyes and started ranting about how she was the reason her parents were dead. In barely a whisper, she said, "Had I not been in the life of killing people, my parents would not have suffered the same fate as those on the other side of my nozzle. I always knew there was a reason to kill people—finding ways to justify killing rapists, murderers, and pedophiles because UQ made us believe that that was the right and just thing to do. I agree that people who hurt other people should suffer for the trauma they have caused. Trauma. Trauma." Her demeanor changed in a matter of seconds. Her tears dried up as quickly as they had fallen. The sinister look was back on her face.

She said, "You know, after I left that night, I made the decision to start fresh. I decided it was time to get on the right side of the law. I spent some time in Versailles. During that time, I disappeared and wiped all traces of myself from the internet. There was not much to begin with because, while I worked for UQ, I always did this. I attended Yale Law and graduated in the top ten percentile. I passed the bar with a 280, and there was nothing that could stop me from success. Shortly after, I was hired as a lawyer by the same firm I worked for during an internship, and I've been thriving ever since. My parents, rest their souls, would be proud of me." She got up, no longer looking tired, and walked straight to me as I sat back in my chair with a knot in my throat. She pushed the chair against the wall and kissed me aggressively. She bit my lip, and I started to bleed. The horror in my eyes triggered joy in her.

"Oh, baby. I'm sorry. Did that hurt?" she asked menacingly.

"Not at all," I replied, refusing to let her see weakness in me. "I know what you're capable of. I've seen it. Yesterday, remember—," I said, knowing that I was actually face-to-face with her evil side. I took this as an opportunity to get to know her.

"You ain't seen nothing yet, *baby*." She moved her lips right next to my ear and whispered, "Next time, I won't miss."

I wanted to strangle her right there and then. *She did try to kill me.* She moved back, slowly pausing to catch the expression on my face. I grabbed her shirt and pulled her closer to me, moving my lips next to her ear, mimicking the same action she had just done to me, and whispered, "Neither will I." I pushed her back, exited the tech room, and ran upstairs. I listened to make sure she wasn't following me and then went outside to the garden and released the breath that was stuck in my chest. *I'm going to have to kill my wife.*

After our foreboding encounter, I went back upstairs to the bedroom to lie down. It was so hard to sleep around her. I decided to ask one of my security men to sit in the living room so he could alert me when she came upstairs. But I was so exhausted that I missed the notification, and I was still asleep when she walked into the room.

"Babe," she whispered as she rubbed my arm.

"Yes," I said in a groggy voice.

"Guess what I found out—Alice is in Paris. I knew it was her who set me up. We need to run surveillance and see where she is staying. It's time I do what I should have done years ago—end this once and for all."

I sat up partially, confused. "I need another twenty minutes and then I want you to tell me everything."

She kissed my cheek, and I rolled over, putting my hand under the pillow to grab my gun. *Not the evil one—it was Zuri.*

Twenty minutes later, I walked downstairs in a t-shirt and sweatpants to see her in the kitchen making herself a smoothie with frozen fruit. I noticed the security guy was standing by the stairs that led to the basement. I signaled for him to leave, and he left through the garden door. I headed to the living room and plopped down on the couch, still sleepy. I slid my gun from the back of my pants and put it in between the cushions. "Come here, babe," I said as I lay on my back.

She grabbed her smoothie and walked over to me. She put her smoothie down on a coaster and lay next to me with her head on my chest. *How could I kill the love of my life? My soulmate?* "So, tell me what you found," I said as I played with her hair and then rubbed her arm, thinking about the inevitable.

"You remember Alice, right? I killed her uncle when we first started going on missions for UQ. Well, her uncle was her only family, and she swore up and down that UQ and I were responsible for his death, but I denied it for obvious reasons. Anyway, she couldn't let it go, and we fell out. Even though she never made a direct threat, I hacked her computer and read through the information she had, knowing she was going to try to get back at me for her uncle's death. Well, I saw it in her notes: **REVENGE** was written in bold large letters with a double underline."

I listened.

"Back at my safe house, I did a search and saw that she was in Greece. When I did a search again on your computer, I found out she is now in Paris. I dug into some security systems, and she was by the Eiffel Tower earlier today. I don't know how long she's been in Paris, but if she is here, I know it was her who set me up."

I lifted my head to look at her and played into her thoughts. "Babe, you do understand in this line of work, we make a lot of enemies. What makes you so sure it was her?"

She sat up. "We have a lot of enemies, definitely. Out of all those enemies, I only believed three of them ever hated me enough to have the motivation to do something to this extent—none of whom are from our line of work. You were initially on the list of three, but then you showed up, and I knew it wasn't you. The other two were Alice and Simon. Everyone else was low on the scale of revenge.

I started laughing. "Not Simon from high school and college?"

"Yes, that Simon." She smirked because she knew that I always hated Simon, and when he finally left, I was so happy.

"He swore to me he was going to get back at us if it was the last thing he did. Granted, back then, he was young, angry, and naïve. Based on what I found, he is a Christian missionary in Africa now."

"Well, isn't that nice?" I said in a teasing voice.

She looked at me. "You know when I left, I became a Christian—I still am. I know that in this line of work, it seems hypocritical, but I believe in God. I believe in his power. He brought you back to me."

"It's funny that you mention that because I kind of did the same thing. I changed the organization for the better. I'm no longer killing to kill. Things are just different now, and I understand what you mean. I have to thank God because he kept us both alive this long and brought you back to me," I said as I leaned in for a kiss.

We were on the road again heading to the 7th arrondissement—to the Eiffel Tower. Alice's last known location was in that area, according to security cameras. We were strictly there to do reconnaissance, a surveillance and information gathering operation only.

When we arrived, I drove around, giving her the opportunity to try and spot Alice on the street. After several unsuccessful tries, I told her we would have a better chance of finding her on foot. I went ahead and parked the car. "C'mon, let's go for a walk. We know she's around here somewhere," I said. Dressed in all black, I knew we would blend into the nighttime—if necessary. We also had the perfect cover because we looked like a normal couple, maybe on our honeymoon, even though we were far from normal.

I stepped out of the car and then walked to the passenger side and opened her door. I grabbed the Sony A7 IV camera that was sitting on her lap and then reached out my hand to help her out of the car. She stood up and continued to hold onto my hand.

We walked through the grassy area near the Eiffel Tower, and I felt a rush of hope in my heart. It was ever so slight, but it was more fulfillment than I have felt in a very long time. We continued to walk, stopping every few feet to take some pictures of her and the beautiful view. I wanted to capture this moment because I hadn't seen that smile, that walk, that playfulness in years.

She stopped walking to pose for some of the photos and others were off guard. One thing I love about pictures is they can capture one moment in time, and you can relive that moment forever. I wanted to relive this moment with her, capturing the calmness of who she was and knowing that time couldn't alter how she behaved at this exact moment—the picture said it all.

We continued to walk until we got right next to the Eiffel Tower. It was packed and busy and beautiful. We kept walking and then she spotted Alice. Zuri turned around with her back facing her, and I snapped pictures.

She kept posing until I said, "Let's go, bunny. Time to get ice cream."

She skipped over to me, grabbed my arm, and we walked back to the car. We got into the car, and she drove to the other side of the Eiffel Tower while I kept snapping pictures. She kept pointing out Alice and three individuals walking until they entered into the Pullman Paris Tour Eiffel hotel. She looked at me and said, "Let's wait thirty minutes to see if they come back out."

They did not.

So, she called the hotel and stated that Alice was at her restaurant and left her room key along with her credit card. "They are going to transfer me," she said mouthing the words to me. She then put the phone on speaker.

The phone rang and a female answered. "Bonjour."

She sat there analyzing the voice.

"Hello? Bonjour? Is someone there?" the voice said again.

She hung up the phone. "The voice . . . it sounded familiar, but it wasn't Alice. I just can't place it. I need you to drive back to the safe house. I can't focus on driving right now because I have to figure out where I know that voice from."

I got back in the driver's seat, and we headed back to the safe house.

Abruptly, Zuri shouted, "My airplane neighbor!" which startled me. "Yes. It was her. It just hit me. It was her, but how?"

I was confused.

"How did Sophia know Alice? What is their connection? We know how Sophia is connected to Paul—what the hell is going on? This is all connected. It has to be. I knew it. I knew it! This cannot be a coincidence. UQ always taught us that nothing in life is a coincidence. We need to go back and kill them."

I stared at her. "Babe, calm down. Let's dig into this before we move solely based on a theory."

"This is not a theory. This is me finally figuring it out. When we get back to the house, let's do some research. I'm sure we are bound to find a connection between Alice and Sophia. I just know it. I feel it."

We arrived at the safe house, and I parked the car. Reluctantly, I followed behind her as she walked inside and then led the way to the tech room. We both sat down, and she quickly pulled up files she put together on Sophia West and Alice Reese. Both individuals had no immediate family but were born on the same day—at the same hospital—by the same mother. Both of them were taken from their mother and brought to the United States from the Czech Republic under different identities.

Sophia grew up the complete opposite of Alice. She was purchased by the highest bidder, who was a drunk couple who beat her every day. They had no business taking care of a child, but money can make all things possible. Sophia eventually ran away right before her tenth birthday. She spent months living on the street and then she ended up in a shelter before being placed into the foster care system. She was moved around from house to house because no one wanted her—she was labeled as damaged goods. Her sweet innocence was gone, and she was a broken girl. She grew up in the foster care system for eight years and then aged out. In her early twenties, she was lucky enough to find a family who took her in while she worked for them. She took care of their children, cooked, and cleaned.

Alice, alternately, was sold to the highest bidder as well, who cared for her like she was his own daughter. He was an older man who just wanted a family. Upon further research, we found that his biological was killed by a bacterial infection that got into her bloodstream when she was five. A few years later, Alice's uncle was killed during a supposed robbery.

"The robbery . . . It wasn't a real robbery. It was my first hit."

I looked at her and chuckled. *She's back at it again—another story.*

Seeing that I didn't believe her, she swore up and down that UQ told her to never talk about that job. She told me that it was one of the first solo trips she did for UQ. She began recalling the assignment. "I was wearing a black sweatsuit and had a silencer on the handgun. It was simple—two shots to the head, point blank range, and then grab his wallet and keys. The bullets were loaded into the magazine while I wore gloves to ensure no fingerprints were left on the shell casing. The gun was wiped down, and the serial number was scratched off. This gun was untraceable.

"Alice's uncle did the same thing every night—quite predictable. Every night, he would have dinner with Alice, and after dinner on Monday, Tuesday, and Friday, he would go to a poker game where he gambled with some close friends. It was more a night of socialization than gambling. The side door to the gambling spot was in an alley. This area was not very crime-ridden, but it was about to be. As Alice's uncle left the bar on a warm Monday night, I was in the alley. I pulled my mask down and walked out from behind a dumpster. His back was turned to me when I said, *hey, sir, do you have any change you can spare?* Alice's Uncle turned around, and I immediately shot two bullets into his head. He fell down. I grabbed the wallet and then the keys and walked past the body. I took the silencer off of the gun, placed it in my crossbody bag, and then holstered the gun behind my back. I took the mask off and put it in my bag right next to the silencer. I removed the scrunchie holding my bun, shook my hair, fluffed it with my hands, and turned onto the main street. Anyone who saw me would have assumed I just came from the house on the corner. I made a left and walked three blocks before getting into a cab. Nice and easy."

I was astonished at what she said. When we were younger, UQ didn't sanction any hits for this man. I was in the heart of everything—all targets, all victims . . . I knew about all of it. Zuri was not in her right mind. The time period she placed this in was before she even knew Alice. "Explain to me how you put two and two together?" I asked.

"It was her name. After I arrived at my safe house, I was doing research on Alice. After I identified she was in

Greece, I started to dive into Alice's background. I was able to find information about her birth mother, who she never spoke about, but I couldn't find the connection between her mother and her uncle. After her uncle was killed, she finished college and moved away. Before she moved, I would see her on campus with this girl—it was Sophia. I always assumed it was a new friend she made, but it was actually her sister. I never met Sophia because Alice and I had already fallen out by that time. When we were boarding the plane, I thought she looked familiar, but I quickly pushed it out of my mind. When I got on the plane, Sophia was such a nuisance that I ignored her. I was wondering why she kept talking to me as if she knew me. It was because she did. When Sophia came back sweaty and messy, and we found out about Paul, we blamed it on him, but what if she was in the back killing The Butcher, and she and Paul were in on it together?"

She paused as if waiting for me to say something but then she continued when she realized I had nothing to say. "That is why Marcy saw them coming out of the bathroom around the same time. We now know that the love triangle was false. It was probably information Paul planted for my benefit. He had to have known that I would find out some way. So, long story short, Marcy killed one male victim, we know Paul killed the female victim, and now we know Paul and Sophia killed The Butcher—allegedly. She must have found out I was responsible for Alice's uncle's death and took her opportunity for revenge. What better way to destroy a lawyer than by having her break the law while in international airspace?"

I stood up in disbelief. "That makes sense, but it also sounds crazy to me—that she would go to such lengths." As soon as I said that, I knew I should've just kept my mouth shut.

"Yeah, they knew what they were doing when they found a guy like Paul. He was attractive, we had a lot of similarities, and I felt like I really knew him. The only reason I felt that was because Alice knew everything about me. She must have told him what to say and how to act," Zuri said while shaking her head. "I finally figured it out. We got them. We got them. I can clear my name. This can be done with," she said, finally sounding relieved. "And maybe we can work on this again." She gestured vaguely to the two of us.

"I think we can get it right this time. You're the one I always wanted to be with. You're the love of my life. You're my soulmate. You're my everything," I said, knowing that we weren't getting our happily ever after because I couldn't ignore what had to be done. Regardless of my feelings for my wife, Amara's mom, I would do everything in my power to make it back to Amara, and if that meant killing Zuri to keep Amara safe, I would do it.

She stood up, walked over to me, and kissed me. "Let's do it," she said.

I grabbed her and held her tight. I needed to cherish these moments because I didn't know how many more we would have together. *The time was nigh.*

30

But the Greatest of These Is Love

She didn't come to bed that night—I slept like a baby. When I woke up, I knew she had to be in the tech room. I knew I would have to give her sleeping pills tonight or she would go on a seventy-two-hour binge of no sleep. I descended the stairs quietly so I could listen as I heard her voice.

"Hi, this is Sherry calling from the front desk. We're pleased to let you know that we're giving you two complimentary tickets to a Burlesque show, and we'll be sending up a bottle of champagne as a thank-you for staying with us. The tickets have been sent to your email, and the show starts at 6 p.m., with an expected arrival of 5 p.m." She paused. "Thank you for your kind words. It has been our pleasure. Do enjoy the show."

I heard her put the phone down on the table. I slowly turned around ready to walk back upstairs but then she continued talking—to herself.

"Phase I complete. Now, moving on to Phase II."

I went back upstairs to the bedroom. I couldn't be a part of whatever plan she was devising this time. I got back in bed, placed my gun underneath the pillow, and lay with my back facing the door. She entered the room about ten minutes later, and I heard her getting ready. She emerged from the bathroom a few minutes later and closed the room door behind her as she walked down the stairs. I assumed she was heading back to the tech room, but I was mistaken.

I thought I heard the front door open, so I got up—gun in hand—and headed downstairs. I opened the front door just in time to see the car speeding out of the driveway. I quickly ran upstairs and called my head of security, telling him to send someone to follow her. He complied and sent two guys, who took off about one minute after she did.

When we had first arrived in Italy, I had the security team buy two cars—the one she was driving, the BMW M5, the subtle but classy one, and then I had a Maserati Bora—the stealthy sports car. So, I shot my head of security a message, telling him to bring the second car around. I quickly got dressed and headed downstairs. I opened the front door to see my head of security waiting for me. He handed me the keys to the Bora and then updated me on Zuri's whereabouts as we walked toward the car—she drove to Alice's hotel.

Once I was a few minutes away from the hotel, I called the security guys who were still watching her, and they let me know she was sitting in her car, but they didn't know what she was waiting for. I arrived and pulled up to my security guys, signaling for them to hang tight while I figured out what was going on. I parked the car, waiting and watching for her to make her move.

I saw her car door open, and she headed to the hotel, dressed in all black, and then walked through the front doors of the hotel without ever looking back. I quickly started the car and drove by the hotel's front doors. The lobby looked chaotic, but that wasn't my focus. I slowed the car to a near stop and saw her slip into the staircase. *Bingo.* I parked the car, ran into the lobby, and then briskly walked into the staircase, making sure no one saw me. I listened as she walked up the steps. Taking the stairs two at a time, I got as close as I could without her hearing or noticing me. I finally caught up to her on the seventh floor, but she kept going up. I stayed one floor behind her and finally heard the door open to the ninth floor. She got out, and I ran up the final flight, closing the gap. I hung back and could see her from the staircase door window. She used a keycard to a room and then went inside. There was nothing to do but wait.

Over an hour later, I saw her leave the room and head to the elevator. She kept looking back as though someone was watching her. I ran downstairs, calling my security guys on the way down, letting them know to keep watch for her exiting the hotel. I made it downstairs and slowly walked into the lobby. My security guys called me and told me that she had gotten into the BMW and drove off. They were a few cars behind her.

Right when I got into my car, they called me again and let me know that she drove to the park around the Eiffel Tower. I was about six minutes behind. I pulled up just in time to see her fighting . . . no one. I called my security guys and told them to leave because I couldn't have them witness this. It was one thing to see the destruction left behind—it was another thing to experience the chaos that led to it.

Once they pulled off, I got out of the car. It was late, and the area was quiet until she fired a few shots in multiple directions. I thanked God that no one was outside because that would've been a mess that even I wouldn't have been able to clean up. As I continued to watch, it looked as if she was picking up something heavy, I'm assuming what she was seeing as bodies, and carrying them into the BMW. She took one last look around and then got into the car. I followed her as she drove out of the city.

Twenty minutes later, she drove into the wooded area where her old safe house was—the one we deserted. I stayed back, no headlights on, and watched as she torched my car. *Are you fucking kidding me? What the hell?* I could only continue to take in the scene from a distance as she began walking the ten miles back to the safe house as if it was a normal day and she was just taking a stroll.

I drove back to the house—traumatized. I parked the car and sat there for about twenty minutes, allowing my mind to process what I had just experienced. My head of security was standing near the house, waiting for me. When I finally got out of the car, I walked over to him.

"Did you find her? She okay?"

"Honestly, I found her, but no, she is not okay. She'll be coming back to the house on foot. When she gets here, alert me."

"Whatever you say, signore."

"Also, I need a new BMW."

He looked at me, ready to ask why, but thought against it. Even though he was one of my most trusted advisors, he knew that this was not the time to ask questions. He nodded, and I walked into the house.

I headed straight to the kitchen and poured myself my usual drink. I quickly drank it and poured another. Then I poured another. I grabbed a wine glass and poured her a glass of wine, putting two sleeping pills in the glass. I left it on the counter, knowing she would come in and drink it. I took a deep breath and went upstairs to take a shower before she arrived.

I stood in the shower, letting the water fall over my face and body. I inhaled and punched the wall several times. I allowed the pain to run through me, the water washing away the emotion from my body and the blood from my knuckles. I was so angry that I couldn't even cry.

I got out of the shower and tried my hardest not to punch the mirror in the bathroom. I knew if I did, it would bring attention to the fact that something was wrong. I also knew I might have to get stitches because that's what happened on a previous occasion. I took several deep breaths and talked myself off of the ledge. I got dressed and got into bed, making sure my gun was under my pillow. As I began drifting off to sleep, my phone pinged. I turned over and checked it, knowing that this was the notification of her arrival. I knew she would see the wine and drink it all, needing to relax.

When she finally came into the room, she immediately went into the bathroom and turned on the shower. After a few minutes, she walked out, smelling like roses, and got into bed. She snuggled up to me as if the events of the night didn't happen.

I woke up—slightly perplexed—to find myself holding her tightly as she lay on my chest. I looked down to see her eyes open. Temporarily breaking my embrace, she turned over to look at the clock—11:01 a.m. She snuggled back into my chest and then adjusted her head so she could look up at me.

"Good morning, beautiful."

She smiled and said, "Good morning, handsome."

"I could get used to this again. I really do miss waking up to your beautiful face. We never did get to experience the married life—I pray that we do after all this is handled," I said.

"I want nothing more than to wake up to you for the rest of my life," she said as she leaned in for a kiss.

I pulled her in closer, mesmerized by her lips as we kept kissing. I leaned back slightly and looked into her eyes. *God, I want to do this for the rest of my life—wake up to her, make out with her, make love to her.* "I have a surprise for you. I know the timing isn't right, but I think it will help if we have just a few hours of retreat versus the constant stress we've been under. Wear your Saturday best."

She got excited. "Tell me! Tell me! What is it?"

I always loved how excited she got when it came to surprises. "Let's get ready and have some breakfast. Then, we'll head out."

She stood up, put a leg on either side of my body, and started jumping on the bed like a little kid. "I'm getting a surprise! Woohoo!" She fell back on the bed, straddling me, and then gave me a kiss and tried to roll out of the bed—but I stopped her by grabbing her arm. I looked deeply into her eyes without saying a word, assessing if I should do what I was planning to do. She looked at me, confused, then relaxed as I pulled her in for another several kisses. I released her arm, allowing her to get out of the bed. She ran to the bathroom while saying, "I need to soak. I'll be quick."

I didn't know what came over me this morning. I'm not sure if it was the dream I had where all of us—her, myself, and Amara—were together as a family, enjoying a family vacation, or if staring into her eyes gave me hope. Regardless, I knew I was making a big decision, but my heart told me I should take a chance on her. *What the hell am I thinking?*

As a man, I'm supposed to be a provider. What type of man am I if I cannot provide help to my sick wife? What type of man am I if I run when things get tough? What type of father would I be if I murdered my daughter's mother? They say love can heal all wounds, but can it heal the wounds that left my baby girl split into several personalities? If love heals all wounds, can I use it to mend her broken heart? If love really heals all wounds, can it help me heal her trauma? The emotions were swimming through my head as I got up and got ready for what may well be the biggest regret of my life or the biggest success of my life. I put negative thoughts out of my mind, vowing to thrive in this happiness that I planned to create for us because whatever I needed to do, to save her from herself, I would do it.

Fully dressed in an all-black Amiri ensemble, I headed downstairs to cook her some breakfast. *Today is going to be a good last day.* I kept thinking this to myself as I finished up breakfast. As I was putting the finishing touches on her plate, she walked into the kitchen wearing a beautiful black outfit by M.M.LaFleur. My mouth was agape as I tried to hold my composure. I quickly put down the spoon in my hand, making my way up to her so I could kiss her. "You're truly gorgeous."

"You're not so bad yourself, handsome," she said as she dusted off my shoulder with her hand.

"Come, let's enjoy some breakfast," I said, leading her toward her plate and grabbing a stool for her to sit on.

We sat down for breakfast and immediately after we finished, I knew it was now or never. "Now, it's time for your surprise," I said as I walked over to her. She turned around smiling so I could blindfold her. I grabbed her hand and led her to the other side of the safe house. She heard a door open and then I let go. "Are you ready?" I asked.

She nodded, her smile growing bigger. I took off the blindfold and watched her expression of utter shock and surprise. I had a similar setup to our previous engagement. There were red rose petals everywhere on the floor; several dozen bouquets of flowers spread around the room, including orchids and a mix of blue, red, and white roses. Toward the back of the room was a large sign that said, "Will you be mine?"

She turned around and hugged me. I reciprocated, holding her tightly. I released her and held her hands. "I know you've been going through hell, but I want you to know that I'm here for you, and I will support you. We'll get through this, and once we do, we'll be able to do all the things that we weren't able to do back then. I've spent too much time away from you, and I don't want to lose another moment with you. Even though the current circumstances are bad, I'm grateful because it brought me back to you." I got down on one knee and re-proposed to the love of my life. The ring was similar to the ring I gave her the first time, but not quite the same. This was a sapphire-centered square-cut ring with diamonds around the sapphire. She was in shock but quickly gained her composure and said yes.

The day continued with bouts of celebration—eating, drinking, dancing, watching movies, and cuddling. The day ended with me making love to my fiancé.

As I lay in bed, with her head on my chest, I thought about how amazing the day was. I felt my love for her return tenfold. While I knew this was an unrealistic situation, I couldn't help but want my old life back—my wife back. With the uncertainty of the future, I wanted to treasure the present because tomorrow was not promised—for either of us.

Whatever fantasy I was living in ended when I woke up with a sick feeling inside of me as if I had been poisoned. I pushed the feeling out of my mind, out of my body, but it kept rearing its ugly head. I couldn't quite put my finger on it, but it all made sense when my phone rang that afternoon.

We spent the morning making love, and finally, we decided in the afternoon that work needed to be done. She led the way downstairs into the tech room. I double-backed and grabbed my gun, holstering it behind my back because something didn't feel right. It wasn't her this time—it was me.

I headed into the tech room to see that she was accessing the police database to see what updates they may have had. I sat down next to her when my phone vibrated, startling me. It was my head of security calling so I picked up the phone, standing up to leave the tech room and heading up the stairs so I could take the call. She was so enthralled with the information she found on the police database about the murders that she paid me no mind.

"Boss, we have a problem. Brace yourself and come outside." He quickly hung up the phone, which was unlike him.

I walked upstairs and saw him in the garden, standing by the table and chairs that were there. I walked toward him and felt that sickness fill my body again. The first thing I asked when I saw him was, "Is it my baby girl—Amara?"

"No, boss. I need you to sit down."

"Tell me, now!" I said, refusing to sit.

"Capo, it's about your mother and father-in-law. We found them . . . dead."

The breath left my body and my knees went weak. My head of security ran and caught me, pulling out a chair so I could sit down. I grabbed the chair handles so tightly that all the blood rushed out of my hands.

"Boss? Boss?"

"What happened to them?"

"They were shot in the head, point blank range."

I put my head in my hands and allowed the tears to fall down my face. I was tired. These last few weeks with Zuri were magical, but realistically, my life was perfect without her. I should've never brought this infection of a woman into my life—my daughter's life. I built a life of my own, without her, and instead of chasing after a fantasy, I should have been focused on reality. She's a cancer, a disease, that only brings pain and death into my life. The moments of happiness are not worth the fiery destruction that she leaves behind.

"I'm going to kill her—once and for all." I stood up, unholstering my gun, and loaded a bullet into the chamber.

"Boss! No!" my head of security said, standing between me and the side door.

I pushed him out of the way, but he stopped me again, putting himself between me and the door. At that moment, I saw her walking inside, heading to the door to come join. She had seen the little tussle that was taking place.

"Boss, signore, please, think about your daughter. There are other ways to handle this," he whispered as she got closer.

I took a deep breath just as she opened the door.

"Baby, are you okay?" she asked with a bit of concern in her voice.

"Fine. Please go back downstairs."

"Okay . . ." she said, eyeing me suspiciously. She closed the door and walked away, looking back a few times.

Once she walked back out of sight, I turned around and sat down, staring into the sky. I knew the evil one did it—I felt it in my soul. She must have realized that her parents were still alive and killed them. If I didn't know any better, I would say she was coming after anyone who did her wrong. Or anyone she believes, real or unreal, did her wrong.

She had taken away everything, and if I didn't stop her now, she would take away the only thing that mattered to me—Amara. I sat there, hoping it was all a bad dream. *How do I tell my daughter that both of her grandparents were murdered? How do I even begin to explain to her that her mother was the one who did it? I can't destroy my daughter's perception of her mother—I won't do it. As a father, I must protect and provide, and sometimes, that means keeping the truth and telling a lie.*

I stood up after about twenty minutes of sitting on that chair, letting the emotions get the better of me. I dusted off my pants, holstered my gun, and looked at my head of security. "I need you to do two things for me—urgently. First, put a bounty on her head. Dead or alive, she should be turned in to the police—$500,000. Second, call the FBI, MI6, and the Parisian detectives. Leave an anonymous tip, letting them know that she will be exiting the Pullman Paris Tour Eiffel Hotel at 8 p.m. tonight. Alert me when these two things are taken care of."

My head of security nodded and immediately picked up the phone to complete the tasks. I gathered myself and walked back into the house. I went upstairs to the bathroom, straightened my clothes out, and headed back downstairs to the tech room. When I entered, she looked perturbed.

"Look!" she yelled to me, pointing at the screen.

I read the message and pretended to be furious. There it was—the half-a-million-dollar bounty I put on her head. "I will get this taken care of right now," I said as I grabbed my cellphone from my back pocket.

"Wait, I think it's time I turn myself in. I'm one of the best damn lawyers in the U.S. I can defend myself, prove my innocence, and I can do it sooner than this bounty will be fulfilled. If I turn myself in, which is all they want, we can control the narrative. While I do that, I need you to take care of this and have it called off. I imagine that the person who posted this is someone who was either close to The Butcher or part of one of the organizations that is searching for me. This has to be someone who is connected to both sides."

I put up a fake fight, excited that my plan was working out for me with little effort. "I cannot and will not let you do that. Hear me out, I know you're stubborn, I know you'll do what you want, but you need to understand that we can change the narrative without you ever having to turn your-self in. I've been thinking, you got rid of Sophia, Alice, and those men, which means we have a perfect opportunity to pin the murders on them. We need to go back to their hotel room and see if we might be able to find evidence that will link them back to the murder. If not, then we plant it and get the hell out of there."

She sat there, thinking for longer than usual. "That's not a bad idea. Not a bad idea at all. Let's do it. This way, my name will be clear, the bounty will be clear, and we can get out from under this bullshit. I will check the hotel database and see if the rooms are still reserved. If so, let's get over there. It will give us an opportunity to check, plan, and strategize," she said as she started typing away.

"I'll get some things packed for the trip and figure out an entrance and exit strategy," I said as I walked out of the room with a big smile on my face. This nightmare was about to be over.

We headed out just before dark. The plan was to walk in through the front of the hotel like we had done before. There was a big event happening at the hotel, and I was banking on the lobby being packed.

We arrived at the hotel in the midst of the chaos. Parking alone was horrendous. As we got out of the car and approached the front lobby, it was mayhem. We walked hand in hand toward the front as a normal couple. She had dyed her hair black to alter her appearance, but the cameras would pick her up this time around because they knew she would be there and who they were looking for.

We arrived at the doors and saw there was a checkpoint due to the event. She walked ahead of me, showing security a room key that she had taken the last time she was here, and they let us in—no questions asked. She led the way and headed for the elevator. The plan was for me to stay in the lobby and keep watch.

Twenty-four minutes later, she called my phone and said, "I found a USB drive. *Bingo*."

"Meet me downstairs," I said, abruptly hanging up the phone. A minute later, the elevator dinged, and she walked off, heading straight toward me. The lobby was still crowded, but it seemed even more so now. "Let's go," I said, reaching out for her hand. I pushed open the hotel door, allowing her to go through first. I noticed two things as I opened the door—the sound of a helicopter approaching the hotel and the feeling of a midsummer's breeze. Immediately, cop cars rounded the corners of the hotel street and sirens were blaring. Police officers stepped out of their cars with their guns drawn, pointing directly at her. The helicopter that I had heard was right above us, shining a bright light down on her. I took a step back to separate myself from her.

"Hands up!"

"Get down!"

"Do it now!"

Voices were shouting from multiple directions. I watched her look from left to right as dozens of agents and police officers walked toward her, guns lifted.

She slowly knelt on her knees with her hands raised. Agents, MI6, and FBI were swarming her. They pushed her down onto her stomach and handcuffed her wrists behind her back. Two individuals, I couldn't see what agency they were with, hoisted her up. She turned when she heard me yelling to her, "Don't say anything! I'll get you a lawyer!"

I tried to hide my excitement because, not only was she finally going to get the help she needed, help I knew I couldn't provide her, but this meant safety and freedom for me, Amara, and the syndicate.

She held her head high, smiling, and looked back at me. "I am a lawyer."

Not anymore.

31

But Joy Comes in the Morning

She sat in a jail cell convicted of the murder of a diplomat, a teacher, and an unidentified male. She ended up hiring her lawyer friend to defend her, but it did her no good. I paid off a lot of people and spent a lot of money to send her to unité hospitalière spécialement aménagée—specially adapted hospital units—UH-SAs. This type of psychiatric ward is what she needed.

I went by to visit her weekly, specifically to check in on her well-being and to let her know it would be alright. I told her that the USB drive that she discovered in Alice's hotel room was heavily encrypted with software that I had only seen once on a mission in Central Europe. I told her I had my team working to break into the USB drive, but every time we got close, there was another firewall blocking our access.

It took two weeks before they deemed her unwell, finally triggering another personality within her. Once diagnosed, they kept her sedated for a number of days, giving them time to run tests on her. After tests were run and she was deemed physically healthy, then came the work on her mind.

I kept asking for information on her therapy sessions and well-being, as her husband, but no one would tell me what was going on. After I used my name, Mariano, they finally realized who I was and quickly obliged. *So, what happens to those who don't have the type of pull and status that I have?* The file I was given said that my wife suffered from schizophrenia. I grew agitated because I specifically told them it was dissociative identity disorder, formally known as multi-personality disorder, but they refused to listen to me. I knew the truth, but it was such rare a disorder that it was heavily overlooked and misdiagnosed. I also believe that they realized they were not equipped to accurately diagnose her because they were not equipped to handle it. Their reasoning was sound but flawed. They thought it was schizophrenia because she was talking to people who were not there, which I witnessed on multiple occasions too. Regardless, I accepted the diagnosis and allowed them to do what they needed to do.

Finally, after a few weeks, they noticed that she was having visual hallucinations, which caused her to see people or things that were not physically present. In further sessions, they identified three identities that she had within herself.

Through these last few weeks, I was reintroduced to each of her personalities. At times, she was playful and loving—that was Hope Amara Sarah Mariano. She was who I remembered her to be and who I grew up with. At times, she was a lawyer trying to negotiate her way out of prison—that was Zuri Sierra Dawson. She admitted feeling lost and confused, especially believing she was being framed for these murders. At times, she was evil, trying to harm herself and trying to harm me, not only with the bomb but also when she shot me and UQ. Her evil side scared me the most. She refused to give us the name of her evil side, but I would find out soon enough. As therapy sessions continued, her evil side seemed to be her focal point, taking center stage and dominating the show.

After the doctors notified me of the evil side being more frequently present, I instructed them that I would sit in on a few sessions. Now that she was locked away, worrying about her felt humane. As irrational as it sounded, I still wanted to better understand all sides of her. I just had to know that my baby was okay first.

Out of all the sessions I sat in on, this particular session was when I knew I couldn't be there for her anymore—to emotionally and physically support her. I stood in front of the one-way mirror and watched as Zuri kept saying that she was being framed, over and over again. When the doctor demanded answers about the murders, something I asked him to do, her face, eyes, and demeanor changed. We had successfully triggered the evil one—she was back.

"I would do it again and again—until I could bathe in their blood. Killing is like a meal—you need food to nourish your body the way I need killing to nourish mine. It starts with breakfast time, the most important meal of the day. I start my killing bright and early. Usually, a jogger or a mailman. Then lunchtime, the best meal of the day, a businessman who is too busy on his phone or too busy staring at my ass to know that I'm a threat. Then dinner time, the tastiest meal of the day, a drunk guy who picks me up at the bar. Great sex and then while he's "resting"—I slit his throat. Oh, the warmth of the blood—more satisfying than an orgasm. Then finally, desert, which is my little secret."

I walked out of the room as the hairs on my skin rose. I couldn't help her more than I already had. She was not well and that irrational need to help her quickly dissipated. I couldn't be around her anymore—it was sickening. I most definitely couldn't bring her around Amara. That woman in there, no longer Hope, Amara's mother—was dead to me. Amara was my only focus, a vow I made to myself, from that point forward.

I had been away from Amara for almost nine months, trying to help my wife, but I could do it no longer. I had neglected parts of my life for the love of my life, which is my biggest regret. It was time to go home.

It felt good to walk through the front door and see my beautiful daughter run straight into my arms. I picked her up and hugged her tightly, not wanting to let go. I basked in that moment for as long as I could before I had to tend to my responsibilities as a father. I had to tell Amara that her grandparents were dead. I couldn't bring myself to tell her that day, so I did it the following morning.

"Hey, Mara, come here," I said as she walked out to the pool in time for our morning swim. "I need to tell you something, and just know that it breaks my heart to break this news to you."

"What's going on, Dad?" she said with concern in her voice as she sat down on the chair across from me.

I grabbed her hands. "It's grandma and grandpa . . . Baby girl, uhm . . . They're dead."

I could see the gut punch that I had delivered to her. She sat there squeezing my hands as the tears began falling down her face. It hurt me so much. I pulled her in for a hug, and she began sobbing into my shoulder. It took twenty minutes for me to calm her down. Once I did, I explained to her that it was a robbery gone bad. I let her know that they caught the person, and they would be locked away for life. That definitely brought some joy to her, knowing that this person got what they deserved. *As parents, we do what we need to, what we have to, to protect our children.*

We held a funeral for Hope's parents a few days after I broke the news to Amara. We buried them with the rest of the family at the end of the estate. It was a sad day, but I did the best I could to put them in their Sunday best. We had to have a closed casket due to the bullet holes in the center of their foreheads, which destroyed Amara because she wanted to see them one last time. We had a very private funeral because I couldn't bring myself to broadcast this tragedy.

The next few weeks, I worked hard to return back to normalcy. The syndicate was fine while I was away—I made sure of it—but there was still some in-person business I needed to take care of.

Every now and again, while in the throes of dealing with a conflict, I would think about her. I had come to terms with sending her to prison because that is where she needed her to be—a place where I needed her to be—so she couldn't hurt anyone. A place where she could heal and maybe learn how to live a normal life, as normal as it could possibly be. I fought the urge to call the UHSA every day, but I called periodically to check on her and get updates. I kept paying the facility to ensure she had the best treatment that money could buy in a situation like this.

A few weeks turned into a few months and then a few years. Amara and I were back to our new normal routine of morning swim practices, after-school bike rides, and evening dinners. It was amazing how she was growing into a beautiful young lady. I cherished these moments dearly. The business was going well, and I was back on top of the world. The hell I went through became a distant thought, memories that I consistently pushed toward the back of my mind.

But I should've known better.

It happened to be a cold rainy day when these moments of joy and light came to a halt. Amara and I were watching *The Incredibles* in our home movie theater, and right when Frozone asked his wife for his super suit, my phone rang.

"Boss, we have a problem."

"Be right out," I said as I hung up the phone. I got up and told Amara to keep watching the movie. I walked outside, and my head of security walked toward me.

"What happened?" I said, fearing that Hope had killed herself.

"She escaped."

32

Lilith Rises

I took a deep breath as I stepped out of the UHSA—Centre Hospitalier Guillaume Reg-nier—CHGR. It was a great day to be alive and a great day for death. Four dead guards, a dead doctor, and a dead inmate, and I was finally free. It had been a long time since I felt this way—not since I murdered those three individuals on the plane headed to Paris. I was in the loony bin for some time, thanks to Massimo, but there I was, a free woman.

Also, how rude of me. Allow me to introduce myself. I am Night Doom, better known as Lilith Mare. Just a little bit about me, I have two goals in life—to hunt and to kill. I may have been sidelined, but that's okay. My goal still stood. I went to Paris to hunt Massimo, and now it was time to kill him.

I walked over to Rennes Saint Jacques Airport and saw a red two-door 1987 Ferrari 275 GTB4 sitting in the parking lot. *What are the chances?* Sadly, there was no driver, so I hotwired the car and then drove off, enjoying every part of the drive. No more hiding due to Hope, and no more running because of Zuri. It was time for me to finally have some semblance of freedom.

First things first, I needed to get a warm bath and some sleep in a nice bed. That first night was a night for me to bask in my freedom and get some rest because we had a lot to do tomorrow.

As I drove, windows down, I let the air soothe my soul. I arrived at Rue Touillier, a road lined with what looked like apartments and houses. I pulled onto the side of the road, parked the car, and started walking. I just needed to find one place, preferably one that was occupied so I could have a little fun before I went to sleep. But if not, then just some peace and quiet. There was a house that had a full mailbox, looking as if someone hadn't been there in a few weeks. I tried the door, and it was unlocked. *Some people are so stupid. Do they not think about burglars?*

I walked in, and the apartment was empty. I was a bit annoyed because I did have an urge to kill, but I was also exhausted. I knew if I killed when I was exhausted, I might be sloppy. First thing I needed was a change of clothes, so I went through the dresser in the bedroom and found some woman's clothing. There were only a few outfits in the dresser, making me believe that it must have been a man's house.

I took a shower, washed my hair, and let the water cleanse me. After my shower, I was feeling drowsy, so I laid down on the couch and fell asleep. A few hours later, I was awakened by a noise. I realized the guy who lived there had come home. Needless to say, he should have stayed out, because now he's dead, and I am back on the road, feeling refreshed and exhilarated. Where was I headed, you ask? Welp, I was driving to fulfill my ultimate purpose, my final kill—Massimo.

Three days later, I arrived in Italy. The drive was nice and serene. Several roadblocks, a few dead people—but I made it.

33

<hr>

To Everything,
There Is a Season

Now that she escaped, I couldn't find her anywhere. Traffic cameras didn't pick her up, and no one knew where she was. Once they realized she escaped, they sent search teams to look for her, but she disappeared. I will say, when she wanted to stay hidden, she did. There was a part of me that was scared, which was out of character for me, but for good reason. I was worried because I remembered her threat to kill me. This was not over. She was out for blood, and if there was one place she was going to come, it was here.

A few days after she escaped, we got an alert that she was in Italy. For the first time, I hated that I was right. *I knew it.* I cannot describe to you the fear I felt for myself and for Amara. All my life, I had to fight for myself. It was one of the most important lessons UQ taught me—how to survive. Fear wasn't something that I felt. I stopped fearing anything or anyone when I was ten years old. But nothing had truly scared me the way my wife scared me—not even when I was being beaten up by my abusive father. My wife, though, she was neither predictable nor stable, and this would prove to be a very challenging situation.

When Amara went to bed that night, the night we found out she was in Italy, I called an emergency meeting with my entire security team. We met in the basement cellar where I mapped out coverage of exit points, entrance points, and the entire land. I knew she was coming for me—I felt it in my soul. My biggest goal, though, was Amara's safety.
It mattered more to me than my own safety. I would do everything in my power to ensure that she lived a long-fulfilled life. UQ always told us to prepare for the worst and expect the worst, so I gave clear instructions to my security team and her nanny—just in case I didn't make it out of there alive. They were the same instructions I delivered to them before I left to find Hope the first time around.

After the debrief, I dismissed my team. I sat down at a desk and looked at the battle plans drawn before me. *I knew I should've killed her.* I could feel a tightness growing in my chest. I worked to purge her from my system, and there she was again, resurfacing. I reached into my pocket and pulled out my wallet. In one of the folds was a picture of Hope, standing near the Eiffel Tower. That moment that I worked so hard to capture was in front of me. I closed my eyes and remembered how it felt to see her playful and happy—it brought a smile to my face. The smile slowly turned to a frown as the thoughts of the hell I went through with her came flooding back. At a point in my life, her smile was all I needed to continue living, that laugh was all I needed to feel happy, and she was all I needed to feel complete.

They say you never get over your first love—I agree. Years have gone by, and I still cannot wrap my head around the way Hope makes me feel. Ironically, she gives me hope. She gave me hope and made me believe that even when things were bad, they were better than they could be. I put the picture in my wallet and then leaned my head forward into my hands. I stood up and flipped the table in front of me. I was enraged. This love shit was over. The woman I loved was no longer there. This was war and only one of us would come out alive.

I walked upstairs and checked on Amara—she was sound asleep. I tiptoed into the room, standing next to her so I could kiss her forehead. I loved watching her sleep. In moments like these, she looked a lot like her mom and acted like her too—in a good way. I backed away from the bed and sat in the chair in the corner of her room. *Serenity.* I stared out the window, looking at the peacefulness of the estate. It was a full moon, beautiful and bright. Thoughts of Hope swarmed my mind again. Hope loved watching the moon at night. Some nights, we would lay down a blanket outside. She would put the back of her head on my chest, and we would stare at the moon until we fell asleep, getting woken up by the 7:00 a.m. sprinklers every time.

I was startled when Amara called out to me. I must have fallen asleep, which I tended to do at least once a week since I came back from helping Zuri. "Good morning, Dad! Rise and Shine," she said as she sat up, wiping her eyes.

"Good morning, my ray of sun! Go brush your teeth and head downstairs for breakfast. I'll be down soon." I wiped my eyes and looked out the window. The sun was shining bright. I checked the time—8:02 a.m. I got up and went to my bedroom. I usually slept in the guest room, which was a habit I picked up since Hope left that night. As I walked into the bedroom, I could smell her perfume. I asked the maid to spray Hope's perfume on my pillowcases each time she cleaned—it always filled the room with the smell of sweetness. I closed the door behind me and let the smell overtake me. The memories flooded back in my head like a wave at sea. I just wanted this nightmare to be over and wished that I could just have my wife back in my arms—like before. My phone vibrated, pulling me out of my fantasy. "What is it?"

"She's here. We found her on the cameras."

I hung up the phone and went downstairs to my office. I opened the closet and pulled out a fresh set of clothes—a plain black collared shirt and a pair of black slacks. I changed my clothes, putting on my pants, and then reaching over to grab my bulletproof vest, putting it on underneath my shirt. I placed my shirt on top, leaving it unbuttoned, as I grabbed two handguns and two additional magazines for each. I holstered one handgun on my hip and the other behind my back. I put the additional magazines in the two empty slots on each side of the vest. I closed the closet door, buttoned up my shirt, and went downstairs. I yelled for Amara, and she came running.

"Darling, I need you to go stay in the movie theater until I come get you. Lock the door, and stay in there with the nanny. We have a code red."

She hugged me tightly and said that she loved me. I kissed her on the forehead and called for her nanny, signaling for her to take Amara into the theater. I grabbed the nanny's arm. "Do not open the door for anyone but me—no one."

She looked into my eyes. I could see the fear in hers, but she knew what needed to be done. She nodded, acknowledging the severity of the situation.

I watched as they went into the theater and then followed behind to ensure I put in the security code and had the room locked down. When UQ built this theater, it was supposed to be a hideout. I decided to renovate it and make it into a bunker. The door and walls were bulletproof. I had a mini kitchen in there as well as a full bathroom. The bunker was stocked with enough movies, food, and water to ensure that several people would be safe, fed, and hydrated for seventy-two hours. It was the safest place for them.

I walked out the side door of the house and straight to my security guys.

"We see her walking through the estate. She stopped by the small house at the far end of the estate. She's nearing the war room."

"We'll go by foot. Two of you with me, the rest of you stay alert. I want you spread out around the mini house. Don't let her get away. Cover all exits. No one makes a move until I say so. She's looking for me."

I headed back into the house with two of my men. We went upstairs to my office, and I shifted one of the books on the shelf. A side door slid open, and we went down the winding staircase. At the bottom of the staircase was a mile-long hallway, lit dimly, that would lead us straight into the war room. UQ had built this underground tunnel, and only a select few people knew about it.

When we were about three-quarters of the way down the hallway, I grabbed my phone and checked the hidden camera I had inside the mini house—no one had access except me. I saw her looking around the house, seeming to admire what she saw, and poking her head into each room. She walked into the living room and saw a few pictures sitting on the side tables next to the TV. Walking past one of the tables, she grabbed one picture and then the next one. She stared at them for a while and then picked up her phone. She stopped suddenly, and I saw her walking toward the war room door.

She looked around and then put her ear to the wall. *I think she hears us.* She felt around the walls and then I saw her slide the bookcase. *Damnit. Why is she so smart?* She opened the door and hesitated before walking down the stairs. I saw her reach behind her back. *She has a weapon.* Then I saw a flashlight turn on. I breathed out a sigh of relief.

When she made it to the bottom of the stairs, she turned the light on. I had to switch back to the general security cameras to see what she was doing next. Fully linked to the cameras, I watched as she kept looking around. A few seconds later, she reached behind her back. This time, it was a gun. She held the gun in front of her as she walked toward the two doors at the end of the hall.

She stopped at the first door. Slowly opening it, with her gun raised, she reached into the room to turn on the lights. I saw her take one last look into the hallway and then disappear into the room, closing the door behind her. That room is where I would also spend my time watching her.

I waited for her to emerge from the room as I positioned myself for her to enter through this door. I knew she would come here next after reviewing whatever documents I had left in there. I sat down in one of the chairs and told my two security guys to stay close by but unseen. Once they were in position, I shut off the lights, leaving the room pitch black as a way to disorient her.

The light from the hallway slightly illuminated the room when she entered, but darkness overtook it when she closed the door behind her. Once the door was fully shut, I turned on the light. "Hey, baby," I said. "Fancy seeing you here."

Her confused eyes adjusted. "You son of a bitch. How could you?" She turned to the left and faced me. "It was you. It was you all along!" Like clockwork, she started whispering to herself.

I hadn't seen her in years, and she looked—different. I could see that the facility took a toll on her. She was skinner than I had ever seen her—she didn't look unhealthy, just different. I could see that she put on makeup and dressed in her casual wear. At that moment, in that light, I couldn't put my finger on what was different. Regardless, she was still beautiful to me.

She loudly yelled, "Wait!" and startled me. "What do you mean be a mother? A mother to that little girl I saw you in the picture with upstairs? Who is she? You expect me to raise a daughter that is not mine? Are you insane?"

I don't know if at that moment I was happy that I knew how to play her game or if I was alarmed by how quickly I could jump into her game—all I knew was that I was sick of the game, and I wanted out. *Here we go again.* "Oh, baby! She is your daughter. I could never have a child with anyone else," I said. I grabbed a picture from my desk and turned it to face her. "This is your daughter. She's amazing. I promised her that, one day, I would bring you back to her, and here you are. When I went to get you, after the plane situation, I knew I had to fight for you, for us, so we could be together. Then I wanted to bring you back here so you could meet her, but, you know . . . Listen, I'm sorry about what happened. Regardless, I'm glad to see that you're doing well, and I hope that you don't hold any resentment toward me—"

She started crying as I was talking, and it was bizarre to me because I had forgotten about these constant tears. Then the tears stopped abruptly, and she pointed the gun at me.

I moved closer to the gun and said, "You're not going to shoot me. I'm the love of your life remember, and we have a child who needs the both of us."

She stopped to think. "How old is she?"

"She is ten, about to turn eleven, and baby, she's brilliant, intelligent, and she's beautiful, just like her mom," I said, smiling.

The anger in her voice took me by surprise. "Are you serious? My daughter is almost eleven years old, and you kept her from me? Does she know who I am?" She paused briefly and then I heard the change in her tone and saw her eyes darken, the evil one was now back. "I thought I killed her. I'm surprised to know Hope's weak, fragile self was able to keep that baby alive. She begged me after we ended up in the mental hospital—courtesy of you—and said, *Lilith, please don't hurt my baby. She's innocent*—as if I cared. I really did try to kill that little girl. Oh, well. All I know is I'm going to kill you first and then I'm going to find that little girl and kill her. It's time I finished what I started."

I could see her mind racing as if she was thinking about her next move. She lowered the gun with a bravado that I thought to be annoying and slid it to the other side of the room. She then turned around to face me.

At that moment, I just wanted to shoot her. I don't understand why, deep down, I constantly struggled with killing her. If she died by her own hand, I wouldn't feel as bad, but there was something about shooting her that I couldn't do. I left my gun on the table and walked over to her. It's hard to fight for the woman you love when she is being taken from you. It's even harder to fight her knowing what she meant to me—still means to me.

Once we were within a few feet of each other, our fists went up like clockwork. *When the guns go down, the fists go up.* She waited, not wanting to make the first move—like always. I decided to do what she couldn't and took a step forward, releasing a right punch. I intentionally missed because I didn't want to hurt her, and I also wanted her to believe that this was going to be an easy win for her. *Make your opponent feel like they have the upper hand and then surprise them when they let their guard down. Another UQ lesson.*

She charged at me and punched me in the face—twice—and then she proceeded to kick me. When she kicked me, I grabbed her leg and threw her backward.

She lost her footing but managed to keep herself upright. In the quick second she took to adjust her stance, I ran to her, picked her up by her throat, and threw her backward. She fell on her back, *hard*. Unphased, she rolled onto her side and did a swing kick at my legs. I fell back, not expecting her to do that. A sharp pain went up my spine. She used this as an opportunity to get on top of me, releasing punch after punch, blow after blow.

The way she was fighting, punching, it was Hope. I knew it from our fighting days. Or maybe it was Zuri because she had the same skill as Hope. Either way, I let her punch me because this was the only pain that I could tolerate, the only pain that I could manage when it came to her—physical pain. It felt better than the emotional pain of seeing my wife transform into three different people, one of which was a complete stranger to me and wanted me dead.

I allowed her to get one last punch in before I was ready to do what needed to be done. I grabbed her arm and kneed her at the same time, throwing her off of me. I was not fighting back, just deflecting because I knew she hated when I did this.

We both got up and continued fighting. The thoughts in my head halted as I fell back into our training days. After a few minutes of this, something changed. She became sloppy and angry—this was not Zuri or Hope. This was Lilith. I wasn't going to fight Lilith. It wasn't worth the risk. I moved closer to her as she stepped back. I double-punched her in the stomach, causing her to keel over. Then, I roundhouse kicked her in the plexus. She stumbled back, shocked. "This is done," I said as I ran toward her, using all my force to grab her. I slammed her into the wall and then grabbed her by her neck and started banging her head against it. I dropped her, and she caught her breath. I kicked her, punched her, and watched as she balled up.

"Stop!" she shouted.

Damnit, Hope or Zuri, is back. Something overtook me in that moment. Something in me couldn't stop hurting her—I ignored her cries and continued kicking her. After the fact, I felt remorse for my actions, but at that very moment, all I felt was rage. I don't know if it was because I was sick of the destruction she left behind or if it was the threat she made on Amara's life that took me over the edge, but it was an out-of-body experience for me. I kept punching her, only stopping right before she was about to lose consciousness. I walked over to grab the gun she had thrown away and pointed it at her. "Get up, now!"

Defeated, she crawled closer to the wall and used it as an anchor to help her get to her feet. I could tell she had no energy left to keep fighting me. "Massimo, please . . . I surrender," she said.

I lowered the gun and started pacing. The thoughts that had subsided while we were fighting came rushing back like a hurricane. "The night you left, I hated you more than I hated my parents. They abandoned me, but you, you're the one who knew me better than I knew myself, and you took something so dear to me. You broke my heart more than they did. I gave you everything. I gave you every part of my being. I loved you more than I loved myself. You took away the only family I ever knew. You took him and then you left me to pick up the broken pieces. So, I did."

Her eyes squinted as she looked out into the distance. I turned around and heard her say, "How could this be? You're supposed to be dead. Grandpa, is that you?"

I looked in the distance and saw my head of security walking toward us. It wasn't UQ—just her mind playing another trick on her. I turned back around as her face went from shock and disbelief to anger. She tried to charge me, and I shot her in the arm—a flesh wound. She fell back, yelling, "I hope you both die!"

I walked up to her and hit her in the head with the butt of the gun, knocking her out. I held the gun in my hand and stood there, waiting for my head of security to arrive. He put his hand on my shoulder and said, "I know I stopped you before back at the safe house in France, but I won't again. You know what you have to do. You have UQ's blessing. Do it for Amara's safety, for your sanity, for the family."

"Yes. This has to end now. I'll take care of it."

I released the magazine to see how many bullets were left and then slid the magazine back in. I loaded a bullet into the chamber and then holstered the gun behind my back. I picked her up, knowing she was not dead yet, and took her to one of the bedrooms upstairs in the mini house. I laid her limp body down. *Has it really come to this*?

I went to the bathroom to grab some supplies to wrap her arm and stop the bleeding. The bullet had just grazed it. I wasn't sure why I was even fixing her up. Maybe it was just habit. Maybe I was trying to prolong what was to come. After I finished wrapping her arm, I went to the kitchen to prepare for the inevitable. I went under the sink and pulled out the extra-large gas canister. I placed it on the counter and then I sat down and got back up and sat down again. I could've shot her in the head or chest instead of shooting her in the arm and then knocking her out, but I think I wanted one last moment with Hope. I wanted to bring that personality to the forefront and talk to her one last time. I just wanted one last time to say goodbye to the love of my life, the only one of the personalities I could ever love—Hope. I didn't have the chance before, but I could now . . . if I could just get to Hope.

I left the kitchen and headed back into the room to check on her. She started to move when I entered. She slowly opened her eyes. "Massimo," she said in the softest voice. "You okay, baby?" she asked me.

I don't know how, but Hope was back.

I ran to her bedside, thanking God for this one last opportunity, "All good, bunny. You were in an accident, so I was just making sure you were okay," I said as I knelt beside her. At any moment, Hope could turn into Lilith or Zuri. I just didn't know what to expect.

She sat up and winced in pain. I watched as she looked at her arm. "Ow! This hurts, baby, but thank you for wrapping it for me. What happened? Oh, wait . . . I remember. Lilith. I'm sorry, babe. I don't know how she got so strong, but she did. At first, I could control her but then, she started controlling me."

Surprised by what she was saying, I grabbed her hand and said, "I know, babe. It's not on you, though, and it doesn't matter now. All that matters is that you're here with me." I stroked her cheek and then stood up and sat on the bed next to her. "Hope, I want you to know that I'll always love you. You have seriously changed my life for the better. When we met, I remember thinking how cute you were. Then we grew older, and I remember thinking how sexy you were. Now, here we are, and I'm thinking how beautiful you are. If I failed you at any point, forgive me. I promise to do the best I can to raise Amara, and you won't have to worry about her. I promise you, I will take care of her and will shower her with enough love for the both of us."

Her eyes were kind and soft as she looked at me, confused. "Baby, I don't understand. I'm not going anywhere."

I grabbed her hand and continued, "I'll never try to replace you. Amara will know you as her mom and only you. I promise to keep our legacy going, but I want your permission."

"Permission to do what?"

"Permission to use your eggs so we can have another child."

"Baby, I understand. You know about what Lilith tried to do to Amara?"

"Yes, babe. I know. So that is why I'm asking for your permission to do this—please?"

"Yes, of course, babe. I promised you at least three," she said, giggling to me. She sat up fully, tolerating the pain, to move closer to me so she could gently kiss me.

I kissed her back. *Please don't change. Please don't change. God, allow me just five more minutes.* We kissed a little while longer while I tried my best to delay the inevitable. Those few moments I had with her, it was everything to me. I pulled back and looked at her one last time. I kissed her forehead and stood up, making my way to the door. *It was time, and she knew it. She had accepted it.*

As I grabbed the doorknob, I felt a force against my back. I yelled, unsure of what just happened. I turned around swiftly to see Lilith holding the lamp from the bedside table in one hand and my gun in her other. I looked into her dark and soulless eyes.

"Where are you going, Massimo? We have unfinished business."

The pain shooting through my back was slightly debilitating. I couldn't feel my legs as they gave out from under me.

"Get up," she said, stepping back and away from me.

"I can't. I need a second."

She waited impatiently as I tried to stand, using the door handle to help me up. I could feel my legs again. I don't know what she hit, but I was in extreme pain.

"Open the door and walk."

I opened the door and slowly walked down the hall. With each step I took, my legs gained more feeling. The pain was still there, but I could tolerate it. We made it to the kitchen.

"Hands up," she said with the gun still pointed at me.

I turned around to face her and raised my hands. I inched toward her, watching to see what she was going to do.

"I'll see you and Amara in hell," she said, smiling.

The anger that rose inside of me shot through me like adrenaline. I rushed her and swung my hand around, knocking her arm back. She was taken by surprise. I grabbed her arm with my left hand, blocking her elbow. I used my right hand to grab her shirt and push her chin to the side, a bit of Krav Maga. I kneed her three times, and she was disoriented. I used my right hand to turn the gun and punched it out of her hand. Her finger was still near the trigger, so I broke it. She yelled in pain. I grabbed the gun, backed up, and pointed it at her head.

"Fuck you," Lilith said to me as she was bent over, holding her finger.

"Right back at you." I shot her in the leg, causing her to fall down. I walked over to her and stood over her body as she groaned in pain.

A glimmer of Hope surfaced. "I love you," Hope whispered. "Do it, babe. I forgive you. Do it, before she comes back."

I gave her one last look, and I shot her in the head. I watched as the life instantly left her body. The woman I loved dearly was gone, and life would go on without her, the way it had for so many years before.

I stepped over her and grabbed the extra-large gasoline canister off the counter. I poured gasoline over her body and over the furniture in the house. I threw the canister on the ground and grabbed my lighter. This was the same lighter she gave me a few days after we got engaged. Engraved on the lighter read, "Death will be the only thing that will keep us apart." I nodded when I read the words again. I dropped the lighter on her body and walked out of the house.

"Clear out," I told my security team. They dipped their heads and walked back toward the main house. I made it halfway back, limping in pain, when I heard an explosion. I didn't bother turning around. That was the past, and I was walking toward my future.

I got back in the house and went straight to the movie theater. I put in the passcode and opened the door. I poked my head inside to see Amara and the nanny eating while watching *Cinderella.*

Amara ran to me and yelled, "Daddy!"

I picked her up and held her tight. As she put her head on my shoulder, I began to sing:

I'll be your knight in shining armor
if you'll be my serenity.
A fire lit on a candle, for whenever you can't see.
A piece of a puzzle that's always been missing—
been missing.
I'll be the one standing there with a hanky
whenever you're crying,
Standing there telling you to keep on trying.
Just thought that I should let you know—
just thought that I should let you know.

Acknowledgements

The *RedEye to Paris* was my first work of fiction. Turning a small idea into this book you see before you today was an amazing process. I just want to take this time to thank those who made it possible.

I would like to thank my editor, Mozelle Jordan. Thank you for your feedback, corrections, and editorial help. If it wasn't for you, this book would not have developed into the work of art it is today.

I would like to thank my friend, Lily G., for giving me the zeal to write and the idea to turn my thoughts into a novel.

I would like to thank S.A. Jones for the constant support, guidance, feedback, and motivation. Your support helped push me forward, and your kind words led me to nourish and grow this book.

To all my family and friends who encourage me no matter what the endeavor is—a special thanks to you all.

And I want to give a final shout-out to God—he is last but definitely not least. Thank you for giving me the mind, strength, focus, ideas, and resources to be able to develop a book and see it through from start to finish.

For all those people who sometimes feel like they can only do one thing in life, my answer to that is *no!* Do not limit yourself or limit the power that God has given you. Be all that you can be, and do all that you want to do. Step into your power and grace and enjoy the success that comes from giving 100%.

Until next time. Signing out—Tiffany A. Domorad

About the Author

Tiffany Akita Domorad is a pseudonym. The woman behind the name is a lawyer and currently resides in New Jersey. Born and raised in New York City, Tiffany found a love for reading when she realized that she could get lost in a different reality while being present in her own and a connection to writing when she found it allowed others into her own mind. Throughout the years, she has leaned into these passions, having her work published in academia, specifically her master's thesis, and as a poet in Stars of our Hearts: Chronicles and Who's Who in American Poetry. The Redeye to Paris is Tiffany's first fictional work, and she is currently working on her second. Tiffany-like the cliché states-loves long walks on the beach and traveling the world. In her spare time, you can find her reading murder mysteries, self-help books, and romance novels. When she is feeling active, she enjoys swimming and hiking, and on lazy days, watching movies and TV shows. As she did when she was younger, Tiffany hopes that while you read her books, you, too, can get lost in a different reality while still being present in your own.